Entertainment Weekly

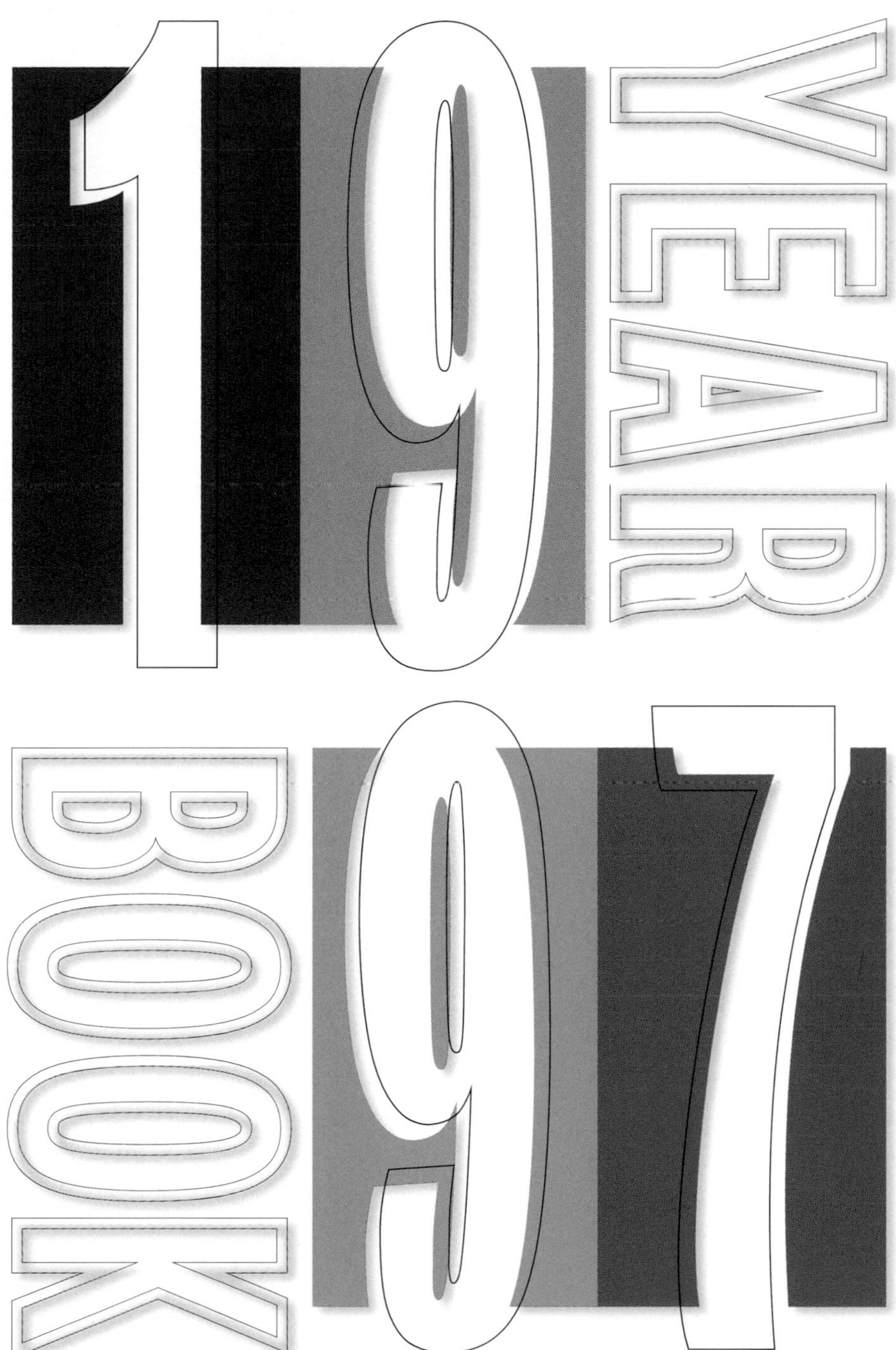

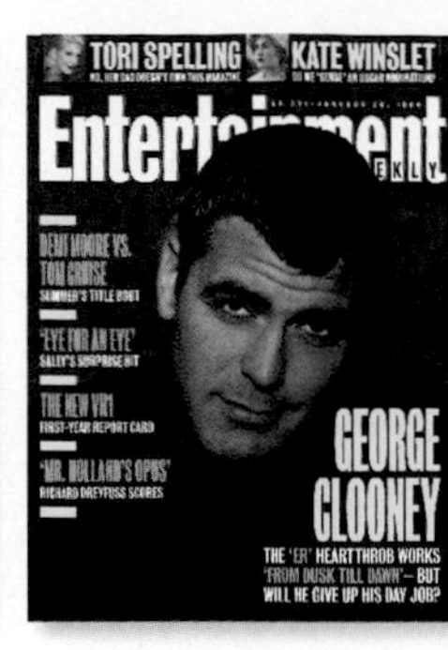

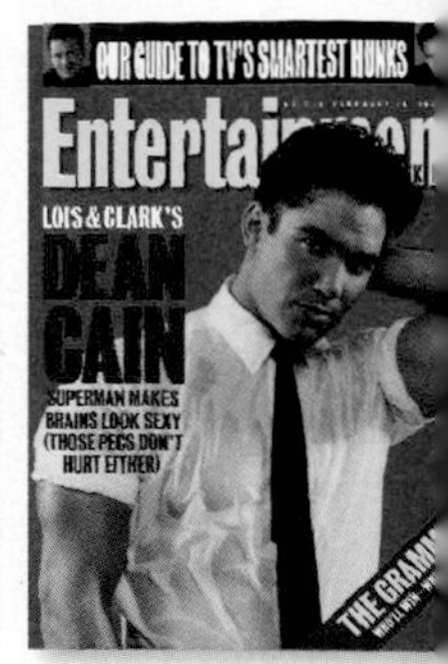

Entertainment WEEKLY 1997 YEARBOOK

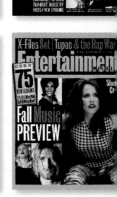

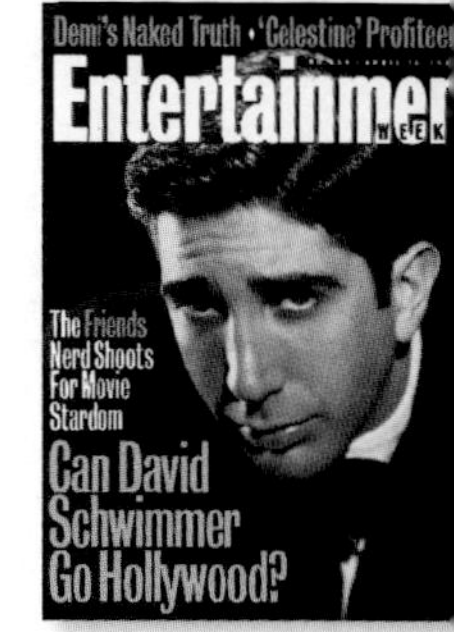

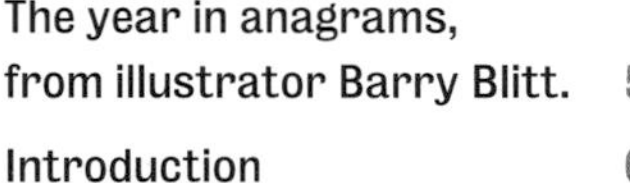

PICTURES OF THE YEAR

THE YEAR IN ENTERTAINMENT

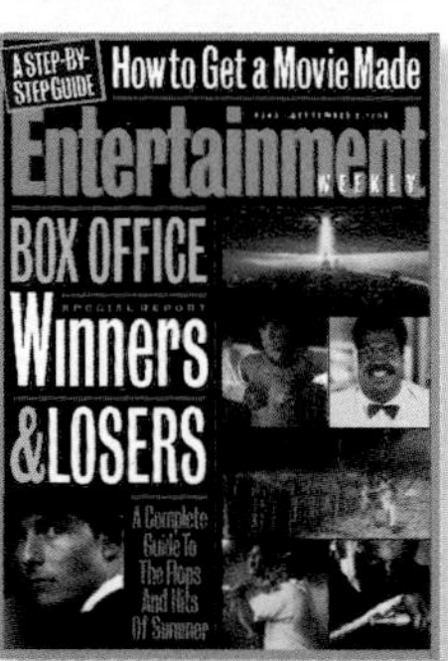

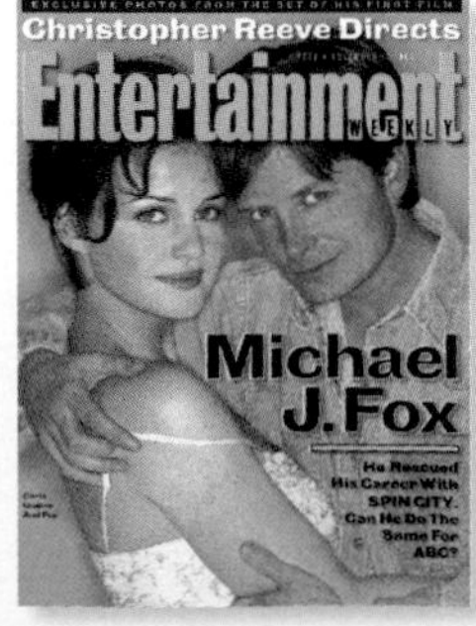

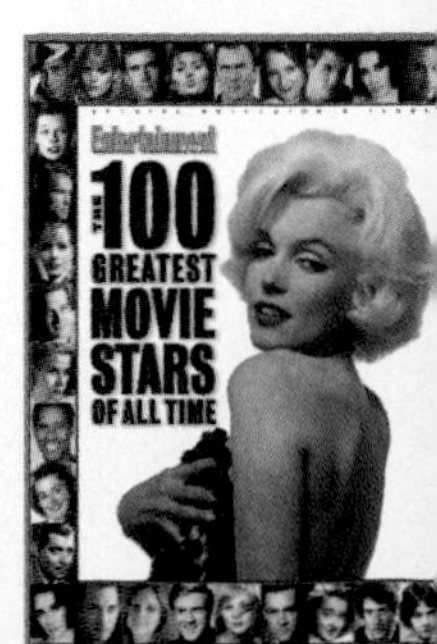

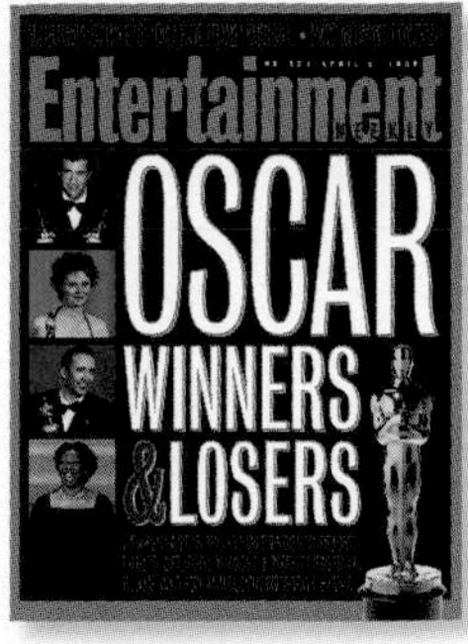

ENTERTAINERS OF THE YEAR

They made talk nice and music nasty. They saved lives and shook up Broadway. In a year when cows flew and the White House exploded, these stars were champagne supernovas.

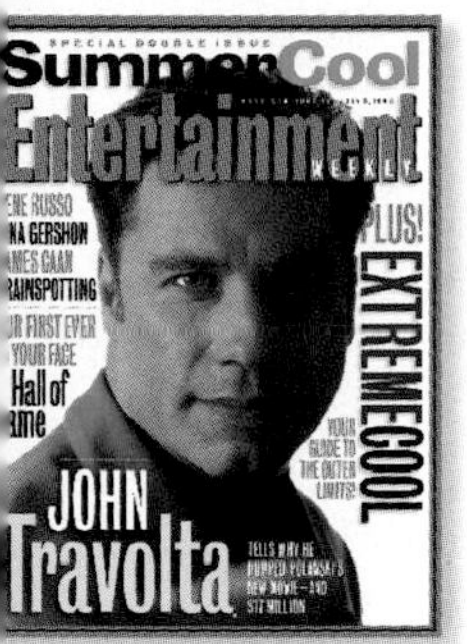

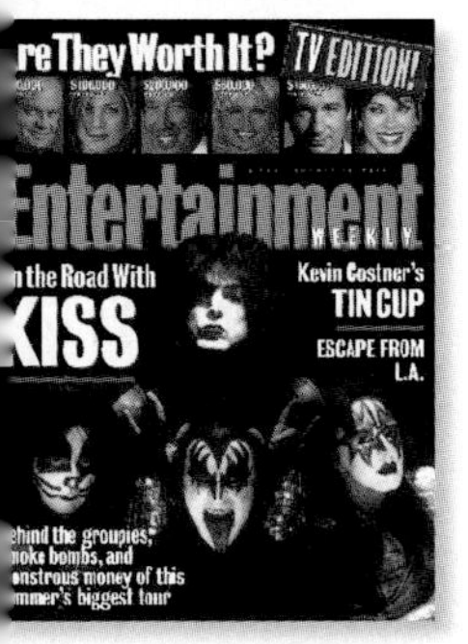

THE YEAR IN REVIEWS

Indie films broke through, *NYPD Blue* stayed tuned, Brit pop rocked: Our critics pick 1996's best—and worst.

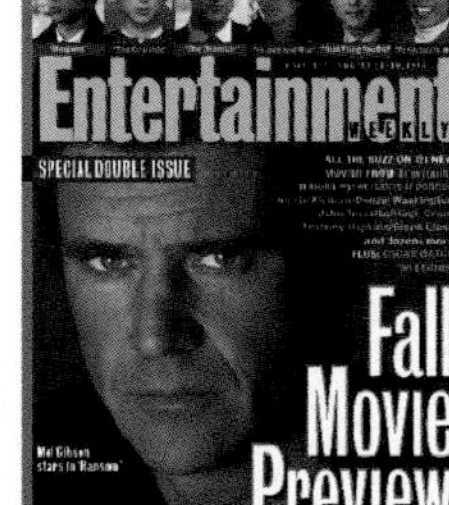

BOWING OUT

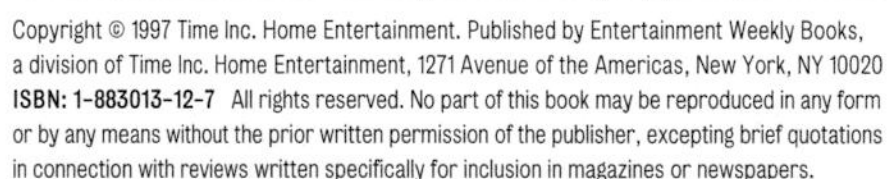

 Published by Entertainment Weekly Books, a division of Time Inc. Home Entertainment, 1271 Avenue of the Americas, New York, NY 10020
ISBN: 1-883013-12-7

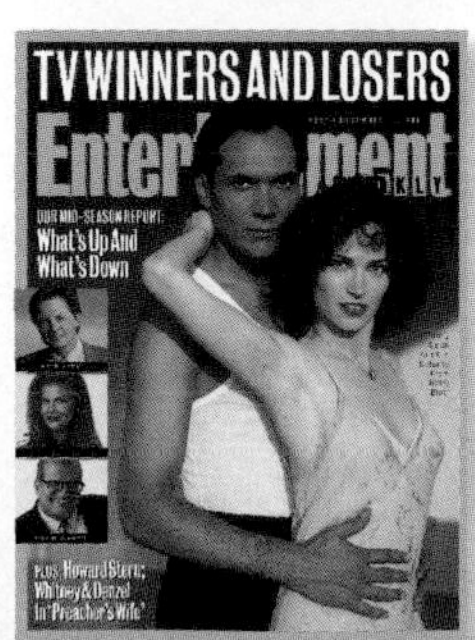

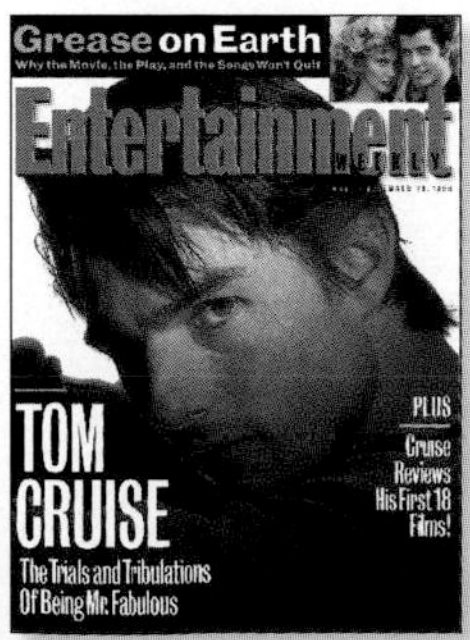

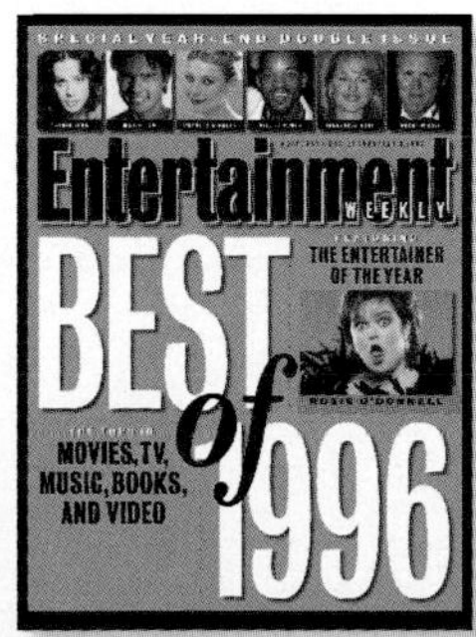

1997 YEARBOOK

EDITOR
David Hajdu
EXECUTIVE EDITOR
Alison Gwinn
SENIOR EDITORS
Marion Hart, Ann Kolson, Bonnie Vaughan
ART DIRECTOR
Don Morris
PICTURE EDITOR
Julie Mihaly
DESIGN ASSOCIATES
Josh Klenert, Jennifer Starr
ASSOCIATE EDITORS
Robin Honig, Wook Kim, Alice King, Joe Neumaier
ASSOCIATE PICTURE EDITOR Stella Kramer
REPORTERS Veronica Byrd, Mitch Frank, Thomas Hudson, Kristi Huelsing, Beth Johnson, Chris Nutter, Joseph V. Tirella, Cheo Tyehimba, Louis Vogel
EDITORIAL PRODUCTION Sue Barnett
COPY CHIEF Steven Pearl
COPY EDITORS Elizabeth Gehrman, Henry Hample
EDITORIAL ASSISTANT Kipp Cheng
IMAGING Ray Battaglino, George L. Beke, Paul Bodley Jr., Kevin Christian, Evan J. Dong, John Goodman, Robert D. Kennedy, Bill Lazzarotti, Lisa DiSapio Motti, Tom Roemlein, George Sumerak, Daniel C. Thompson

ENTERTAINMENT WEEKLY CONSUMER MARKETING
CONSUMER MARKETING DIRECTOR
Alexander H. Sareyan
ASSISTANT CONSUMER MARKETING DIRECTOR
William J. Stutzman
CIRCULATION DIRECTOR Monica Ray

TIME INC. HOME ENTERTAINMENT
MANAGING DIRECTOR David Gitow
DIRECTOR, CONTINUITIES David Arfine
DIRECTOR, NEW BUSINESS DEVELOPMENT
Stuart Hotchkiss
FULFILLMENT DIRECTOR Michelle Gudema
PRODUCT MANAGERS Robert Fox, Michael Holahan, Jennifer McLyman, John Sandklev, Alicia Wilcox
EDITORIAL OPERATIONS MANAGER John Calvano
PRODUCTION MANAGER Donna Miano-Ferrara
ASSISTANT PRODUCTION MANAGER Jessica McGrath
PRODUCTION CONSULTANT Joseph Napolitano
FINANCIAL MANAGER Tricia Griffin
ASSISTANT FINANCIAL MANAGER Heather Lynds
ASSOCIATE PRODUCT MANAGERS
Ken Katzman, Daniel Melore, Allison Weiss, Dawn Weland
ASSISTANT PRODUCT MANAGERS
Alyse Daberko, Charlotte Siddiqui
MARKETING ASSISTANT Lyndsay Jenks

EDITOR IN CHIEF: Norman Pearlstine
EDITORIAL DIRECTOR: Henry Muller
EDITOR OF NEW MEDIA: Daniel Okrent
TIME INC.
CHAIRMAN: Reginald K. Brack Jr.
PRESIDENT, CEO: Don Logan

Entertainment WEEKLY

MANAGING EDITOR
James W. Seymore Jr.
EXECUTIVE EDITOR
Richard Sanders
ASSISTANT MANAGING EDITORS
Peter Bonventre, Jeannie Park
GENERAL EDITOR
David Hajdu
DESIGN DIRECTOR
John Korpics
PHOTOGRAPHY DIRECTOR
Mary Dunn
L.A. BUREAU CHIEF
Cable Neuhaus
PICTURE EDITOR
Doris Brautigan
SENIOR EDITORS: George Blooston, Doug Brod, Mark Harris, John McAlley, Maggie Murphy, Mary Kaye Schilling
DIRECTOR OF RESEARCH SERVICES: Annabel Bentley
SPECIAL PROJECTS MANAGER: Alison Gwinn
MANAGING ART DIRECTOR: Michael Picón
STAFF EDITORS: Cynthia Grisolia, Tina Jordan, Albert Kim
CRITIC-AT-LARGE: Ken Tucker
CRITICS: David Browne, Ty Burr, Bruce Fretts, Owen Gleiberman, Lisa Schwarzbaum
WRITER-AT-LARGE: Dana Kennedy
SENIOR WRITERS: Rebecca Ascher-Walsh, Jess Cagle, Jeff Gordinier, David Hochman, Gregg Kilday, Benjamin Svetkey, Bret Watson, Chris Willman
SENIOR ASSOCIATE EDITORS: Lauren Kunkler, Caren Weiner
ASSOCIATE EDITORS: Doug Brantley, Marion Hart, Dulcy Israel, Joe Neumaier, Mitchell Vinicor, Tracy A. Walsh
STAFF WRITERS: Steve Daly, A. J. Jacobs, Kate Meyers, Degen Pener, Tom Sinclair
CORRESPONDENTS: Casey Davidson, Christopher Nashawaty, Jessica Shaw, Dan Snierson
SENIOR BROADCAST CORRESPONDENT: Lisa Karlin
COPY CHIEF: Ben Spier **COPY EDITOR:** Steven Pearl

DESIGN
ASSOCIATE ART DIRECTORS: Joe Kimberling, Rina Migliaccio
ASSISTANT ART DIRECTOR: Bobby B. Lawhorn Jr.
DESIGNERS: Stacie Reistetter, Julie Schrader
DESIGN ASSISTANT: Erin Whelan

PICTURES
PICTURE EDITOR, SPECIAL PROJECTS: Sarah Rozen
ASSOCIATE PICTURE EDITOR: Alice H. Babcock
ASSISTANT PICTURE EDITORS: Michael Kochman (L.A.), Richard B. Maltz, Michele Romero
ASSISTANT: L. Michelle Dougherty

NEW MEDIA
COORDINATOR: Stan Olson

RESEARCH SERVICES
REPORTERS: Tim Purtell (Deputy), Martha K. Babcock (Deputy, Special Projects), Beth Johnson, Kirsten McCumber, Tiarra Mukherjee, Cheo Tyehimba, Louis Vogel
INFORMATION CENTER MANAGER: Rachel Sapienza
DEPUTY: Stacie Fenster **ASSOCIATE:** Sean O'Heir
ASSISTANT: Alexandria Carrion

PRODUCTION
MAKEUP MANAGER: Robin Kaplan
PLANT OPERATIONS MANAGER: Karen S. Doyle
PRODUCTION MANAGER: Sue Barnett
STAFF: Ray Battaglino, George L. Beke, Paul Bodley Jr., Kevin Christian, Evan J. Dong, John Goodman, Don Gordon, Robert D. Kennedy, Bill Lazzarotti, Lisa DiSapio Motti, Ann Griffith O'Connor, Lauren Planit, Eve A. Rabinovits, Tom Roemlein, Leona Smith, George Sumerak, Daniel C. Thompson

TECHNOLOGY
MANAGER: James S. Mittelmark
SENIOR TECHNOLOGY COORDINATOR: Godwin Mensah
TECHNOLOGY COORDINATOR: Jeffrey Cherins

ASSISTANTS
Kristen Baldwin, Kipp Erante Cheng, Shirliey Y. Fung, Anna Holmes, Alexandra Jacobs, David Karger, Erin Richter, Gary Eng Walk

ADMINISTRATION
ASSISTANT TO THE MANAGING EDITOR: Rita Silverstein
STAFF: Carole Willcocks

CONTRIBUTORS
WRITERS: Pat H. Broeske, Erica K. Cardozo, Nisid Hajari, Glenn Kenny, L.S. Klepp, Ann Kolson, Gene Lyons, Lois Alter Mark, Jim Mullen, Alanna Nash, Richard Natale, Lawrence O'Toole, Michael Sauter, Stephen Schaefer, Heidi Siegmund Cuda, Bob Strauss

PRESIDENT
Michael J. Klingensmith
PUBLISHER: Michael J. Kelly
EXECUTIVE DIRECTOR OF MARKETING AND BUSINESS DEVELOPMENT: Marian L. Schwindeman
DIRECTOR OF CONSUMER MARKETING: Alexander H. Sareyan
CIRCULATION DIRECTOR: Monica Ray
DIRECTOR OF FINANCE & ADMINISTRATION: George H. Vollmuth
ASSOCIATE PUBLISHER: David S. Morris
PRODUCTION DIRECTOR: Carol A. Mazzarella
DIRECTOR OF PROMOTION AND PUBLIC AFFAIRS: Daniel J. Osheyack
PUBLIC RELATIONS DIRECTOR: Sandy W. Drayton
TIME INC. EDITORIAL SERVICES
EXECUTIVE EDITORS: Joëlle Attinger, José M. Ferrer III
DEVELOPMENT EDITOR: Isolde Motley
DIRECTOR: Sheldon Czapnik
GENERAL MANAGER: Claude Boral **PHOTO LAB:** Thomas E. Hubbard
RESEARCH CENTER: Lany Walden McDonald
PICTURE COLLECTION: Beth Bencini Zarcone
TECHNOLOGY: Thomas Smith **MARKETING:** James Macove
TIME INC. EDITORIAL TECHNOLOGY
VICE PRESIDENT: Paul Zazzera **DIRECTOR:** Damien Creavin

1996 — The Year in ANAGRAMS
BY BARRY BLITT AND BOB SLAPCOFF
KATHIE LEE GIFFORD
THE FRAGILE KID FOE
TICKLE ME ELMO
E.T. COME KILL ME
MADONNA AS EVITA
A NAME'S NOT A DIVA
TV STAR ELLEN DEGENERES
EVER-GENDERLESS TALENT
I AM DENNIS RODMAN
MR. INSIDE MADONNA
CLINTON BEATS DOLE
O, BLAND LIE CONTEST

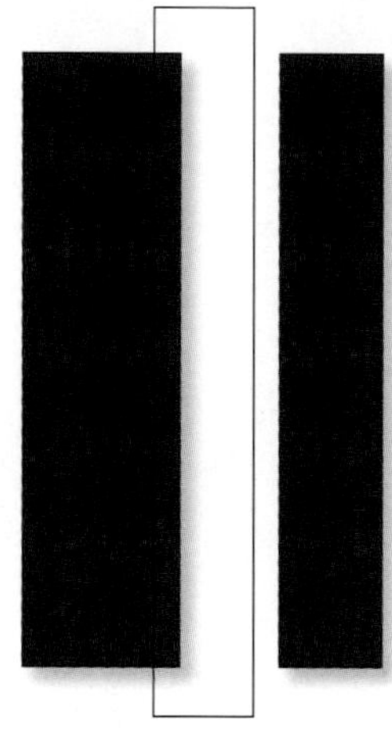

SN'T ONE OF THE MOST COMMON RAPS against pop culture and the media's coverage of it that we're always looking to put a cynical spin on everything? Yet what struck us here as we looked over an entire year's worth of movies, TV, music, video, books, CD-ROMs, and Jenny McCarthy is that so much of what went on in the past 12 months had the earmarks of hopefulness, energy, even—dare we say it—idealism. Positivity was positively popular. For a bundle of optimism, look no further than EW's Entertainer of the Year, Rosie O'Donnell. The instant success of her new daytime talk show almost single-handedly put the kibosh on sensational, lowest-common-boobominator chat shows. Many were canceled or took ratings dives; one of them, Jenny Jones', got lots of attention on Court TV; all the while, Rosie's feel-good, be-smart style took hold. She and Oprah Winfrey, another talker rewarded for taking the high road (celebrating that most outmoded of things—books!—to enormous impact), proved the country hungers for good examples and good work. (*And* good works: In a year when public figures as various as Tonya Harding, Mark Harmon, and John Grisham came to the aid of people in trouble, Tom Cruise performed no fewer than three rescues—no doubt a celebrity record.) O'Donnell spent much of her first year confessing to a crush on Cruise, whose *Jerry Maguire* was one of many films that restored our faith in a vanishing breed: a good story well told. Like moviegoers, EW has bemoaned the fact that the craft of the screenplay has faded, making such solidly constructed films as *Maguire*, *Breaking the Waves*, and *Big Night* especially heartening. As for the summer blockbusters, even these mega-budget thrill rides were exercises in affirmation: *Twister* suggested honest folks could triumph over nature. And what was the biggest hit—*Independence Day*—if not an F/X-inflected hymn to American can-do, derring-do, and do-you-believe-those-grosses? But pop culture accentuated the positive in higher-quality work as well. Some of the best fare came from idiosyncratic artists pursuing quirky visions within big entertainment systems: Think *The X-Files* (Fox risked moving it to Sunday and hit the ratings jackpot); Beck (cunning oddball comes up with one of 1996's most praised albums, *Odelay*); Frank McCourt's memoir, *Angela's Ashes* (moving, rich prose lives!); the *Monty Python and the Quest for the Holy Grail* CD-ROM (a game that goes one step beyond the 1975 movie); and video's *The Beatles Anthology* (boomer nostalgia as cogent scholarship). Now, it would be insulting to the memory of slain rapper Tupac Shakur—whose death was one of the year's most dramatic music stories—to say that there was anything positive about his violent demise in September. Yet it already seems likely that his legacy will glow: Shakur's hip-hop served as an example to millions of the dangerous contradiction inherent in the glorification of the gangsta lifestyle. In early 1995, Shakur began (along with other key rappers, including producer Dr. Dre) a dialogue with his listeners about the moral and commercial implications of rhymed hostility. That's just one bit of the serious show business news our yearbook places in perspective. You'll find all the year's most provocative people, events, and artifacts inside these pages. We've souped up our Year in Entertainment section, now a month-by-month rundown of the year's events, and expanded all our critics' best-of-the-year lists. It's, like, all here: reportage and lists, hard numbers and flash. A year whose pop culture contained both the Macarena and Madonna's bambino. A year that gave middle-aged women their due in the hit *First Wives Club* and granted romantically desperate young men a chance to be "money" with *Swingers*. Any year that begins with the breakup of Michael Jackson and Lisa Marie Presley's marriage and ends with the TV industry's imposing ratings on itself (as well as—hmmm—a new Jackson spouse, this time with the promise of a baby) is a year to reckon with.

PICT

OF Y

THE

URES

EAR

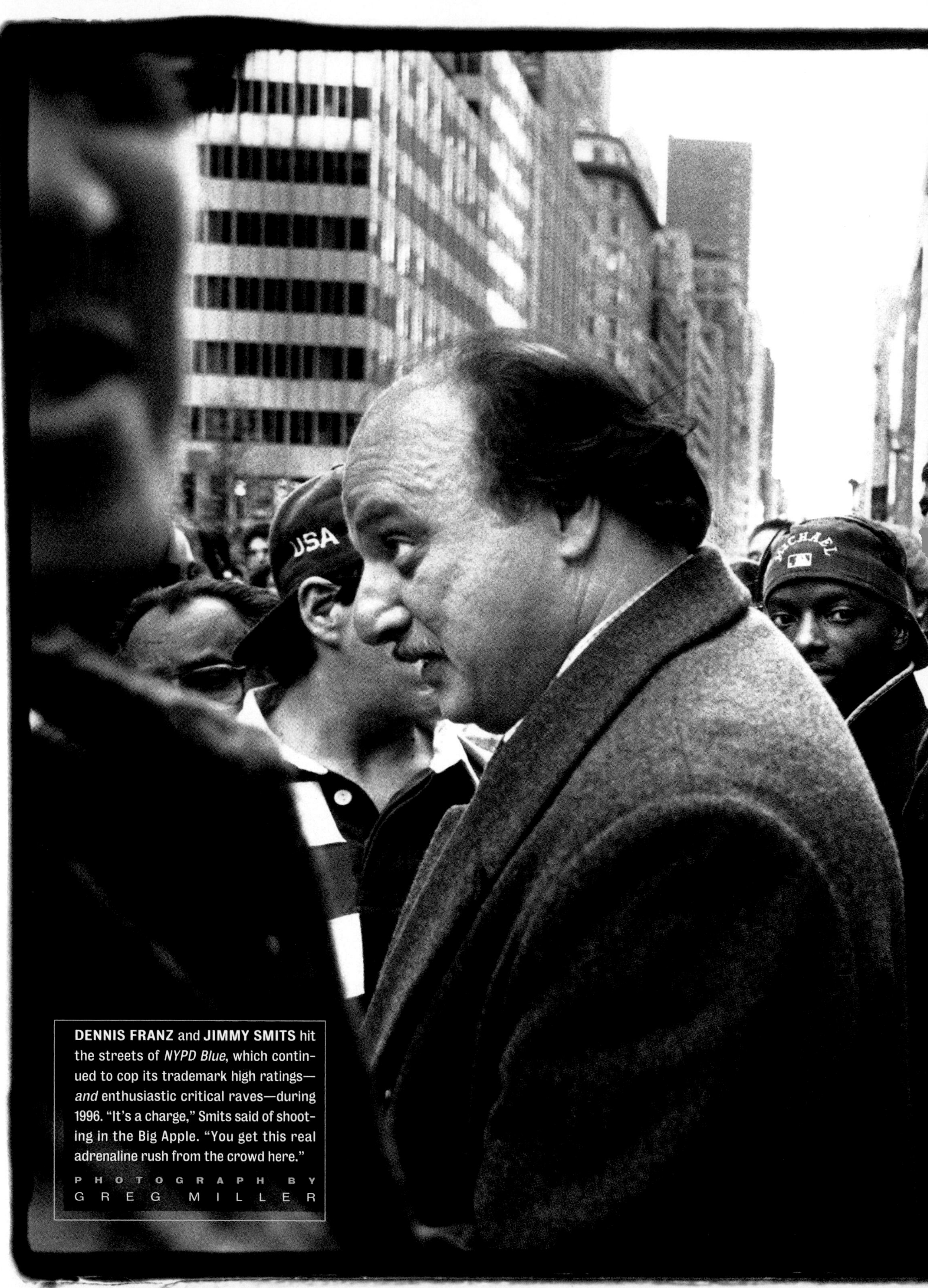

DENNIS FRANZ and **JIMMY SMITS** hit the streets of *NYPD Blue*, which continued to cop its trademark high ratings—*and* enthusiastic critical raves—during 1996. "It's a charge," Smits said of shooting in the Big Apple. "You get this real adrenaline rush from the crowd here."

PHOTOGRAPH BY GREG MILLER

NICOLAS CAGE won an Oscar for his turn as *Leaving Las Vegas'* madcap but suicidal drunk. "He's very sensitive about the perception that he's wacky," said director Mike Figgis, "because his performance isn't that. It's all hard work."

PHOTOGRAPH BY RUVEN AFANADOR

JOAN OSBORNE must have had God on her side in 1996, which saw her cleverly ironic hit "One of Us" lodge itself firmly in the top 10 for a couple of months and the bluesy rocker take home five Grammy nominations—a blessing in itself.

PHOTOGRAPH BY JOSEPH PLUCHINO

HOMEBOYS IN OUTER SPACE hang on the 23rd century set of the fledgling UPN network's first foray into sci-fi comedy. So what do you get when you cross *Star Trek* with *In Living Color*? Say "cheese," everyone.

PHOTOGRAPHS BY DAVID STRICK

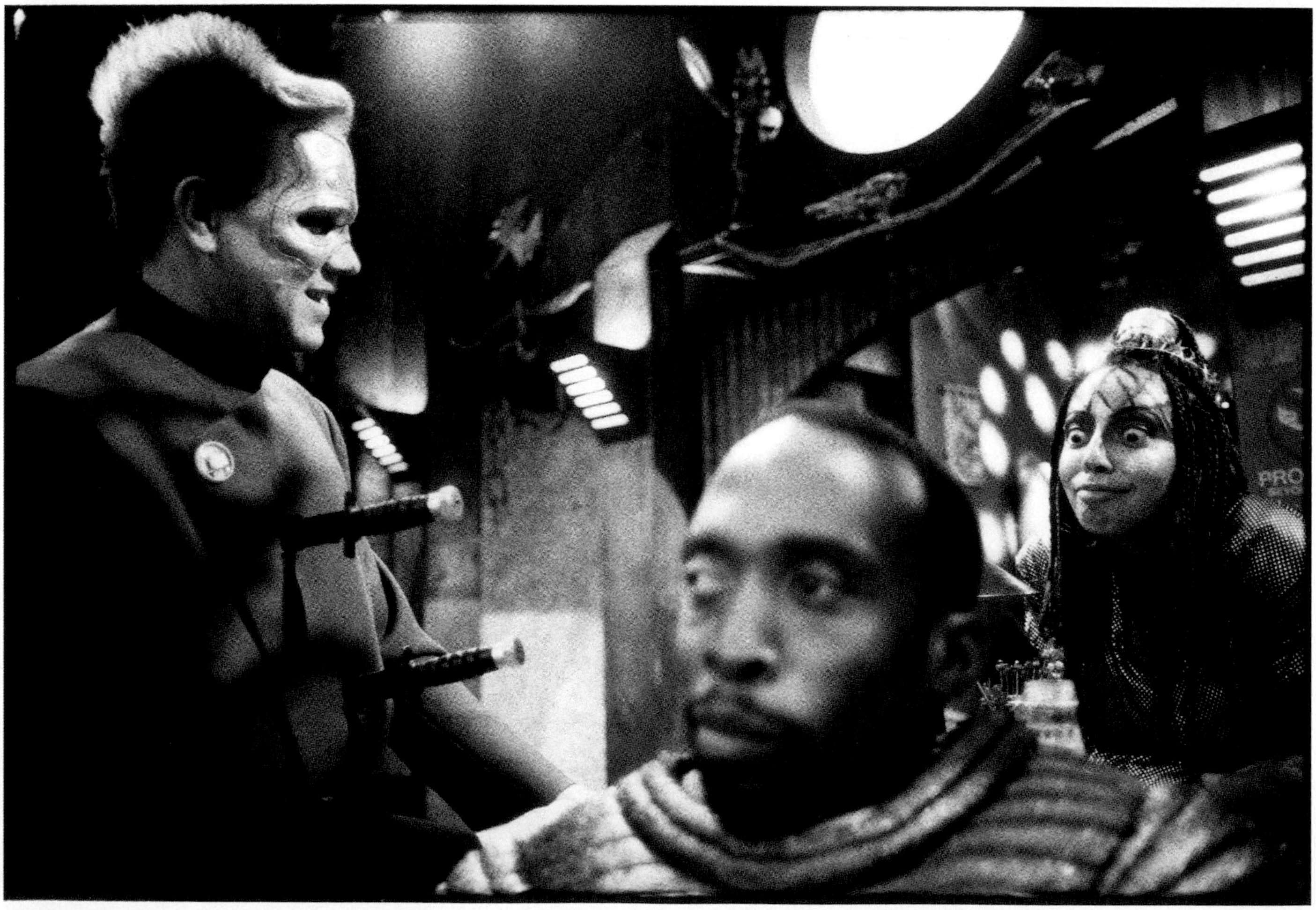

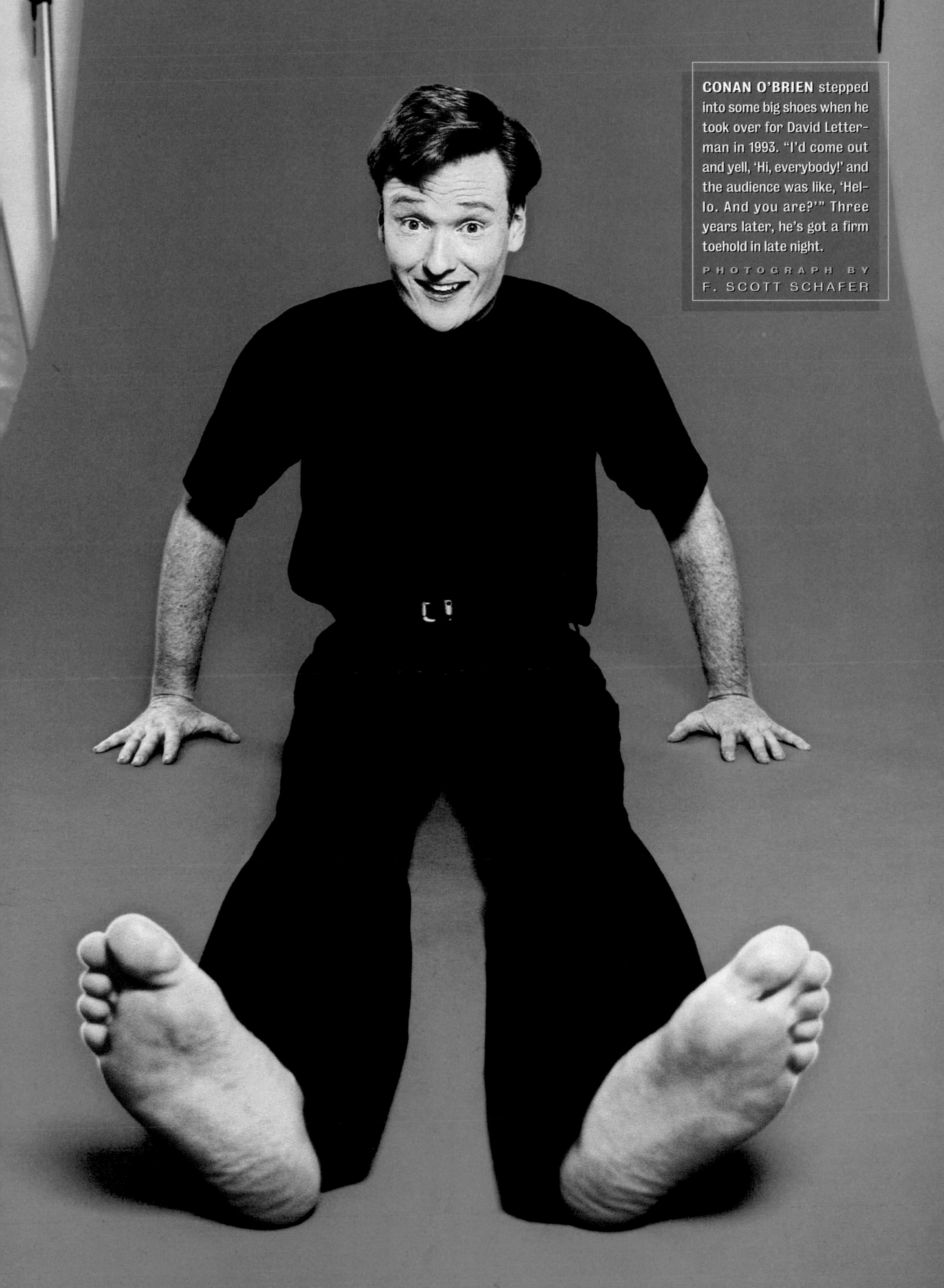

CONAN O'BRIEN stepped into some big shoes when he took over for David Letterman in 1993. "I'd come out and yell, 'Hi, everybody!' and the audience was like, 'Hello. And you are?'" Three years later, he's got a firm toehold in late night.

PHOTOGRAPH BY F. SCOTT SCHAFER

HEATHER MATARAZZO, a poised teen who stretched as a long-suffering geek trying to survive seventh-grade hell in *Welcome to the Dollhouse*, reported that the R-rated film is just "a G-rated version" of what really goes on in junior high.

PHOTOGRAPH BY
JOSEPH PLUCHINO

TERRY McMILLAN came off the success of *Waiting to Exhale*, the movie, with No. 1 best-seller *How Stella Got Her Groove Back*, about a 42-year-old single mom who finds love with a much younger Jamaican cook. (It didn't hurt that she was writing from experience.)

PHOTOGRAPH BY
JEFFERY NEWBURY

RIGHT: OUTLINE

JOI said as a child "I had a big head, and kids called me Tweety bird." But now, with a cut on the *Fled* soundtrack, an upcoming CD, and a spot on the Fishbone tour, the artist, whose daughter was born in June, looks more like the cat than the canary.

PHOTOGRAPH BY CLEO SULLIVAN

GINA GERSHON, who rose from *Show-girls'* ashes as *Bound*'s butch ex-con, said of her love scene with costar Jennifer Tilly: "The only difference with a girl is you talk about the sales at Barneys first."

PHOTOGRAPH BY ROBERT TRACHTENBERG

OUTLINE

GEORGE CLOONEY kept pedal to metal with two films, quick changes from *ER* scrubs to cape and codpiece as the next Batman, and a real-life campaign against the stalkerazzi. What drives him? "I've seen that it *will* go away."

PHOTOGRAPH BY
DAVID JENSEN

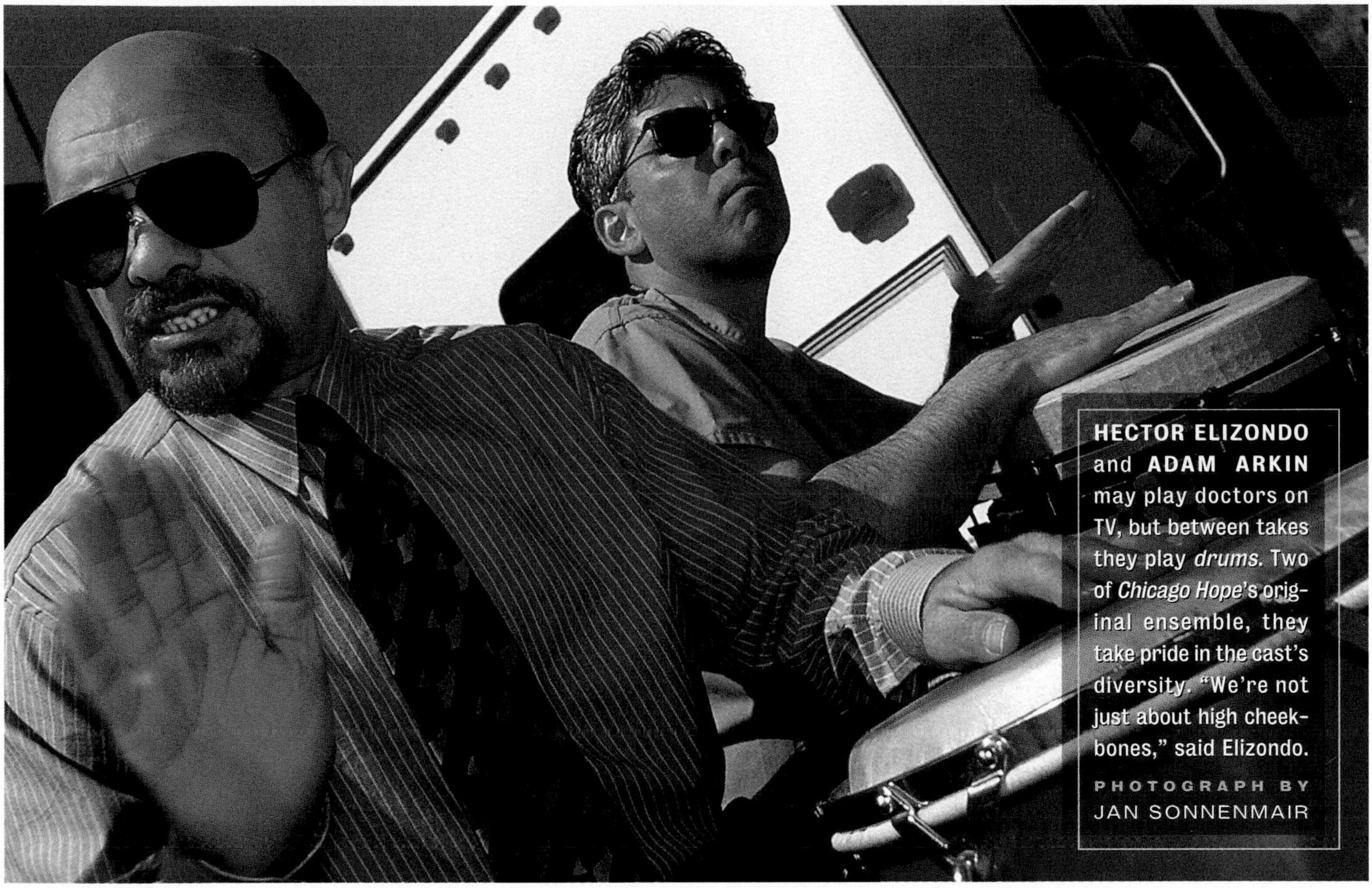

HECTOR ELIZONDO and **ADAM ARKIN** may play doctors on TV, but between takes they play *drums.* Two of *Chicago Hope*'s original ensemble, they take pride in the cast's diversity. "We're not just about high cheekbones," said Elizondo.

PHOTOGRAPH BY JAN SONNENMAIR

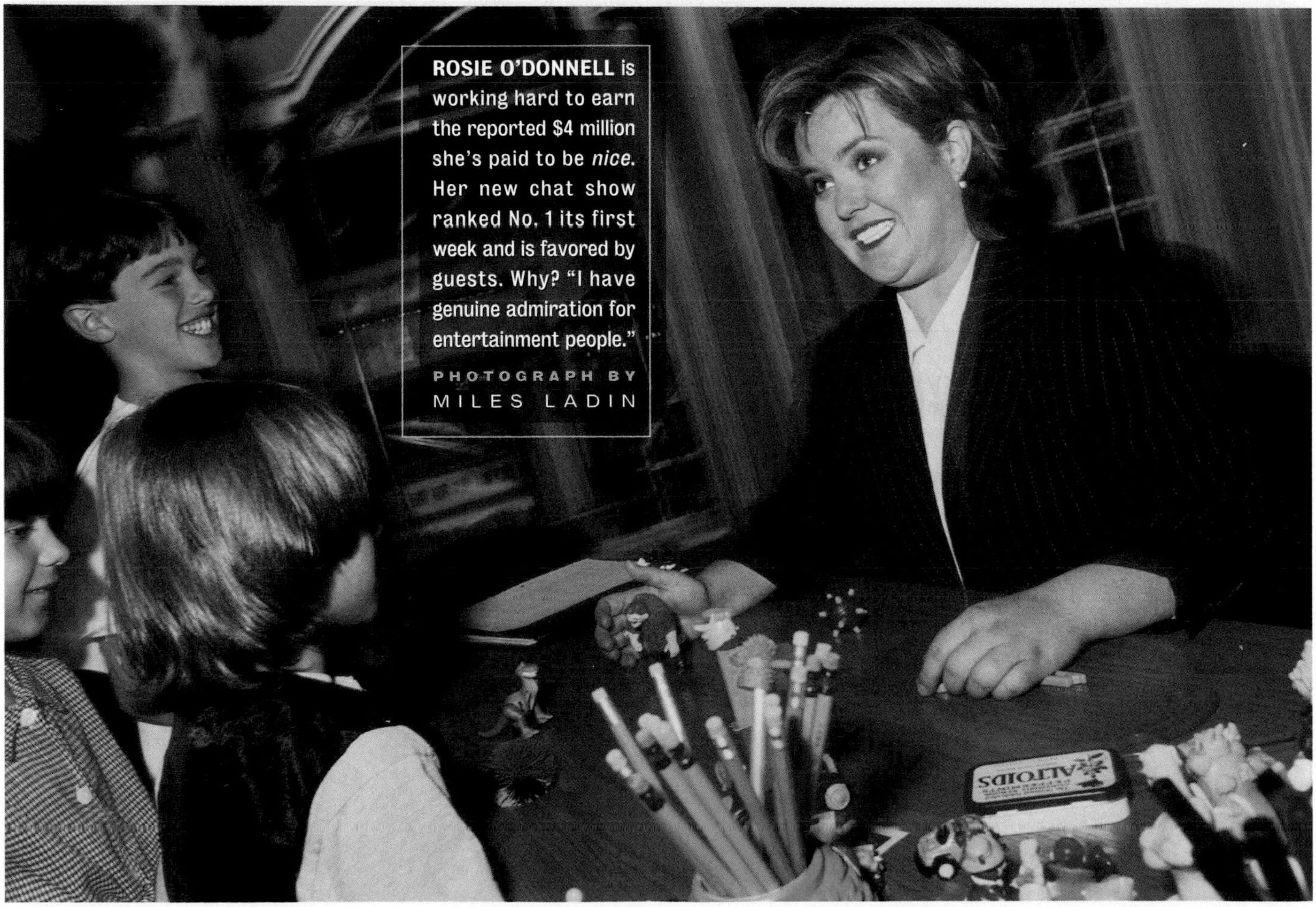

ROSIE O'DONNELL is working hard to earn the reported $4 million she's paid to be *nice*. Her new chat show ranked No. 1 its first week and is favored by guests. Why? "I have genuine admiration for entertainment people."

PHOTOGRAPH BY MILES LADIN

JOHN LITHGOW, known for villains light-years from his *3rd Rock From the Sun* alien, likes his enviable spot in the sitcom universe, where "the jokes bounce back and forth between the brain and the groin, pausing now and then at the heart."

PHOTOGRAPH BY STEPHEN STICKLER

VING RHAMES, of the basso profundo and laser stare, presided over 1994's *Pulp Fiction*, but it was his *Mission: Impossible* cyber-spy that certified his Holly-wood-heavy cred. "I didn't choose acting," said the Juilliard grad. "It chose me."

PHOTOGRAPH BY JEFFREY THURNHER

OUTLINE

LIV TYLER, the 19-year-old ex-model with a rock & roll pedigree, graced Bernardo Bertolucci's *Stealing Beauty* and Tom Hanks' *That Thing You Do!* in '96. "One minute she was a little girl," said Bertolucci, the next, "she was a femme fatale of 25."

PHOTOGRAPH BY JEFFREY THURNHER

OUTLINE

JENNIFER TILLY followed her Oscar-nominated turn as the hardly drab Olive in *Bullets Over Broadway* with *Bound*'s even more colorful and *crafty* moll, Violet. Bucking her sex kitten rep, Tilly said, "I've [never] played anybody as smart as her."

PHOTOGRAPH BY STEPHEN STICKLER

JIMMY SCOTT: With *Heaven*, his aptly named album of spiritual music, a new generation heard the otherworldly voice that made Scott a '50s jazz legend. "This world disappointed me," he said, "but there ain't no disappointment in heaven."

PHOTOGRAPH BY DANNY CLINCH

OUTLINE

CELINE DION didn't take her '96 success (a No. 1 single, "Because You Loved Me," from the top-seller *Falling Into You*) lying down. "I'm not in competition with Mariah, Whitney, or Barbra," said the soprano. "I'm in competition with myself."

PHOTOGRAPH BY SANDRA JOHNSON

RETNA

FRANCES McDORMAND *became* pregnant police chief Marge Gunderson, out to solve a triple homicide in *Fargo*. Off screen, she traded a prime Broadway role to potty-train new son Pedro. As Marge says, "There's more to life." You betcha!

PHOTOGRAPH BY KATRIN THOMAS

NATHAN LANE's regal queen bee rattled Robin Williams in *The Birdcage*, while his solo turn hosting the embattled Tonys—where he won for *A Funny Thing Happened on the Way to the Forum*—firmly landed him in the catbird seat.

PHOTOGRAPH BY RAFAEL FUCHS

JULIANA MARGULIES is sitting pretty with her RN Hathaway having risen from the dead to become the heart of *ER*'s operation and movie offers rolling in. Not that she's ready to give up her day shifts: "I'm holding out for the quality parts."

PHOTOGRAPH BY JON RAGEL

DENZEL WASHINGTON exudes "an extraordinary inner life" for the camera, said his *Courage Under Fire* director Ed Zwick. The actor has said he had no black role models when he began his singular career. Future thespians need look no further.

PHOTOGRAPH BY MICHEL HADDI

SANDRA BULLOCK hasn't much time to kill, but the star, whose *Speed 2* will net her $11 million, savors each minute. On the set of *A Time to Kill*, she recalled urging her cohorts to appreciate their good fortune. "I get all sentimental sometimes."

PHOTOGRAPH BY DAN WINTERS

PHISH: With noodling guitars and lyrics pressing fans to "toss away stuff you don't need in the end/But keep what's important, and know who's your friend," rock's largest living cult band owes more than just a nod to the Grateful Dead.

PHOTOGRAPHS BY
DANNY CLINCH

OUTLINE

SEINFELD: The gang of four pushed humor to the brink with the full-body dry heave, proof that abstinence makes one either *very* smart or *very* stupid, and death by cheap glue. No looking back for them—except maybe in everlasting syndication.

PHOTOGRAPH BY DAN WINTERS

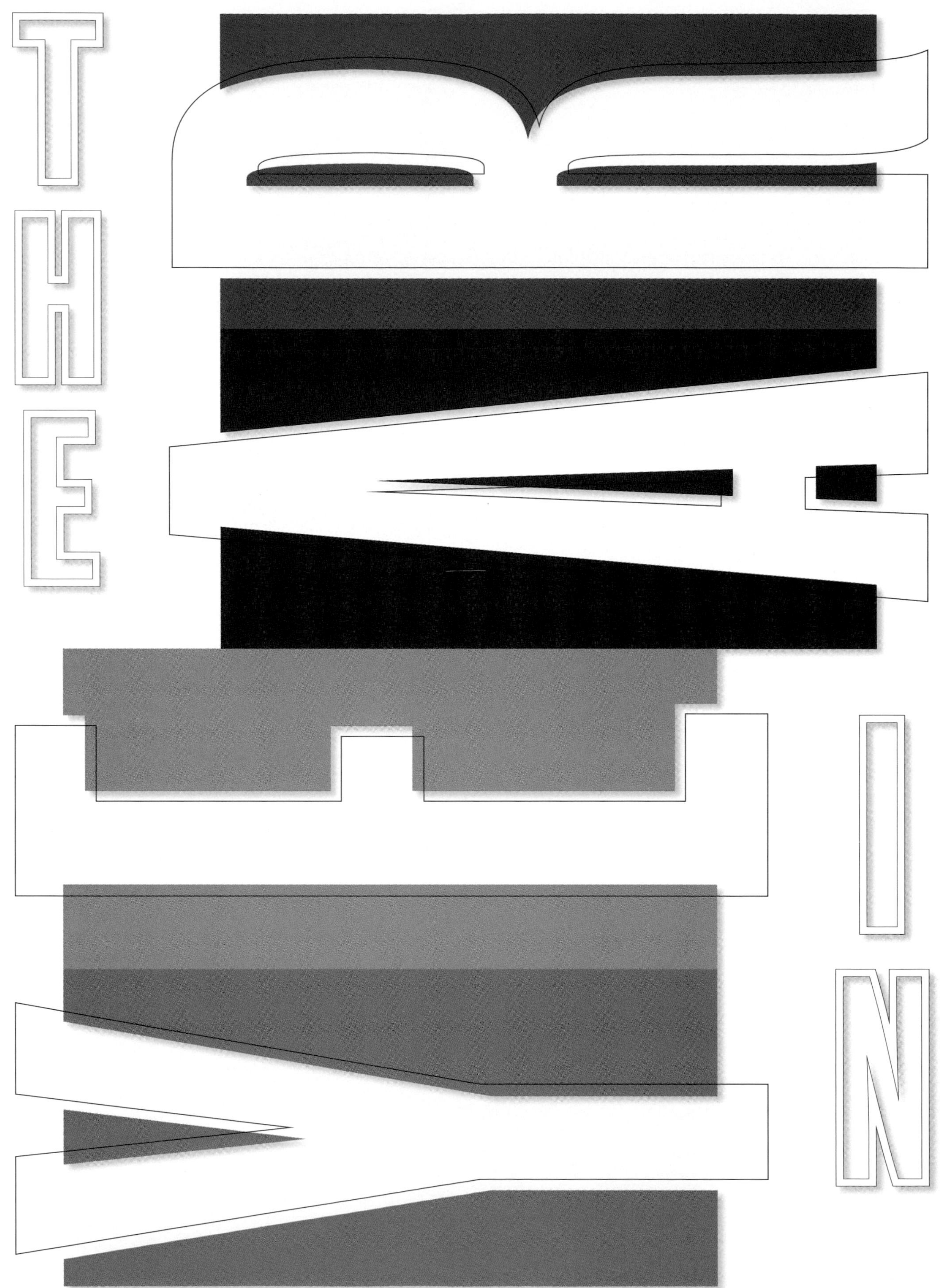
THE
YEAR
IN

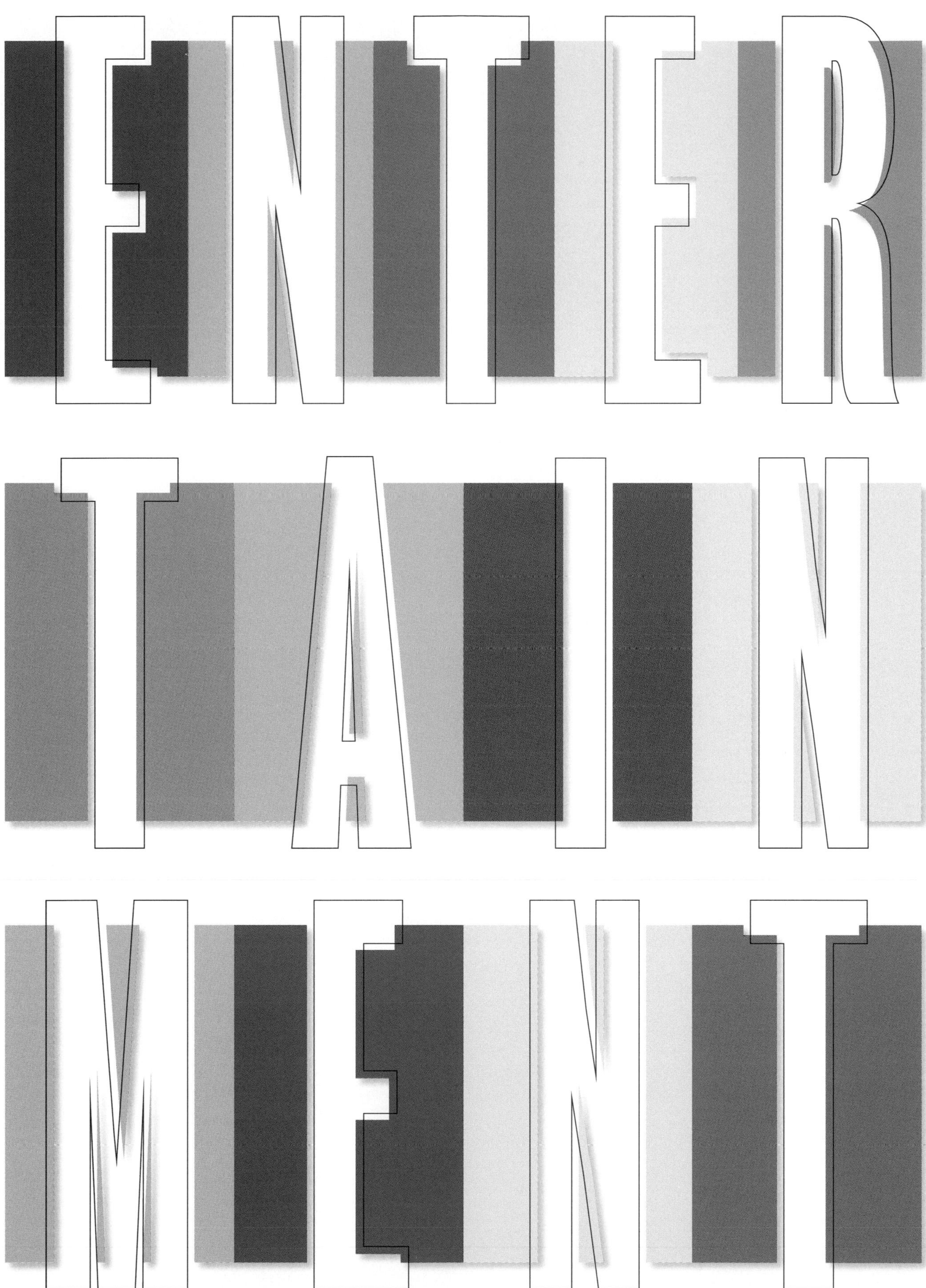
ENTER
TAIN
MENT

Super Bowling For Dollars

WHO WON Super Bowl XXX, the Cowboys or the Steelers? Better question: Who cares? It was what aired afterward that kept us glued to the set, when NBC ran a one-hour show featuring the sexy *Friends* sextet. Packed with stars—Julia Roberts, Brooke Shields, Jean-Claude Van Damme, and Chris Isaak—Super *Friends* drew 52.9 million viewers, making it TV's highest-rated series episode since *Cheers'* 1993 finale. The twentysomethings even ruled commercial breaks, wrapping a three-week Diet Coke ad blitz (theme: Which Friend drank the stolen soda?).

The Buddy Bowl buzz lasted longer than your average caffeine jolt. Shields' surprising comedic debut won her the NBC sitcom *Suddenly Susan* (at press time, TV's No. 3 series). Though Roberts didn't reap any extra box office heat (February's *Mary Reilly* grossed only $6 million), she found (fleeting) love with Friend Matthew Perry. The series finished its second season as TV's second-highest-charting sitcom, fueling Warner Bros.' $4 million-plus-per-episode syndication deal. But continued hawking of the franchise begat a July backlash, when all six stars demanded and got roughly $75,000 per episode for their third season. And though the show remains a Nielsen gem, ratings have dipped nearly 15 percent this season. Hmmm...maybe you *can* have too many Friends after all. —*Dan Snierson*

I Want to Sell You

THE GLOVES didn't fit, the jury voted to acquit, and on Jan. 24, 1996, O.J. Simpson went on Black Entertainment Television for an hour-long chat about his "grueling ordeal." Pleading he was prohibited from answering questions about the case by the contract for his new video *O.J. Tells* (*not* his lawyers, who'd insisted he back out of his post-verdict interview with NBC), Simpson urged viewers to ▶

MUST-SEE BET: O.J. won high ratings

Lisa to Jacko: 'Beat It'

WE WERE shocked—*shocked!*—to learn that Michael Jackson and Lisa Marie Presley's connubial bliss had come to an untimely end when Mrs. Jacko filed for divorce Jan. 18, citing irreconcilable differences. "It's going to be a very simple, clean divorce," said her lawyer, dashing hopes we might see the couple on Court TV battling over Bubbles' bones or Elvis' movie residuals. Rarely one to be seen sulking, a grinning Jackson was off globe-trotting in search of more kiddie-packed photo ops. His soon-to-be ex, who'd recently taunted cynics to "eat it," also stayed mum, though a *Vogue* fashion spread highlighted her Perma-bond pout, which may have been a telling mood signifier—or just genetic. —*Chris Willman*

WINNER

WOMEN IN ROCK

Sisters were doin' it at the Grammys—Alanis Morissette and Mariah Carey snagged six noms each, Joan Osborne five—and on *Billboard*'s charts, where divas dominated the top three with the *Waiting to Exhale* soundtrack, Mariah's *Daydream*, and Alanis' *Jagged Little Pill.*

LOSER

MADONNA

Not usually one to shy away from an open mike or a dishy public appearance, the recalcitrant plaintiff was ordered under threat of arrest by a fed-up L.A. judge to testify against her stalker Robert Dewey Hoskins, who was convicted and is now appealing.

buy the $29.95 tape for the truth. The program rated about 10 times higher than BET's average, a success the cable network hopes to repeat when the Simpson civil trial finishes. "We will certainly request another interview," says Jefferi Lee, BET's president. "The story in black America is much larger than guilt or innocence. There's a system on trial." *—Kristen Baldwin*

HITS

MOVIES *12 Monkeys*
TV *3rd Rock From the Sun* debut (NBC)
BOOKS Dean Koontz's *Intensity*
MUSIC *Waiting to Exhale* soundtrack
VIDEO *The Indian in the Cupboard*
MULTIMEDIA *The 11th Hour* CD-ROM

MISSES

Sandra Bullock's *Two If By Sea* (Warner Bros.) ◆ *Champs* debut (ABC) ◆ Linda Davies' *Wilderness of Mirrors* (Doubleday) ◆ Linda Fiorentino's *Jade* (Paramount)

MONITOR

BIRTHS A daughter, Caroline, was born to *Today*'s Katie Couric, 39, and husband Jay Monahan, 40, Jan. 5.... Jasmine Page, to Martin Lawrence, 30, and wife Patricia, 25, Jan. 15.
RESCUES After a campaign to rescue him from a cramped tank in Mexico, the ailing *Free Willy* star, Keiko, was overnighted via UPS to a spacious new home in the Oregon Coast Aquarium on Jan. 7.... *Chicago Hope*-ful Mark Harmon, 42, pulled a teen from a burning Jeep that crashed into a gate outside his Brentwood home on Jan. 3.
AXED TV took out the trash as daytime talkers Gabrielle Carteris, Danny Bonaduce, and Charles Perez got the hook.
BIKINI BRIEF Breaking a hallowed tradition of unveiling its swimsuit issue on TV, SPORTS ILLUSTRATED gave cybergawkers at Time Warner's website first peek, Jan. 22.
HUBBUB Random House published Anonymous' thinly veiled roman à campaign, *Primary Colors*, on Jan. 22, igniting a Beltway version of Clue: Which Clinton insider committed the breach? Dee Dee Myers in the briefing room, George Stephanopoulos in the Oval Office, Mark Miller in the newsroom, James Carville in the war room—or Bob Woodward in the garage with *The Washington Post*?

EVENTS At Sundance, *Welcome to the Dollhouse* took the Grand Jury Prize, and *Shine* sparked a very public bidding war—Miramax cochair Harvey Weinstein was bounced from Mercato Mediterraneo, a Park City, Utah, eatery, for cursing the movie's rep, who'd closed a deal with Fine Line.
FEUDS Ending a quest to headline the big-screen *Evita*, Madonna arrived in Buenos Aires on Jan. 20 for filming to a less-than-stellar welcome. Locals expressed themselves with graffiti—"*Viva Evita! Fuera Madonna!*"—and a former Perón aide threatened to kill her.
DEALS Inking a reported $80 million, four-album deal with Virgin Records, Janet Jackson, 29, bested her bro *and* Madonna as music's highest-paid performer.
—Jason Cochran

FEBRUARY

Clooney Steps Up to Bat

DR. FEELGOOD: *ER* hunk trades scrubs for cowl

HOLY EKG! How did *ER* heartthrob George Clooney—with nary a box office hit to his name—wind up playing Bruce Wayne in *Batman & Robin*, the fourth movie in Warner Bros.' main-artery franchise?

Two words: team playing. As director Joel Schumacher has since attested, the rubber suit's previous occupant, Val Kilmer, behaved like a very dark knight indeed while making 1995's *Batman Forever*. So Warner released Kilmer when conflicts arose with his shooting schedule for Paramount's *The Saint*—ironically, a title role Clooney had lobbied to play. "I loved that Phillip Noyce [*Clear and Present Danger*] was directing," Clooney told EW last January. "But that wasn't a project they were going to give me."

At least not back in the fall of 1995, before his Very Special storm-drain rescue on *ER* won huge ratings and, later on, several Emmy nominations. That November-sweeps episode, along with early buzz on *From Dusk Till Dawn* (which went on to okay box office business), helped Clooney land the action lead in DreamWorks SKG's Fall '97 release *The Peacemaker*. With more movie offers rolling in, Warner brass, whose TV division produces *ER*, made the bold casting move—one that would keep their hardworking star happy, and on the lot, since *Batman & Robin* was to shoot a few soundstages away from the *ER* sets.

With tens of millions riding on his next two films, is Clooney sweating bat bullets? As he put it to EW, "If the series goes away and the films flop, I've reached a point in my career where I could live off dinner theater for the rest of my life. That is a great place to be." —*Steve Daly*

DOWN BY LAW: *Murder One* was a ratings no-show

Swept Away at ABC

FOR THE precariously perched ABC, the February sweeps wrought an alien invasion of the worst kind. Proving one person's junk is another's treasure, NBC turned its rival's reject about goofy aliens starring John Lithgow into the mid-season's only new hit. While the Peacock landed in first place with the top five series (including *ER* and *Seinfeld*) and an adaptation of *Gulliver's Travels*, ABC's aging slate—orbiting at No. 1 the year before—ran out of gas while its rookies (*Hudson Street*, *Murder One*, *High Incident*, *Second Noah*) never revved up. ABC crashed at No. 3, even losing to CBS. Call it *Whacked by an Angel*. —*DS*

WINNER

JACKIE CHAN

The Hong Kong chop-socky sensation finally kicked his way to U.S. box office stardom when New Line's *Rumble in the Bronx* opened at No. 1 with $10 million. Quite a leap from his lackluster U.S. debut in 1980's *The Big Brawl*.

LOSER

ANNA NICOLE SMITH

Reports surface that the not-so-merry widow had declared bankruptcy to scrape up the hefty legal fees to battle the family of her late hubby, J. Howard Marshall II, over his $500 million fortune.

Not-So-Fine Romance

FOR A FEW days in a New York courtroom, the drama and camp of *Dynasty* gripped audiences again, as a teary Joan Collins, in high dudgeon over a blow to her literary integrity, fought to keep the $1.3 million that publishing giant Random House paid her in 1990. As an advance on a $4 million, two-book deal inked at the height of her fame, the sum befit the pop-culture pull of the star, who already had one novel and an autobiography to her name. But seven years after *Dynasty* ended, testimony from editors—who branded Collins' submissions, *Hell Hath No Fury* and *The Ruling Passion*, "unprintable"—suggested the queen of primetime mean had lost some of her bite, and, perhaps, her way with words. Still, the jury sided with Collins, stating her contract required "complete," not "acceptable," manuscripts. At press time things were continuing to look up for the author. Random House dropped an appeal to the court's decision, and Joseph Pittman, editor of Collins' *Infamous*, an April '96 Dutton reprint of a British novel released in '95, is keeping an open mind: "If she writes more fiction, we'll certainly consider it." —*Alexandra Jacobs*

WRITER IN THE STORM: Collins

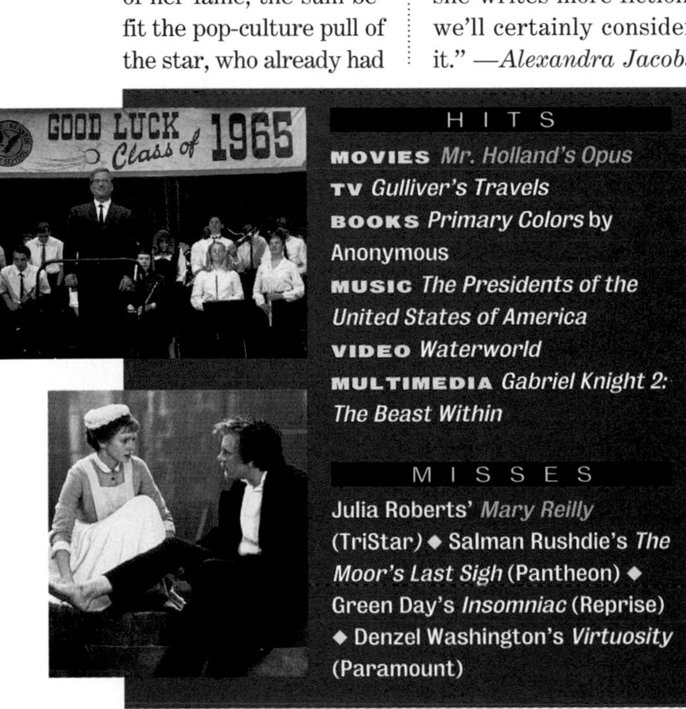

HITS

MOVIES *Mr. Holland's Opus*
TV *Gulliver's Travels*
BOOKS *Primary Colors* by Anonymous
MUSIC *The Presidents of the United States of America*
VIDEO *Waterworld*
MULTIMEDIA *Gabriel Knight 2: The Beast Within*

MISSES

Julia Roberts' *Mary Reilly* (TriStar) ◆ Salman Rushdie's *The Moor's Last Sigh* (Pantheon) ◆ Green Day's *Insomniac* (Reprise) ◆ Denzel Washington's *Virtuosity* (Paramount)

MONITOR

MARRIAGES ⚥, 37, wedded one of his dancers, Mayte Garcia, 22, on Valentine's Day.
SPLITS Elizabeth Taylor, 63, filed for divorce from Larry Fortensky, 44, on Feb. 5.... Halle Berry, 27, and Atlanta Brave David Justice, 29, filed for divorce on Feb. 25.
ACQUITTALS An L.A. judge cleared Snoop Doggy Dogg, 24, and his former bodyguard on Feb. 20 in the '93 death of a man shot by a passenger in the Jeep the rapper was driving. Snoop was acquitted of manslaughter in March.
ARRESTS Former Milli (or Vanilli) Rob Pilatus, 31, was caught by L.A. police on Feb. 4, after breaking in to a car, then verbally assaulting the resident of a neighboring house (this time with his own voice). He pleaded no contest and was sentenced to three months in jail and rehab.
HUBBUB On Feb. 19, 32-year-old Pulp lead singer Jarvis Cocker stormed the stage in protest during Michael Jackson's performance at the Brit Awards. "Jackson sees himself as some Christlike figure," he later explained. "The music industry allows him to indulge his fantasies because of his wealth and power."

DOGG HAD HIS DAY: A proud Snoop with his pup

DEALS Christopher Reeve snagged $3 million to write his memoirs for Random House.... On Feb. 8, director Mike Nichols bought the movie rights to *Primary Colors* from "Anonymous" for a reported $1.5 million.... Shortly after recording "One Sweet Day" with Mariah Carey (wife of Sony Music president Thomas Mottola), Boyz II Men announced on Feb. 13 that though they'd stick with Motown Records, they would begin producing on their own label, Stonecreek Recordings, for Sony.... On Feb. 21, MCA paid $200 million for half of the Interscope Records division Time Warner dropped in 1995 after its gangsta acts, including Tupac Shakur, Dr. Dre, and Snoop Doggy Dogg, drew fire.
KNOCKOUT NBC's Feb. 4 *Gulliver's Travels*, with Ted Danson, 48, and Mary Steenburgen, 42, drew more viewers than CBS and ABC combined from 9 to 11 p.m. in 32 metered markets. —*JC*

MARCH

Oscar Mild

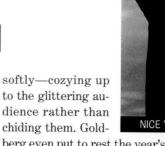

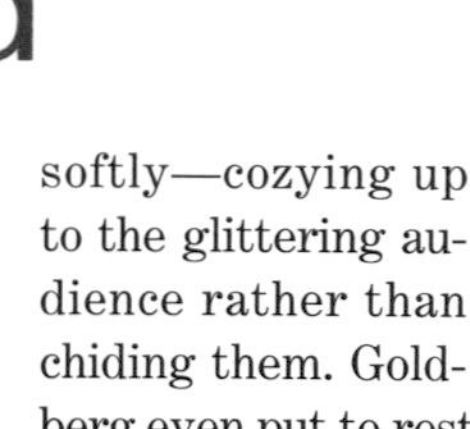

NICE 'N' EASY: Goldberg jabbed gently

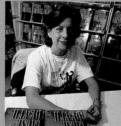

BEAR IN MIND that in the preceding year David Letterman had hosted the Oscars and subsequently admitted freely that he'd screwed up royally. So when Whoopi Goldberg took the stage at the Dorothy Chandler Pavilion to host the 68th Annual Academy Awards, she went softly—cozying up to the glittering audience rather than chiding them. Goldberg even put to rest the year's incipient controversy—a feeling that blacks were underrepresented among the nominees—when she made deflating jokes about the Rev. Jesse Jackson's Oscar boycott.

This was a broadcast that accepted genuine emotions, a shrewd Academy Awards telecast rather than the traditional merely crass one. For many, the most moving moments were Christopher Reeve's appearance and Kirk Douglas' heroic acceptance of a Lifetime Achievement award in the wake of a stroke. Oh, yeah: Big winner? *Braveheart*. Big loser? *Babe*. Best acceptance speech? Kevin Spacey, best supporting actor for *The Usual Suspects*, who saluted his sobbing mother with eloquence and sweet humor. Best-rewarded actor? Tom Hanks, who snared his third Oscar in three years for his voice work on *Toy Story*. —*Ken Tucker*

BRAVE HEART: Tears outnumbered sequins when Reeve spoke at the Oscars

WINNER

PATRICIA CORNWELL

The best-selling mystery writer cashed in with a $24 million, three-book deal with Putnam. Happily, Jim Carrey didn't seize the opportunity to up *his* asking price.

LOSERS

GEORGE WENDT & JOHN RATZENBERGER

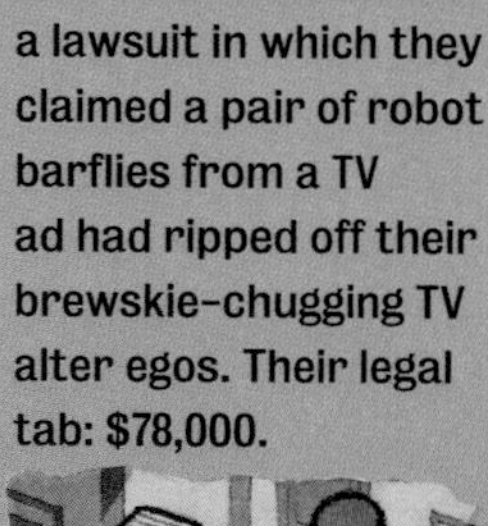

The *Cheers* alums lost a lawsuit in which they claimed a pair of robot barflies from a TV ad had ripped off their brewskie-chugging TV alter egos. Their legal tab: $78,000.

The Axeman Cometh

WHEN BASEBALL teams slump, they fire the manager. When late-night talk shows slump, they fire the executive producer. So on March 11, after a yearlong ratings slide, David Letterman axed Robert "Morty" Morton, his coworker for 14 years, since the early days of his late-night show. Using a bizarre metaphor, Dave likened the event to an infected limb that "had to come off." But *Late Show*'s emergency surgery—a new executive producer (ex–head writer Rob Burnett) and a flashy new set were brought in—hasn't reversed its fortunes. Morty, meanwhile, landed a rich production deal with ABC, where his squeeze, Jamie Tarses, is entertainment president. It remains to be seen who'll have the last laugh. —*Bruce Fretts*

BATTERY NOT INCLUDED: Baldwin won his anti-stalkerazzi case, hands down

Photo Finisher

TEAM STALKERAZZI took a big hit from Team Celebrity when Alec Baldwin was acquitted on March 22 of one count of battery brought by photographer Alan Zanger. Zanger filed the suit after the actor struck the photographer when he tried to capture shots of Baldwin, wife Kim Basinger, and their newborn daughter, Ireland. Baldwin gave persuasive testimony in court, saying "anyone with a shred of human decency would understand there are times in your life when you want your privacy respected." But with price tags in the hundreds of thousands of dollars for single shots of hot stars, respect and privacy aren't factors in *this* business. —*Jessica Shaw*

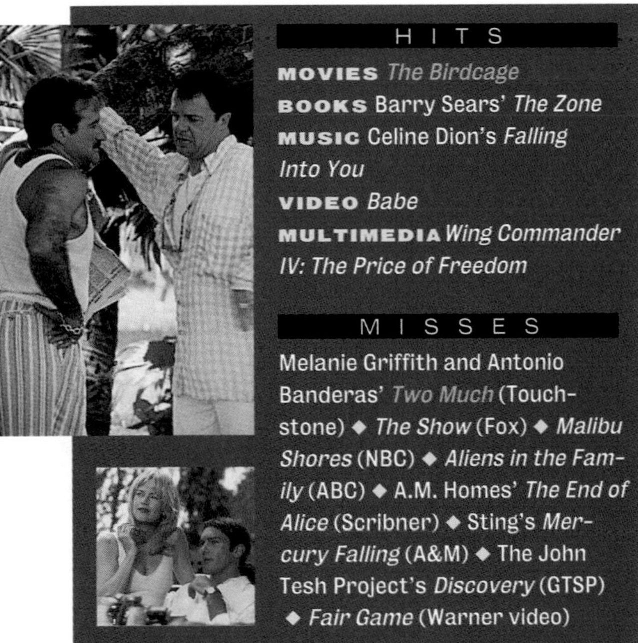

HITS

MOVIES *The Birdcage*
BOOKS Barry Sears' *The Zone*
MUSIC Celine Dion's *Falling Into You*
VIDEO *Babe*
MULTIMEDIA *Wing Commander IV: The Price of Freedom*

MISSES

Melanie Griffith and Antonio Banderas' *Two Much* (Touchstone) ◆ *The Show* (Fox) ◆ *Malibu Shores* (NBC) ◆ *Aliens in the Family* (ABC) ◆ A.M. Homes' *The End of Alice* (Scribner) ◆ Sting's *Mercury Falling* (A&M) ◆ The John Tesh Project's *Discovery* (GTSP) ◆ *Fair Game* (Warner video)

MONITOR

MARRIAGES A fistful of rice: Clint Eastwood, 65, wed California TV anchor Dina Ruiz, 30, on March 31. **ENGAGEMENTS** Brooke Shields, 30, and Andre Agassi, 25, made a love match after a two-year-plus courtship. **BIRTHS** A bald, bouncing baby girl, Brigidine Roisin Waters, was born to singer Sinéad O'Connor, 28, in early March.... Katey Sagal, 40, *Married...With Children*'s Peg Bundy, and husband Jack White welcomed Jackson James on March 1. **ADOPTIONS** Six pack: Steven Spielberg, 49, and Kate Capshaw, 42, added Mikaela George, born Feb. 28, to the fold.... Thomas Haden, the second adoptive child of Jamie Lee Curtis, 37, and Christopher Guest, 48, was born March 13. **DEBUTS** Model twins activate! Amber Valletta and Shalom Harlow, both 22, took over MTV's *House of Style* on March 11.... The Bubba Gump Shrimp Co. restaurant, inspired by the Oscar-winning *Forrest Gump*, opened in Monterey, Calif., on March 29. **EXITS** On March 26, CBS announced the end, after 12 seasons and 11 Emmy nominations, of *Murder, She Wrote*, starring Angela Lansbury, 70.... Phil Collins, 45, called it quits with Genesis after 25 years. —*JC*

CRUISE PATROL

Va Va Va Vroom

IN SANTA MONICA, Calif., on March 4, Tom Cruise, 33, stopped at the scene of a car accident, waited for EMS with an injured pedestrian, and paid her nearly $7,000 medical bill.

PAMELAPALOOZA

No Nudes Is Good News

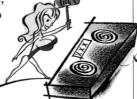

ON MARCH 29, Pamela Lee, 28, and husband Tommy Lee, 33, filed a $10 million suit to try to stop *Penthouse* from printing stills from a homemade sex video stolen from their Malibu love nest. The suit failed.

APRIL

'Rent' Strikes

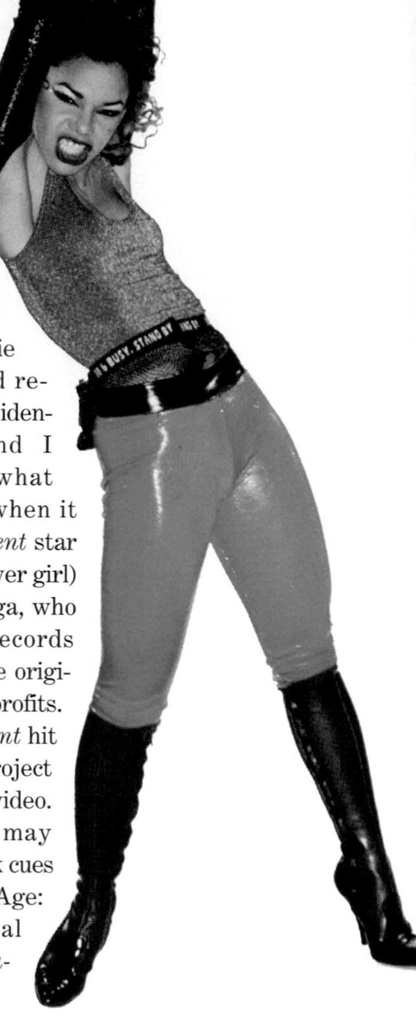

IT ALL HAPPENED fast. First, on Jan. 25, 35-year-old composer Jonathan Larson died of an aortic aneurysm. The next day, *Rent*, his edgy poperetta based on *La Bohème*, debuted Off Broadway. Then came the gushing reviews, the buzz, the April Broadway transfer. Before anyone knew what had happened, *Rent* was the hottest ticket in America. On the backstage walls of the Nederlander Theatre, *Rent*'s celebrity graffiti accumulated faster than its raves ("You are all amazing!" Lauren Bacall scribbled). While tap scion Savion Glover pounded Broadway into the Urban Age on April 25 with *Bring in 'Da Noise, Bring in 'Da Funk*, *Rent* led the way with prizes: the Tony, an Obie, the Pulitzer. DreamWorks recorded a cast album, Bloomingdale's rushed out a line of *Rent*-inspired thrift-shop-like fashions, and Miramax inked a reported $2.5–5 million movie deal. Musicals had returned. "People can identify with it, and I suppose that's what *Oklahoma!* did when it came out," says *Rent* star (and *Newsweek* cover girl) Daphne Rubin-Vega, who got a Mercury Records deal and, like all the original cast, a cut of the show's profits. Just a few months after *Rent* hit Broadway, Larson's final project came out: a cowritten kids' video. Its title, *Away We Go!*, may seem trivial, but Larson took cues from the musical's Golden Age: That was also the original name of a show called *Oklahoma!* —*J. Cochran*

WINNER

JANEANE GAROFALO

The self-deprecating Gen-X comedian scored with grade-A cameos on *Ellen* and *Dr. Katz*, and blossomed into an alternative big-screen sex symbol in *The Truth About Cats & Dogs*.

LOSER

MARLON BRANDO

The kissin' bandit put his foot in his mouth with an anti-Semitic rant on *Larry King Live*, saying Hollywood "is run by Jews"—that's why we don't see Jewish stereotypes in film. What a meshuggener.

The Comeback Kidder

ON APRIL 24, *Superman* star (and manic-depressive) Margot Kidder, 47, was found cowering in a Glendale, Calif., backyard, sparking tabloid stories and messages of support from the likes of screen beau Christopher Reeve. Within a week, Broadway producer David Merrick announced he wanted Kidder for the lead in his play *Stieglitz & O'Keeffe*. By September she seemed on the road to recovery, with an appearance on Barbara Walters' *20/20* and a guest spot on *Boston Common*. But despite her good fortune, even Kidder's most sincere well-wishers had to wonder: Did their Lois Lane have to fall this far to rise again? —*Dave Karger*

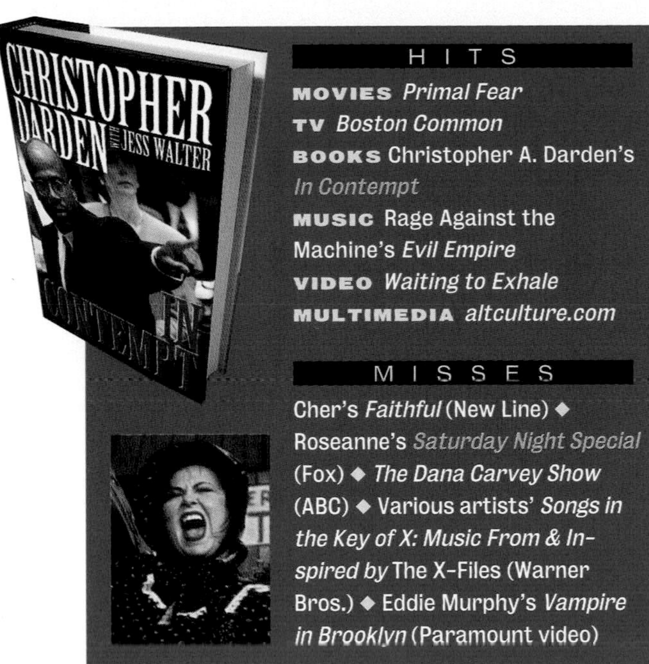

HITS

MOVIES *Primal Fear*
TV *Boston Common*
BOOKS Christopher A. Darden's *In Contempt*
MUSIC Rage Against the Machine's *Evil Empire*
VIDEO *Waiting to Exhale*
MULTIMEDIA *altculture.com*

MISSES

Cher's *Faithful* (New Line) ◆ Roseanne's *Saturday Night Special* (Fox) ◆ *The Dana Carvey Show* (ABC) ◆ Various artists' *Songs in the Key of X: Music From & Inspired by* The X-Files (Warner Bros.) ◆ Eddie Murphy's *Vampire in Brooklyn* (Paramount video)

Outrageous Fortunes

THE GREAT Jackie O. auction of 1996 whetted national taste buds for even the merest morsel of Camelot. From April 23 to 26, prices for House of Kennedy tchotchkes like golf clubs (sold to Arnold Schwarzenegger for $772,500) and frayed throw pillows (three for $25,300) flew to the moon and back. The media, alternately enthralled and appalled, went into a frenzy too: The sale scored the cover of TIME and two full editions of *Larry King Live*, and filled pages of the New York City tabloids for days running. But after the bidding bacchanalia ended, the feeling quickly crept in that the rush to sell and buy a piece of Onassis' sphinxlike aura had cheapened both us and her. —*Degen Pener*

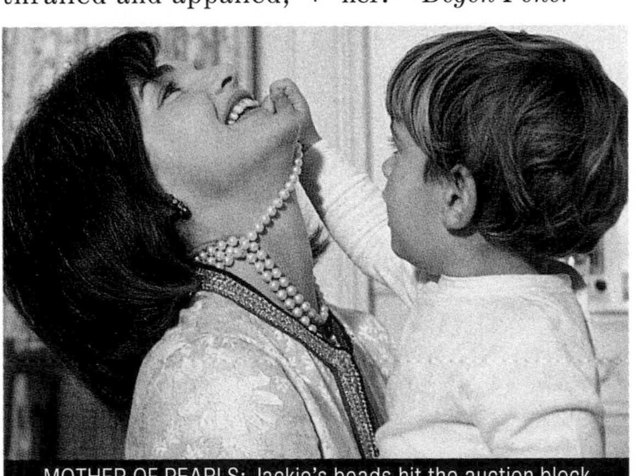

MOTHER OF PEARLS: Jackie's beads hit the auction block

MONITOR

MARRIAGES Dennis Hopper, 59, took his fifth trip down the aisle, with actress Victoria Duffy, 29, April 12.... After eight years and two kids, Robin Wright, 29, and Sean Penn, 35, finally made it legal on April 27.

ENGAGEMENTS Widower Hume Cronyn, 84, popped the question to children's book writer Susan Cooper, 60.

MAMMA MIA! Leon, Madonna

EXPECTING Madonna, 37, announced she was with child, due in October. The proud papa-to-be: her boyfriend of 18 months, personal trainer Carlos Leon, 29.

DEALS The future's Rosie: Warner Books ponied up more than $3 million to comedian Rosie O'Donnell, 34, for her memoirs.

SHAME Probably wanting to be home alone, Macaulay Culkin, 15, dialed 911 to file a harassment report after dad Kit slapped him for not cleaning his room.

RESCUES Christian Slater, 26, fled an April 14 fire at a friend's home carrying two mutts to safety.

REHAB On April 24, Stone Temple Pilots canceled a trio of free shows. Five days later, lead singer Scott Weiland, 28, checked in to a treatment facility for heroin and cocaine addiction.

FEUDS On April 5, illusionist David Copperfield, 38, sued Butterfield & Butterfield and Batmobile owner Michael Eisenberg, complaining the car he'd bought at auction for $189,500 was a promotional vehicle and not the one used in 1989's *Batman*. On April 8, Eisenberg countersued to force Copperfield to pay up anyway. —*JC*

WOODY WATCH

Pulp Friction

WOODY HARRELSON, 34, withheld $10,000 in taxes as a protest against the government's recently overturned logging ban. The flora- and fauna-loving actor was incensed by his belief that tax dollars are being used "to desecrate nature."

MAY

Kathie Lee Plays Bawl

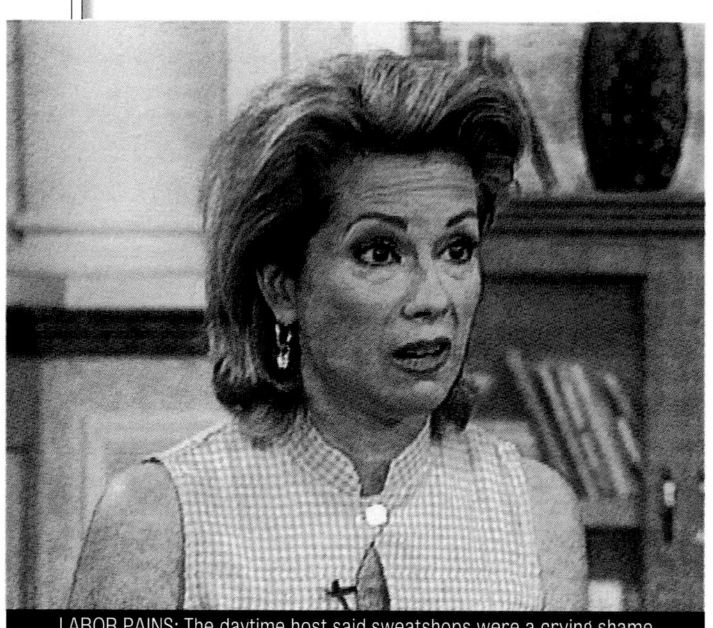

LABOR PAINS: The daytime host said sweatshops were a crying shame

DON'T CRY for me, Kathie Lee Gifford said in so many words: I can do it myself. It was that kind of *annus horribilis* for the doyenne of daytime. On May 1, Gifford appeared on *Live With Regis & Kathie Lee*, quivering with tears of indignation. The National Labor Committee had loudly announced that her down-market clothing line was once stitched by Honduran children toiling for 31 cents per hour. "You can say I'm ugly, you can say I'm not talented," she whimpered. "But when you say I don't care about children...how dare you?"

They dared. Three weeks later, the story broke that Gifford's budget togs were also being sewn in a sweatshop in Manhattan's garment district, albeit by adults. This time Gifford skipped the tears, hired a pricey flack, and dispatched good-guy husband Frank to the factory to hand out $300 apiece to the nonplussed workers.

But the saga may have a sweeter ending than even Gifford's Christmas specials. Joining forces with Labor Secretary Robert Reich, Gifford began a crusade against sweatshops the world over. It's enough to make you promise you'll never say she's ugly, or untalented, or doesn't care about children again. *—Dana Kennedy*

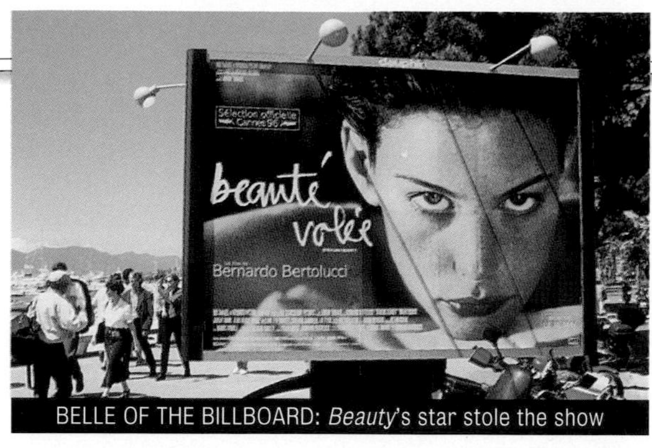

BELLE OF THE BILLBOARD: *Beauty*'s star stole the show

Livin' Large at Cannes

SURE, THERE were a few prizes awarded at the Cannes Film Festival—top honors went to two memorable odes to dysfunction, *Secrets & Lies* and *Breaking the Waves.* But was the competition the real news? *Mais non.* Cannes 1996 will go down as the week the world fell in love with 18-year-old Liv Tyler, known for frolicking in Aerosmith's "Crazy" video (frontman Steven Tyler is Liv's proud pop). While Tyler's blue-eyed mug loomed large over the Croisette via *Stealing Beauty* billboards, the genuine article was sweetly courting the 4,000 members of the press, who dubbed her "Liv Taylor." *Vive la* hype! *—D. Karger*

Julie—Madly, Deeply

"MARY POPPINS Hoppin' Mad!" blared a New York tabloid, and for once, it didn't overstate the case. After a matinee performance of Julie Andrews' Broadway smash, *Victor/Victoria*, the 60-year-old star announced she was rejecting her Tony award nomination for Leading Actress in a Musical because everyone else in the troupe—including her husband, director Blake Edwards—had been "egregiously overlooked." The Tony committee rejected her rejection, keeping her on the ballot, but Tony voters rejected Julie too, giving the award to *The King and I*'s Donna Murphy. Nonetheless, the flap handsomely pumped up *Victor/Victoria*'s already strong box office sales. *—SD*

MONITOR

WINNER

CHRISTOPHER REEVE

The Man of Steel signed on to direct HBO's AIDS drama *In the Gloaming*, to voice King Arthur in Warner's animated *The Quest for Camelot*, and to pen a Random House autobiography.

LOSER

SUSAN LUCCI

Proving once and for all that she's the Rodney Dangerfield of daytime TV, the *All My Children* soap star lost the Outstanding Lead Actress Daytime Emmy for the 16th time. You go get 'em next year, Susan!

"I am not comfortable with sexuality as a person, let alone touching myself in front of Local 357, you know what I mean?"

Janeane Garofalo on her sudsy phone sex in *The Truth About Cats & Dogs*

HITS

MOVIES *Twister*
TV *Mad About You's* season finale (NBC)
BOOKS Terry McMillan's *How Stella Got Her Groove Back*
MUSIC Fugees' *The Score*
VIDEO *Leaving Las Vegas*
MULTIMEDIA *Warcraft II: Tides of Darkness*

MISSES

David Schwimmer's *The Pallbearer* (Miramax) ◆ *Ruby Ridge: An American Tragedy* (CBS) ◆ Jay McInerney's *The Last of the Savages* (Knopf)

BIRTHS Paul Newman, 71, and Joanne Woodward, 66...grandparents? The Newmans' own daughter Lissy, 34, gave birth to a son, Peter Stewart Elkind, on May 18.

MARRIAGES Public displayers of affection Antonio Banderas, 35, and Melanie Griffith, 38, officially bonded in a London civil ceremony on May 14.... Actor Wayne Knight, 40—*Seinfeld*'s peevish mailman, Newman—wedded his longtime girlfriend, makeup artist Paula Sutor, 43, on May 26.... Rocker Stephen Stills, 51, tied the knot for the third time when he married Kristen Hathoway, 29, his children's ex-nanny, on May 27.

THE BUCK STOPS: TV pooch dies

PASSINGS Buck, the shaggy briard, perhaps the most civilized cast member of *Married...With Children*, bow-wowed out on May 25 at the age of 13 (that's 91 in dog years).

LAWSUITS Mel Gibson, 40, was in the doghouse when neighbor Terry Adamson filed a complaint on May 17, saying Gibson's unleashed Australian cattle dog attacked her outside the star's Malibu home a year earlier. The issue was settled out of court.

AILING Felled by an aortic aneurysm, actor George C. Scott, 68, bowed out of Broadway's *Inherit the Wind* on May 2, forcing the play to close. The illness came shortly after his former assistant Julie Wright, 26, slapped him with a reported $3.1 million sexual harassment lawsuit. The actor denied the charge.

OUTBURSTS Martin Lawrence, 30, was restrained by L.A. cops on May 7 after they found him screaming "Fight, don't give up!" at a Van Nuys intersection. His doctor said Lawrence had forgotten to take his medication and blamed exhaustion and dehydration. Police discovered a concealed handgun but the actor was not charged.

EXITS *Entertainment Tonight* cohost John Tesh, 43, announced on May 14 that he would leave the show to focus on his music.

DEALS After a fierce bidding war for the movie rights to Anne Rice's 1989 novel *The Mummy*, Twentieth Century Fox wrapped it up with a reported $3 million bid on May 8. —*JC*

JUNE

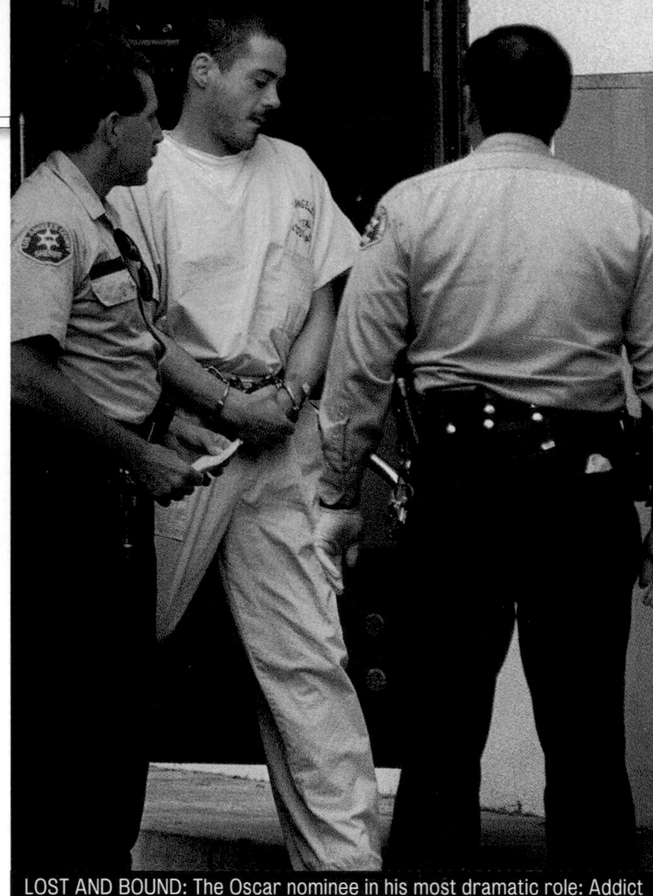

LOST AND BOUND: The Oscar nominee in his most dramatic role: Addict

Downey And Out in L.A.

IT WAS HARDLY shocking to learn that another hip, young, talented actor was using drugs. But when Malibu sheriffs stopped Robert Downey Jr., 31, for speeding on June 23, they nabbed an extraordinary haul: heroin, cocaine, and crack, not to mention an unloaded .357 Magnum. While most celebrity addicts acknowledge their recovery after the fact (as Downey had following previous attempts at rehab) or reveal themselves to the world on the obituary pages (as did River Phoenix), the Oscar-nominated Downey would have to answer for his crimes and face his demons in the spotlight. But first, he would engage in some very public evading of the issue: Three weeks after his arrest while free on a $10,000 bond, he was found snoozing in a surprised neighbor's bedroom; four days later, he fled his court-appointed detox center. After completing several months of court-ordered rehabilitation, Downey finally answered for himself in November, clowning about his arrest and drug addiction on *Saturday Night Live* and discussing it openly with Diane Sawyer—both television appearances taking place under the strict supervision of his rehab counselors. He told Sawyer he didn't want to become the "poster boy" for recovery, and sympathetic audiences rooted for him to stay on the straight and narrow. Even if he didn't get the irony. *—Jess Cagle*

1996's Tour de Force

"YOU WON'T BE seeing any flannel shirts," snorted Gene Simmons, 46, at the press conference announcing the reunion tour of the makeup-shrouded '70s group Kiss. The fans who'd sneaked in roared, and they weren't alone. The tour got rolling on June 28, when Detroit's Tiger Stadium became the first of 92 mostly sold-out venues on 1996's must-see tour. Mascara-dotted diehards and curious Gen-Xers saw it all: the fire, the "blood," the deliriously dopey odes to rock and babes, and, of course, the Tongue. More than just nostalgia, the shows vindicated Kiss as both an institution *and* an influence. And the money—more than $100 million—wasn't bad either.*—David Browne*

DOMINANT GENE: Still hot after 20 years

WINNER

CHRISTIANE AMANPOUR

The CNN reporter signed a reported $1 million-plus deal splitting gigs between the news channel and CBS' *60 Minutes*. Seems Andy Rooney wasn't keen on reporting from Bosnia or Zaire.

LOSER

CENTRAL PARK WEST

After a dismal debut on CBS, Darren Star's sex-and-suds-in-the-city saga was resurrected with much fanfare—*and* Raquel Welch (with Gerald McRaney, below). It was yanked again four weeks later.

The Art of 'Noise'

THIS WAS the year the scrappy downtown musical rocked uptown theater audiences, injecting the Great White Way with a dose of urban energy as *Rent* and Savion Glover's *Bring in 'Da Noise, Bring in 'Da Funk* each scored four Tonys on June 2.

Awards were spread among Broadway's critical hits (Best Play, Terrence McNally's *Master Class*; Best Revival of a Play, Edward Albee's *A Delicate Balance*), but a youthful exuberance was notable: *Rent*'s Wilson Jermaine Heredia won Best Featured Actor in a Musical for his portrayal of a drag queen, perhaps a reflection of Broadway's desire to goose its stodgy image.

While live audiences witnessed the show's smooth proceedings, TV audiences saw a mishmash of videotaped and live portions. In some cases, recipients had to feign surprise at the announcement of their awards. Now, *that's* Tony-worthy acting. —*Kipp Cheng*

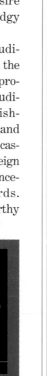

HAPPY FEAT: Glover brought down 'da house

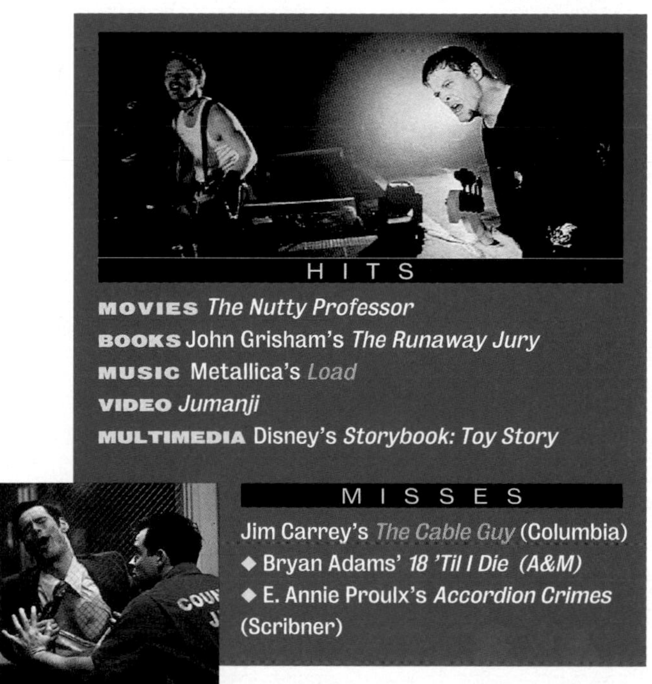

HITS

MOVIES *The Nutty Professor*
BOOKS John Grisham's *The Runaway Jury*
MUSIC Metallica's *Load*
VIDEO *Jumanji*
MULTIMEDIA Disney's *Storybook: Toy Story*

MISSES

Jim Carrey's *The Cable Guy* (Columbia) ◆ Bryan Adams' *18 'Til I Die* (A&M) ◆ E. Annie Proulx's *Accordion Crimes* (Scribner)

MONITOR

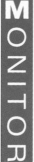

BIRTHS Keypsiia Bluedaydream Gipp was born on June 30 to soul singer Joi, 25, and hip-hopper Gipp.
REUNIONS The Who's Roger Daltrey, 51; Pete Townshend, 51; and John Entwistle, 52 (plus Ringo Starr's son, Zak Starkey, on drums), regrouped to play excerpts from *Quadrophenia* at the June 29 Prince's Trust concert in London, then went on the road. Daltrey wore a bull's-eye eyepatch to conceal a shiner he got during a rehearsal accident.
EXITS Why can't this be love? Van Halen broke with lead singer Sammy Hagar, 48, on June 27.... Keanu Reeves, 31, put the brakes on his participation in *Speed 2*—and on a reported $11 million paycheck.... After a long and stormy relationship, NBC hitmaking exec Jamie Tarses, 32, defected to ABC on June 20.
LAWSUITS On June 6, Jodie Foster, 33, slapped PolyGram with a $54.5 million suit for allegedly reneging on an agreement to cast her as Michael Douglas' daughter in *The Game*. (Douglas, 51, wanted her to play his sister.) The script was rewritten and began shooting in August, with Sean Penn, 35. Foster settled for an undisclosed sum in October.
BREAKTHROUGHS *Slate*, a webzine from ex-*Crossfire* host Michael Kinsley, debuted on June 14. Two months later, a spoof arrived: *Stale*. —*JC*

PAMELAPALOOZA

Heir Time

PAMELA LEE and her husband of 16 months, rocker Tommy Lee, 33, announced the birth of a son, Brandon Thomas, who weighed in at 7 pounds, 7 ounces, on June 5.

WOODY WATCH

Weed It and Reap

WOODY HARRELSON was arrested June 1 for planting four hemp seeds at a hemp legalization rally in Kentucky (ironically, one of America's leading growers of covert pot crops). Harrelson was Jonesing for the legalization of industrial hemp, not the smokable kind.

JULY

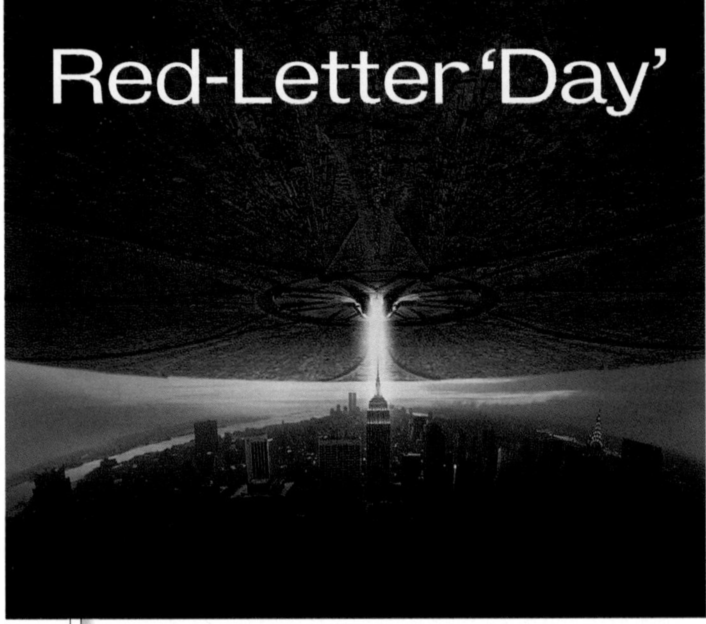

Red-Letter 'Day'

THIS TIME, the hype worked. Nearly six months before *Independence Day* was to open, everyone was talking about it—thanks to one strategically placed Super Bowl commercial in January. And by summer, the *ID* buzz from several cast appearances and a March press screening of eight minutes of footage was so deafening that Twentieth Century Fox decided at the last minute to open the film the night before its July 3 release. The move paid off: The film raked in $11.1 million that night, $50.2 million its first weekend, and $104.3 million its first six and a half days out—beating *Jurassic Park*'s record $100 million dash by three days. And alien mania extended far beyond the multiplex: *ID* renewed interest in alleged UFO landing sites Area 51 and Roswell, N.M., spawned instant sequel talk (*after* Fox had sent director Roland Emmerich and producer Dean Devlin on an all-expense paid vacation to Mexico), and heightened interest in such upcoming sci-fi flicks as Bruce Willis' *The Fifth Element* and Laurence Fishburne's *Event Horizon*. *ID*'s strongest aftershocks, however, rattled studio marketing departments, which, following Fox's lead, began cranking up the hype months in advance for such releases as *Evita* and *Jerry Maguire*. Whether the tactic will launch other movies' grosses into the stratosphere remains to be seen. Devlin, for one, counsels caution: "We only did that one Super Bowl spot. There's a real danger in overexposure." Oh yeah? Prove it. —*D. Karger*

Klein's True 'Colors'

PRIMARY COLORS' Anonymous byline obsessed readers inside and outside the Beltway like no covert identity since Deep Throat. Nailed by a handwriting match, *Newsweek* columnist Joe Klein finally fessed up with "relief and sadness," spurring book sales—and sparking debate over the author's ethics. Klein drew fire for his repeated and very vocal denials, as did his boss, *Newsweek* editor Maynard Parker, for abetting the subterfuge and running speculative pieces on possible scribes. Klein ultimately agreed to take a breather from the magazine, *and* resigned his CBS commentator gig in semi-disgrace. Meanwhile, Mike Nichols' projected film adaptation has ▶

Moore's the Pity

BUFFED WITHIN an inch of her G-string—and in sore need of a hit after *The Scarlet Letter* and *The Juror*—Demi Moore put her best assets forward in late June, bumping and grinding through the much-hyped, then reviled *Striptease*. Though she's never been shy about showcasing her wares, producers quickly distanced the film's story of a scrappy mom who disrobes for a living from *Showgirls'* debacle, insisting Moore's turn was more *tease* than *strip*. Then, after test audiences balked at a rape scene, filmmakers retooled the flick, making it more lighthearted. Though the film opened to $12.3 million, its final take, $32.8 million, didn't justify Moore's record $12.5 million paycheck. Maybe she should leave her clothes *on* next time, lest her price drop to more modest proportions. —*KC*

WINNER

ROSIE O'DONNELL

As penance for a crack Donny Osmond made about her weight, talk's cherubic queen forced the former *Tiger Beat* pinup to don a dog costume and croon a humbling rendition of his 1972 hit "Puppy Love."

LOSER

CALIFORNIA

Golden State, say hi to your new resident Joey Buttafuoco. The Long Island expat went West to improve his alleged prospects for a movie career. Guess he hadn't noticed his 15 minutes had long since come and gone.

proved as fraught as the novel's raucous campaign trail. First Tom Hanks, then John Travolta, headlined the tale of a skirt-chasing Southern governor aiming for the White House, a project Universal Studios wavered on at one point because of financing snafus but then went ahead. And, proving Socks isn't the only political cat with more than one life, Klein himself has been resurrected, having signed in October as the Washington correspondent for *The New Yorker*. —*Marlene McCampbell*

HITS

MOVIES *Independence Day*
TV Summer Olympics on NBC
BOOKS Patricia Cornwell's *Cause of Death*
MUSIC LeAnn Rimes' *Blue*
VIDEO *Broken Arrow*
MULTIMEDIA IBM's, *USA Today*'s, NBC's, and ESPNET's Olympic sites on the Web

MISSES

Woody Harrelson's *Kingpin* (MGM) ◆ Anything on TV other than the Olympics ◆ Bob Woodward's *The Choice* (Simon & Schuster) ◆ ♀'s *Chaos and Disorder* (Warner Bros.) ◆ Matt LeBlanc's *Ed* (Universal)

MONITOR

BIRTHS Parents of two girls, Garth Brooks, 34, and wife Sandy, 31, welcomed a third, Allie Colleen, on July 28.

ENGAGEMENTS Paula Abdul, 34, and Brad Beckerman decided to wed.

DEALS Jason Patric, 30, came on board *Speed 2*, filling the shoes of Keanu Reeves, 31, and beating out Christian Slater and Matthew McConaughey.

EVENTS On July 18, Michael Jackson, 37, helped South African president Nelson Mandela celebrate his 78th birthday.

EXITS Implicated in the fatal July 11 heroin overdose of Smashing Pumpkins keyboardist Jonathan Melvoin, 34, drummer Jimmy Chamberlain, 32, was fired from the band.

LAWSUITS Tom Cruise, 34, adoptive dad of two, filed a $60 million defamation suit against the German magazine *Bunte*, July 30, for claiming he has a zero sperm count; later, after two top *Bunte* executives died in a plane crash, Cruise dropped the suit in exchange for a printed retraction and payment of his lawyer's fees.

FULL NELSON: Jackson saluted Mandela

ARRESTS On July 20, four days after passing out in a neighbor's bed, Robert Downey Jr., 31, was arrested for violating bail by leaving his court-ordered rehab facility in Marina del Rey. After a short jail term, he went back into rehab, followed by three years' probation.

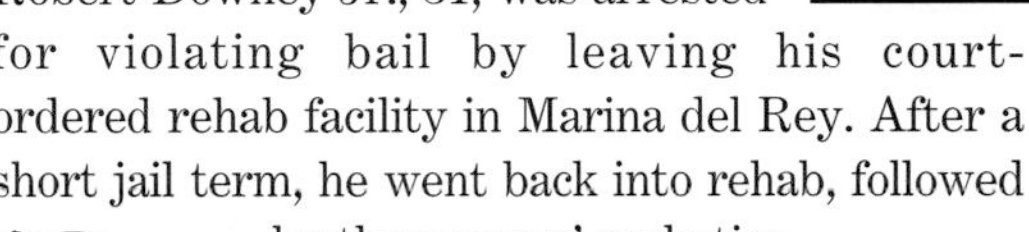

HUBBUB The six Friends went on strike for a larger piece of the show's growing financial pie but stayed on the job. To ensure they'd still be there for you, NBC raised their salaries to roughly $75,000 per episode, with an increase to $120,000 by 1999. —*JC*

CRUISE PATROL

Good in a Pinch

Pressing the flesh outside the London theater where *Mission: Impossible* was about to premiere, Tom Cruise saved a boy from being crushed against security barricades by the overzealous mob.

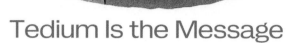

AUGUST

Athletes' Feats

THE OFFICIAL Olympic motto: "Swifter, Higher, Stronger." But for the 1996 Summer Games, it could also have been More Expensive (NBC paid $456 million for the broadcast rights), Better Rated (the Nielsens were 25 percent higher than those for 1992), More Dramatic (a bomb in Atlanta's Centennial Olympic Park killed one and injured 111). Here are *our* awards.

THE GOLD MEDAL FOR CLASS: When he lit the Olympic flame, visibly ailing, ever-courageous heavyweight Muhammad Ali got the Games off to an inspiring start.

THE GOLD FOR DOUBLE-TALK: NBC called some of its coverage "plausibly live." (That's "tape delayed" to you and me.) So as not to spoil the drama, Tom Brokaw refrained from discussing little details—such as Strug's career-capping early evening strained-ankle vault—on the broadcast of the nightly news. The silver goes to party-crasher Nike, which, though not a sponsor, set up shop next to the Olympic Village.

KERRI'D AWAY: Strug (with coach) cleaned up

THE GOLD FOR REVIVING THE COLD WAR: Former *Entertainment Tonight* host John Tesh added scads of members to his hate club with his jingoistic coverage, which included playing up the differences between the U.S. and "*Soviet* systems."

THE GOLD FOR ABSURD TIE-INS: *Jeopardy!* and *Wheel of Fortune* were the official game shows of the Olympics. Nobody unites nations like Vanna White.

THE GOLD FOR CREATIVE SELLING OUT: After the games, gymnast Kerri Strug landed a guest spot on *Beverly Hills, 90210*, three endorsement deals, and two book contracts. The silver goes to teammate Dominique Dawes, who vaulted into Broadway's *Grease!* as the goody-two-shoes head cheerleader, and runner Michael Johnson gets the bronze for snagging a $1 million deal from HarperCollins for his motivational book *Slaying the Dragon*. —*A.J. Jacobs*

Tedium Is the Message

ASIDE FROM the Olympics, it was the summer's most star-jammed TV event: Christopher Reeve spoke, the *Rent* cast sang, and Kevin Costner was spotted in the crowd. Yet the Democratic National Convention racked up abysmal ratings. President Clinton's love-fest held no suspense, and there was nothing like the conflict in Chicago 28 years before. (*Nightline*'s Ted Koppel, who left the Republicans' gathering after two nights, didn't even attend the Democrats' nonevent.) Ironically, in turning their conventions into slickly packaged infomercials, the political parties may have scared off major TV networks forever. The saving grace: Al Gore's lampooning the Macarena marked the beginning of the end of that irksome trend. —*BF*

WINNER

R.E.M.

The quartet were shiny happy people after inking the *second* largest contract in music history (a reported $80 million for five albums) with Warner Bros., behind only Janet Jackson, who's getting $80 million for four albums.

LOSER

MACAULAY CULKIN

A bad year for old Mac grew ever more worse when he put his stalled career on hold and petitioned a judge for reportedly about $2 million of his own loot to buy new family digs and help pay the bickering brood's legal fees.

McCarthy Singled Out

YES, MAKING goofy faces can pay off—especially if you're a hyper, buxom blond. Just ask Jenny McCarthy, the ex–Playboy Playmate who became a pop-cult phenom by rolling her eyes and contorting her mouth on MTV's *Singled Out*. Eight magazine covers later, her *Jenny McCarthy*'s *Surfin' Safari* CD has sold 100,000 copies, in mid-July MTV bought 22 episodes of her upcoming variety show, and NBC's handed her a sitcom deal for the fall of 1997. But...*why*? "There's a saying that there are two types of women—the kind men want and the kind they want to settle down with. Jenny sums up both," says Douglas Pollok, creator of The Unofficial Jenny McCarthy Fan Club website (*www.Jenny-McCarthy.com*). "She's funny. Watching her is like watching *Baywatch* and *Seinfeld* at the same time." —*KB*

HITS

MOVIES *A Time to Kill*
MUSIC The "Macarena"
TV *Seinfeld*
BOOKS Tom Clancy's *Executive Orders*
VIDEO *Homeward Bound II: Lost in San Francisco*
MULTIMEDIA *Final Doom* game

MISSES

NBC's *The John Larroquette Show* and *Wings* on a new night ◆ *Rhythm of the Games*, with Gloria Estefan's Olympic anthem, "Reach" (Arista) ◆ Ellen DeGeneres' *Mr. Wrong* (Touchstone)

MONITOR

MOMS: Etheridge, Cypher

EXPECTING Melissa Etheridge, 35, announced her girlfriend, Julie Cypher, 31, was pregnant.

BIRTHS A daughter, Sophia Rose, was born to Sylvester Stallone, 50, and fiancée Jennifer Flavin, 28, on Aug. 27.... Liam Neeson, 43, and Natasha Richardson, 33, welcomed a second son, Daniel Jack, also on Aug. 27.

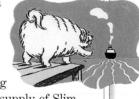

ENGAGEMENTS Oasis lead singer Liam Gallagher, 23, and actress Patsy Kensit, 28, announced they would wed.

AILING Actor Jan-Michael Vincent, 51, suffered a fractured neck and facial lacerations after the car he was driving accidentally rammed his girlfriend's, then hit a traffic light.

LAWSUITS On Aug. 2, Scott Bakula obtained a temporary restraining order against Tina Marie Ledbetter (who was convicted and served three years probation for making terrorist threats against Michael J. Fox in 1989) for allegedly sending unsigned letters accusing him of betraying his fans by leaving his former wife, Krista.

DEALS Woof! Woof! DreamWorks SKG midseason sitcom starring Arsenio Hall fetched a reported $900,000-per-episode license fee from ABC, which beat out CBS, NBC, and Fox for the rights.

HUBBUB Friends of Animals, a Darien, Conn., animal rights group, offered to find a new home for Kathie Lee Gifford's bichon frise after the *Live* star joked she wanted to get rid of it because it was getting fat. The group also sent Gifford a supply of Slim Fast for her children, Cody and Cassidy, "to ward off the possibility that they, too, might one day be callously abandoned for thinner, more aesthetically appealing children." —*JC*

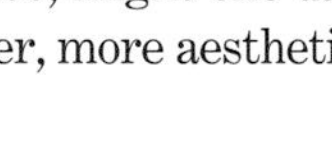

CRUISE PATROL

Life Preserver

Where there's smoke, there's Tom Cruise. Vacationing off the Italian isle of Capri, the ever-vigilant actor helped rescue five people adrift in a life raft who'd had to abandon their boat after it caught fire.

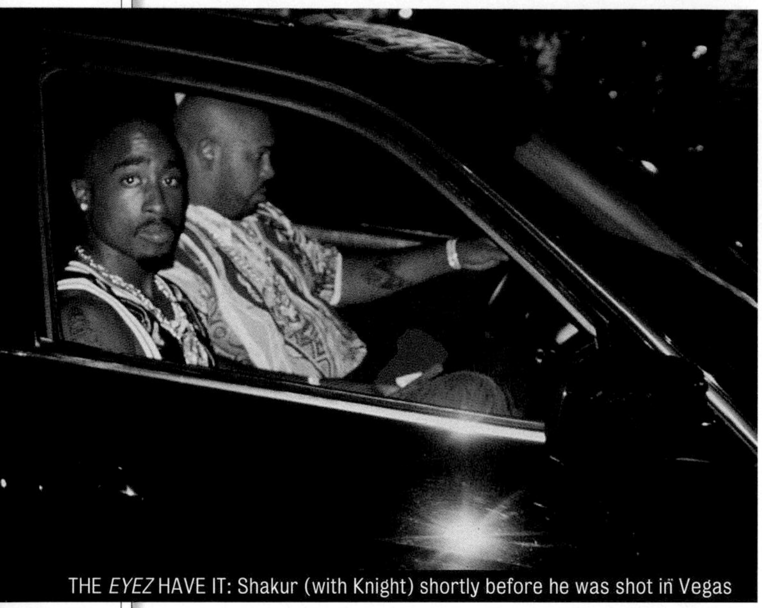

THE *EYEZ* HAVE IT: Shakur (with Knight) shortly before he was shot in Vegas

2 Young 2 Die

IN RETROSPECT, it was the saddest, strangest video of the year. With scenes of a somber Tupac Shakur swaying in heaven after being shot, the rapper's September-released "I Ain't Mad at Cha," from his multi-platinum *All Eyez on Me*, chillingly foreshadowed his own death.

On Sept. 7, Shakur was gunned down by an unknown assailant in Las Vegas after the Mike Tyson–Bruce Seldon fight. He was with Death Row Records chief Marion "Suge" Knight, who suffered a minor injury. Shakur died six days later.

An unlikely gangsta idol, Shakur attended Baltimore's High School of the Performing Arts, and later remade himself into Death Row's prince of darkness. With albums like *Eyez* and the posthumously released *The Don Killuminati/The 7 Day Theory*, he was also a cash machine for the label. Some say Shakur's murder and Knight's legal problems—he was incarcerated in October for probation violations—sounded the death knell for Death Row, and for gangsta rap itself. But with material for at least three more albums in the can, Shakur's voice, at least, is not silenced. His lyrics may offer a clue to his life—and his death: "It's not about East or West," Shakur rapped in "Bomb First." "It's about niggas and bitches, power and money, riders and punks. Which side are you on?" —*D. Kennedy*

Yes—She's a Thespian

MORE CHALLENGING than *Jeopardy!*, more fun than *Wheel of Fortune*, it became television fans' favorite guessing game: Will she or won't she? On Sept. 13, the media leaked that Ellen DeGeneres, star of ABC's *Ellen*, was considering having her pants-wearing character come out as a lesbian. The response was ►

Oprah's Title Wave

OPRAH WINFREY'S connection with books was truly novel. An avid reader, the talk-show host had amply proved her marketing mettle, plugging how-tos from both her chef, Rosie Daley, and trainer, Bob Greene, to No. 1 best-sellerdom. But when she announced on Sept. 17 that first-time fiction writer Jacquelyn Mitchard's *The Deep End of the Ocean* would kick off a monthly on-air book chat, the literary world felt the shock wave of television's mass drawing power (in this case, a loyal 15–20 million viewership). Readers went off *The Deep End*, sending the book to the top of the best-seller lists just a week later. All of a sudden, the queen of daytime television was publishing's most precious asset. —*AJ*

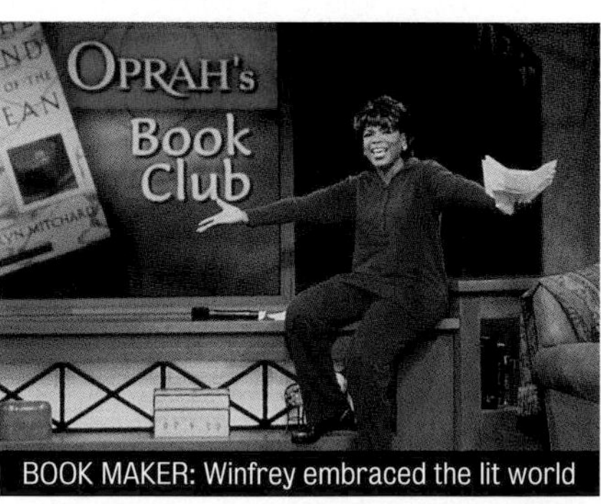

BOOK MAKER: Winfrey embraced the lit world

WINNER

SONDRA LOCKE

Despite ex-beau Clint Eastwood's Teflon image, the would-be director won a jury ruling that the Squint must pony up an undisclosed sum to settle a $2.5 million suit claiming he sabotaged her career.

LOSER

OASIS

Who says blood is thicker than water? The ersatz Fab Four's surly Gallagher brothers came to blows on their U.S. tour, canceled their other gigs here, and sulked home. Mum must have been proud.

fast and furious: buckets of news ink, objections from the religious right, skittishness from advertisers, a resounding silence from nervous ABC parent Disney, and plenty of coy teasing from DeGeneres herself (she peppered the sitcom with hints, including one scene in which she literally comes out of a clothes closet). But if the hoopla was meant to boost the show's ratings, it failed: The Wednesday-night sitcom still got beaten by CBS' *The Nanny*. —*AJJ*

HITS

MOVIES *The First Wives Club*
TV *Suddenly Susan*
BOOKS Tom Clancy's *Executive Orders*
MUSIC New Edition's *Home Again*
VIDEO *The Birdcage*
MULTIMEDIA *Virtual Graceland* CD-ROM

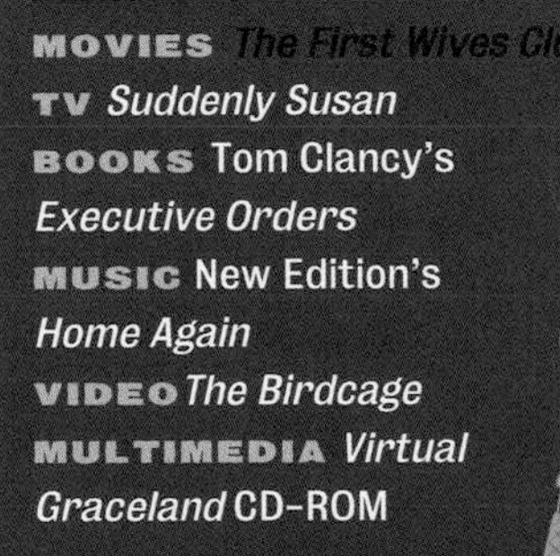

MISSES

Tom Arnold's *The Stupids* (New Line) ◆ Keanu Reeves' *Feeling Minnesota* (Fine Line) ◆ *Dark Skies* (NBC) ◆ *Townies* (ABC) ◆ Lucille Ball's *Love, Lucy* (Putnam) ◆ Tina Turner's *Wildest Dreams* (Virgin) ◆ *The Quest* (MCA/Universal video)

MONITOR

MARRIAGES By *George*, she got him! John F. Kennedy Jr., 35, wed longtime girlfriend Carolyn Bessette, 30, in a top secret ceremony on Cumberland Island, Ga., on Sept. 21.... On-again, off-again pair Jim Carrey, 34, and Lauren Holly, 32, said "I do" on Sept. 23.

BIRTHS A girl, Savannah, was born to Steven Seagal, 42, and girlfriend (and ex-sitter) Arissa Wolf, 21.... Melanie Griffith, 39, and Antonio Banderas, 36, had their first child, Stella del Carmen Banderas Griffith, on Sept. 24.

SPLITS Vanessa Williams, 33, and husband and ex-manager Ramon Hervey, 45, separated after nine years and three kids.... Tom Petty, 46, and wife Jane, 44, on Sept. 9, split after 21 years of marriage.... After a 21-month marriage, Martin Lawrence, 31, filed for divorce from ex–beauty queen Patricia Southall, 25, on Sept. 17.

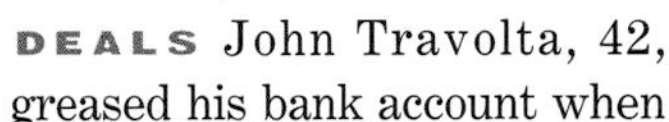

DEALS The force is with them: George Lucas, 52, announced on Sept. 25 that he'll step behind the camera for the first time since 1977's *Star Wars* to direct the first of a trilogy of prequels to the sci-fi classic.

EXITS Leaving to focus on his burgeoning film career, Greg Kinnear, 32, taped his final *Later* for NBC on Sept. 18. (Oops! His next movie, *Dear God*, tanked two months later.)

SEE YA, *LATER*: Kinnear

DEALS John Travolta, 42, greased his bank account when he signed three deals at $20 million a pop: the Clinton tour de farce *Primary Colors* for Universal, the Robert Redford-produced *A Civil Action* for Touchstone, and a big-screen version of *Have Gun Will Travel* for Warner Bros.

REHAB After flipping his car outside his home in Agoura Hills, Calif., and being arrested for suspicion of drunk driving on Sept. 21, Kelsey Grammer, 41, checked in to Betty Ford. For most of his monthlong stay, *Frasier* went on hiatus; Grammer was charged with driving with an expired license. —*JC*

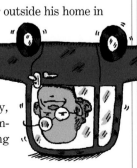

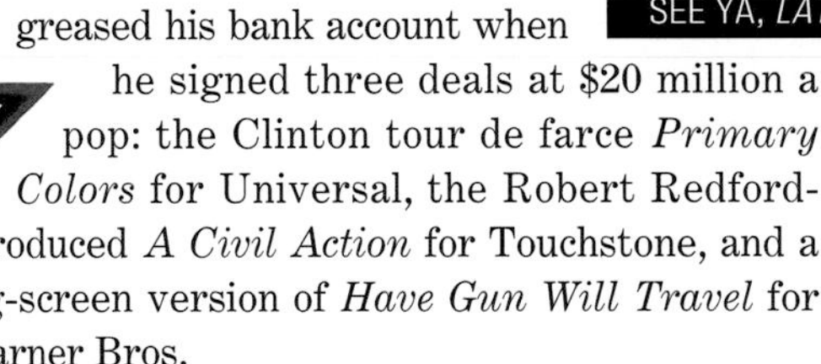

OCTOBER

A Child Is Born

SHE GAVE BIRTH 1996 years, 10 months, and 14 days after that *other* Madonna. The Birth of the Century, MTV called it. But this was no virgin birth. The father is one Carlos Leon, a personal trainer, recent guest star on *Nash Bridges*, and definitely *not* just a sperm donor. The delivery took place in an eighth-floor suite at Los Angeles' Good Samaritan Hospital, where the Maternal Girl was registered as Victoria Hernandez, and Dr. Paul Fleiss (Heidi's dad) delivered the 6-pound, 9-ounce Lourdes Maria Ciccone Leon by C-section after 12 hours of labor. The blessed event was chronicled by reporters, several of whom tried to evade security by posing as patients on crutches.

If that first infant changed the world, this one at least helped Madonna's latest career makeover. First off: an unexpectedly low profile. Despite offers of $250,000 for a paparazzi shot, Madonna kept baby pictures under wraps for months. The tabloids were reduced to digging up lame tidbits (Madonna reportedly took her jealous Chihuahua to a pet shrink). And the new, saintly mama granted her first big postpartum interview to promote *Evita* to the homey *Redbook*, of all places. There she said Lourdes would watch no TV and would read the Bible. *Amen. —AJJ*

Many Unhappy Returns

IS IT LIVE or is it... Spiñal Tap? When Van Halen issued a June press release bidding farewell to Sammy Hagar and welcoming original frontman David Lee Roth to lend his vocal cords to new tracks on the upcoming greatest hits album, *Best Of, Volume I*, the stage was set for the most fleeting reunion in rock history. First, Eddie Van Halen and Roth, who had split from the band in 1985, clashed at September's MTV Video Music Awards. Then Roth, learning that Extreme's Gary Cherone was going to become the official throat for the veteran hard-rock band, fired off an I've-been-duped statement: "It sickens me that the reunion...was nothing more than a publicity stunt." Answered Eddie: "We never said, 'You're in the band.' It was *just* a project." But one that let us dance the night away—if only for half the eve. *—DS*

HALEN FAREWELL: The band with Roth (right)

HITS

MOVIES *Sleepers*
TV *Millennium* debut
BOOKS Ellen Fein and Sherrie Schneider's *The Rules*
MUSIC Van Halen's *Best Of, Volume I*
VIDEO *Twister*
MULTIMEDIA *9* CD-ROM game

MISSES

Chris O'Donnell's *The Chamber* (Universal) ◆ *Public Morals*; *Almost Perfect* (CBS) ◆ Ethan Hawke's *The Hottest State* (Little, Brown) ◆ Jay Leno's *Leading With My Chin* (HarperCollins) ◆ Chris Isaak's *Baja Sessions* (Reprise) ◆ *Moll Flanders* (MGM/UA video)

Shutterbugged

MORE CUTTING than a surgeon's blade, more righteous than Batman's fight against evil, was actor George Clooney's attack on *Entertainment Tonight*. Clooney boycotted the wholesome Hollywood show after its sister series, *Hard Copy*, aired paparazzi footage of Clooney and his girlfriend, Celine Balidran. In a letter to *ET*'s producers on Oct. 28, Clooney claimed the broadcast violated a promise made by the programs' parent company, Paramount, that he'd be left alone by *Hard Copy*. Other actors—including the entire *ER* cast, Whoopi Goldberg, and Madonna—quickly jumped on Clooney's boycott bandwagon. But just one week later, *ER*'s Eriq La Salle appeared on an *ET* segment—proving, if nothing else, that the show will always go on. —*JS*

A PRIVATE AFFAIR: Clooney with Balidran

WINNER

COURTNEY LOVE

Columbia's *The People vs. Larry Flynt* became a film-fest darling, and the unlikely leading lady, Hole frontwoman Love, landed in the pre-Oscar buzz bin for her turn as the *Hustler* mogul's junkie stripper wife.

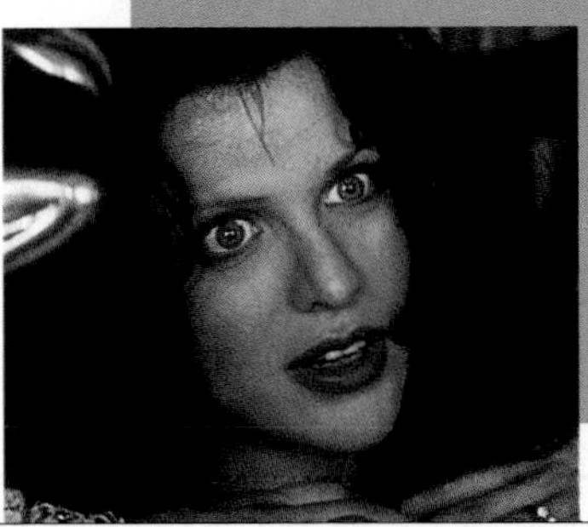

LOSERS

GEENA DAVIS & RENNY HARLIN

The lovebirds continued their red-ink-stained streak, following up the huge fiscal sinkhole *Cutthroat Island* with the $70 million dud *The Long Kiss Goodnight.*

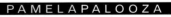

MONITOR

PETERED OUT: Drescher, spouse

MARRIAGES Country stars Faith Hill and Tim McGraw, both 29, two-stepped down the aisle on Oct. 6.

BIRTHS Woody Harrelson and Laura Louie, 30, brought home a second daughter, Zoe.... A son was born to singer ♀ and his wife, Mayte Garcia, apparently on Oct. 16. The infant, suffering from a bone disorder, died a week later; the parents declined to disclose details.

SPLITS Exit whining? Fran Drescher and husband/collaborator Peter Marc Jacobson, both 39, separated after 18 years of marriage.

DEALS Touchstone paid a soaring $8–10 million for film rights to Michael Crichton's then unpublished disaster novel *Airframe*.

DEBUTS Wasted *Ink*: After the unfunny early edition of Ted Danson and Mary Steenburgen's CBS sitcom was yanked from its scheduled Sept. 16 airdate, it was revamped by *Murphy Brown* creator Diane English and redistributed for an Oct. 21 premiere.

REHAB *Grace Under Fire*'s Brett Butler, 38, entered an L.A. outpatient facility for an addiction to painkillers.

EXITS Bruise your illusion: On Oct. 29, Guns N' Roses lead singer Axl Rose sent a fax to MTV announcing Slash was officially out of the band. Rose claimed the lead guitarist hadn't been musically involved since 1994.

INJURIES On Oct. 8, *Xena* warrior princess Lucy Lawless, 28, was rehearsing a sketch for *The Tonight Show With Jay Leno* when she fell off a horse and fractured her pelvis. Leno thanked her for being a good sport. —*JC*

PAMELAPALOOZA

A Kiss-and-Tell-All

PAMELA LEE EARNED an inflated figure of around $800,000 from Warner Books in exchange for her autobiography, to be written—in a book, not as flash cards—with PEOPLE magazine correspondent Todd Gold. Sample chapter: "The History of My Breasts."

NOVEMBER

Marrying Man

IN THE EARLY '90S, Michael Jackson crowned himself the King of Pop; by the end of 1996, he seemed determined to earn the title King of Popping the Question. On Nov. 15, just 10 months after his divorce from Lisa Marie Presley and 10 days after confirming that his dermatologist's assistant, Debbie Rowe, 37, was six months pregnant with his child, the 38-year-old Jackson married the mom-to-be in a quickie wee-hours ceremony following a Sydney concert appearance. "Please respect [our] privacy," he beseeched in the subsequent press release—which, to those weary of Jackson's increasingly bizarre attempts at media manipulation, sounded a little like Br'er Rabbit, *begging* not to be thrown in that publicity patch.

If asked if she and Jackson have sex, at least Rowe won't have to go on television and reply to Diane Sawyer, "Yes, yes, yes!" à la Lisa Marie; the couple's press reps denied reports of artificial insemination, and even the tabloids perpetuating those rumors conceded that Rowe was telling pals the couple tried conceiving the conventional way, too. However it came about, fatherhood may be a wish come true for the former child singing star who's made juvenilia his adult life's pursuit. —*CW*

HITS

MOVIES *Ransom*
TV *J.R. Returns*
BOOKS Toni Morrison's *Song of Solomon*
MUSIC Makaveli's *The Don Killuminati: The 7 Day Theory*
VIDEO *Toy Story*
MULTIMEDIA *Castle Infinity* CD-ROM
THEATER *Chicago* revival

MISSES

Greg Kinnear's *Dear God* ◆ *The Presidents of the United States of America: II* (Columbia) ◆ *Titanic* (CBS) ◆ Olivia Goldsmith's *Marrying Mom* (HarperCollins) ◆ *Director's Chair* (Knowledge Adventure)

NBA Action

THE NATIONAL BOOK Award may be the literary world's Oscar—but with one difference: No one ever accused Oscar of ignoring commercial interests. Long simmering tensions about the NBA's typically esoteric taste reached its peak this year. The 1996 nominees—including winners Andrea Barrett's *Ship Fever and Other Stories* and James Carroll's Vietnam War reminiscence, *An American Requiem*—were so obscure as to draw outrage among publishing execs. Not only did the volumes fail to top best-seller charts, they were notably absent from most critics' best-of lists as well. Who *should* have won? Most insiders picked Frank McCourt's memoir, *Angela's Ashes*, a critical and commercial hit. But as National Book Foundation director Neil Baldwin has said, "The NBA is not about...a fame that has been accomplished." —*AJ*

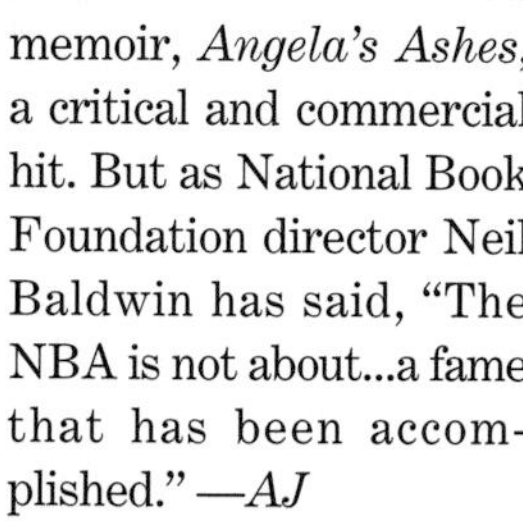

WINNER

HBO

The channel swept Nov. 16's CableAce Awards by winning 28 trophies. Leading the way was Garry Shandling's cynical late-night send-up, *The Larry Sanders Show*, which won four trophies. Hey now!

LOSER

MARION "SUGE" KNIGHT

On Nov. 26, the Death Row Records capo was ordered to remain in L.A. County lockdown for three more months after four alleged parole violations. The gangsta rap mogul faced a possible nine-year sentence.

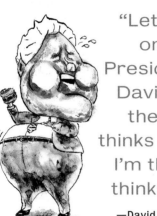

"Let me just say one thing to President Clinton... David Brinkley is the David who thinks you're boring. I'm the Dave that thinks you're fat."

—**David Letterman** on *Late Show*

Working for a Song

HOW DO YOU measure a year in the life? For Lynn M. Thomson, *Rent*'s dramaturge (or theatrical editor), 1996 was measured in the multimillion-dollar suit she filed Nov. 25 against playwright Jonathan Larson's estate. Thomson, 50, got $2,000 for her contributions to the rock musical hit from May 1995 to April 1996, plus royalties of $50 a week, but says her work radically turned Larson's retelling of *La Bohème* into a downtown-to-uptown phenom. Her suit sought 16 percent of the estate's earnings—a tidy sum for a show expected to earn tens of millions. Now *that* would be enough to pay Thomson's rent. —*KC*

MONITOR

MARRIAGES On Nov. 13, *The Crucible*'s Daniel Day-Lewis, 39, joined the World's Most Ineligibles list by wedding Rebecca Miller, 32, daughter of Arthur Miller.

SPLITS Kirstie Alley, 41, let "the big one" get away when she and Parker Stevenson, 44, separated on Nov. 27, after 13 years of marriage.... Citing irreconcilable differences, Robert Nottingham, 32, called it quits with *Murphy Brown*'s Faith Ford, 32, on Nov. 25.... *Beverly Hills, 90210*'s Jennie Garth, 24, filed for divorce on Nov. 22 from her spouse of two years, Dan Clark, 27.

LAWSUITS Love will burn a bridge: On Nov. 27, country star Wynonna, 32, and her husband, Arch Kelley, 43, were accused of sexual harassment and discrimination by Andria M. Surles, who claimed they made "sexually explicit and suggestive comments" while she worked as manager on Wynonna's Tennessee farm. They denied the charges.

EXITS Sherry Stringfield, 29, checked out of *ER*, partly to be with her boyfriend in New York.... On Nov. 23, Bob Hope, 93, capped his 61 years with NBC in *Laughing with the Presidents*, his 284th special.

DEALS Comedian Billy Crystal, 49, who hosted the 1990–93 Academy Awards, was greenlighted for his fifth telecast, in March 1997. —*JC*

WOODY WATCH

A Bridge Too Far

THE LIBERAL gadfly was arrested for the second time in six months: He and eight others who scaled San Francisco's Golden Gate Bridge on Nov. 23 to protest redwood logging were charged with trespassing and public nuisance. The activists filed a motion to drop these charges—a Feb. 1997 hearing is set.

PAMELAPALOOZA

Ciao Time

ON NOV. 19, Pamela Lee made the papers yet again by filing for divorce from Tommy Lee, her husband of 21 months.

DECEMBER

Ovitz And Out

DECEMBER WAS the cruelest month for onetime superagent Michael Ovitz, who quit after a tumultuous 16-month stint at the Walt Disney Co., where he had been second in command to chairman Michael Eisner.

Being No. 2 was apparently the one thing that Ovitz, once called the most powerful man in Hollywood, was unable to master. Though he left with a severance package reportedly worth at least $90 million, he had lost, for the moment anyway, his once-priceless aura of omnipotence.

What went wrong? The smart money said Ovitz clashed with Eisner, alienated colleagues with his imperiousness—and simply didn't have the managerial skills. He made a couple of sticky missteps, such as his involvement with Martin Scorsese's film about the Dalai Lama, *Kundun*. The film upset Chinese officials, who threatened to make it difficult for Disney to expand there. At press time, Ovitz' next move was still a mystery. Could the silence just be Ovitz' way of trying to rebuild his myth? *—D. Kennedy*

The Rating Game

NO IFS, ANDS, OR BUTTS: Except on *Blue*

ON DEC. 18, responding to a perception that *The Nanny* may just be too much emotional dynamite (and sexual innuendo) for average citizens, a ratings system for prime-time television programming was announced. Using guidelines similar to those for movies—TV-G (General Audience), TV-PG (Parental Guidance Suggested), etc.—the ratings were decried by some parents' groups, who found them lacking in content-specific information about the degree of sex, violence, or bad language in any given show. Some producers feared that a show given a TV-14 rating (Parents Strongly Cautioned) would drive away viewers *and* sponsors. Meanwhile, on *NYPD Blue*, backsides continued to be shown, TV-14'd but uncensored. *—KT*

WINNER

INTERSCOPE RECORDS

Less than a year after being dumped by Time Warner and picked up by MCA, the label had five acts (Bush, No Doubt, Snoop Doggy Dogg, Dr. Dre, and Tupac Shakur) in top spots on the pop charts.

LOSER

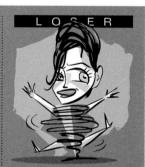

CARLA GUGINO

Breaking up wasn't hard to do for Michael J. Fox. Gugino, his love on ABC's *Spin City*, left after 12 episodes. But then, Courteney Cox did okay after splitting with Alex P. Keaton.

Boy, George!

MOST OF THE entertainment to come out of the White House this year involved Hillary's hairdos or Dick Morris' sex scandal. But Clinton's former senior adviser George Stephanopoulos, 35, did a reverse Ronald Reagan by leaving politics for a big-bucks career in the television, literary, and academic worlds. Besides accepting a two-year poli-sci professor's gig at Columbia University, the young gun was at the bull's-eye of two major bidding wars. With a dozen publishers waving their checkbooks at him, Stephanopoulos nabbed a $2.75 million advance for his memoirs from Little, Brown & Co. And after spurning offers from CNN and CBS, Stephanopoulos agreed to toil as a regular political analyst for ABC on both *This Week* and *Good Morning America*. How's that for politicking? *—Jessica Shaw*

HITS

MOVIES *Jerry Maguire*
TV *Mrs. Santa Claus*
BOOKS Ekaterina Gordeeva's *My Sergei: A Love Story*
MUSIC No Doubt's *Tragic Kingdom*
VIDEO *Tin Cup*
MULTIMEDIA *The Ultimate James Bond: An Interactive Dossier*

MISSES

Sylvester Stallone's *Daylight* (Universal) ◆ Madame Vasso's *Fergie: The Very Private Life of the Duchess of York* (Pinnacle) ◆ *The Cable Guy* (Columbia/TriStar video)

MONITOR

ENGAGEMENTS Chris O'Donnell, 26, popped the question to his longtime girlfriend, Caroline Fentress, 23, a kindergarten teacher.... Acclaimed actors Angela Bassett, 38, and Courtney B. Vance, 36, were engaged.

MARRIAGES Model-actress Angie Everhart, 27 (once a Mrs. Sly Stallone-to-be), wedded Ashley Hamilton, 22, son of George Hamilton and Alana Stewart (and onetime Mr. Shannen Doherty) on Dec. 1. Confused yet?

BIRTHS Destry Allyn Spielberg was born on Dec. 1, a seventh child for Steven Spielberg, 48, and Kate Capshaw, 43.

BANKRUPTCIES Burt Reynolds, 58, filed for Chapter 11 on Dec. 2, claiming more than $10 million in debts.

REHAB On Dec. 5, NBC West Coast president Don Ohlmeyer slipped into the Betty Ford Center to treat his alcohol addiction.

ARRESTS Bum rap? William Drayton, 37, better known as Public Enemy's Flavor Flav, was stopped in the Bronx on Dec. 6 when cops noticed a bulge in his pocket. It was a brick of marijuana, and he was subsequently booked. At press time, Drayton was awaiting trial.

AD HAWK: Lee signs with DDB

DEALS Filmmaker Spike Lee, 39, signed up with the ad agency DDB Needham to give him his own division, SPIKE/DDB. Lee's previous commercials included spots for Snapple, Nike, and Taco Bell.

PAMELAPALOOZA

Sea Ya Later...

IN MORE PAMELA LEE news, the mailloted mom announced Dec. 17 that she'd be bowing out of *Baywatch*. She planned to dive into her autobiography, *Pamdemonium*, and other projects. One major project was resurrecting her marriage to Tommy Lee. She vowed to stand by him as he tried to beat his alcoholism.

FLASHES

ILLUSTRATIONS BY
DAVID COWLES

ALICIA SILVERSTONE

JULY 19

When it came to casting herself in the upcoming *Excess Baggage*, first-time producer Silverstone balked. "I suggested [I fire myself] before we started. But they didn't go for that."

EMMA THOMPSON

JANUARY 12

She starred in *Sense and Sensibility* and wrote its Oscar-winning script, but Thompson knows her limits: "People asked if I wanted to direct, but it would've been a little much...how can you direct in a corset?"

ROSIE
O'DONNELL

JUNE 14

Promising a brave new approach to chat, the new talk queen vowed not to "humiliate the guests...or read off the cue cards like a zombie"—*and* "to cry less than Kathie Lee. Does she weep every day now, or what?"

JIM **C**ARREY

JUNE 7

The *Cable Guy* star on his foray into black comedy: "I'm gonna lose some people on this and gain some, but that's the way you've gotta go." The film's tepid box office confirmed his hunch; fans like him best dumb and even dumber.

CHRIS **R**OCK

MAY 31

"I'm having a *real* hard time finding hair-care products up here," *Politically Incorrect*'s presidential campaign correspondent said of the New Hampshire primary beat. "I have the barbershop take on politics."

DAVID HASSELHOFF

AUGUST 2

Bracing himself for unflattering *X-Files* comparisons, the hunky star of the sci-fi spin-off *Baywatch Nights* predicts, "We're going to get pretty well beat up, but I've been beat up before."

DOWNTOWN JULIE BROWN

AUGUST 2

When she wasn't dishing, the *Gossip Show* host did a *Spy Hard* cameo and "worked with Halle Berry on *B.A.P.s* [Black American Princesses]. It's a small part, but my boobs look great."

WHOOPI GOLDBERG

OCTOBER 18

Last year's Oscar host with the most says she won't step up to the podium again in March. "I did it. I'm done. Two years from now, I might do it again. But I don't need to do it every year."

VING RHAMES

JUNE 14

Mission: Impossible's success hasn't spoiled the journeyman badass. "The only difference between working on a huge-budget and a lesser-budget film is the quality of lunch and dinner."

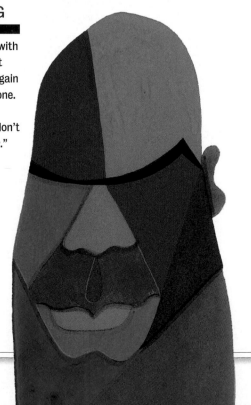

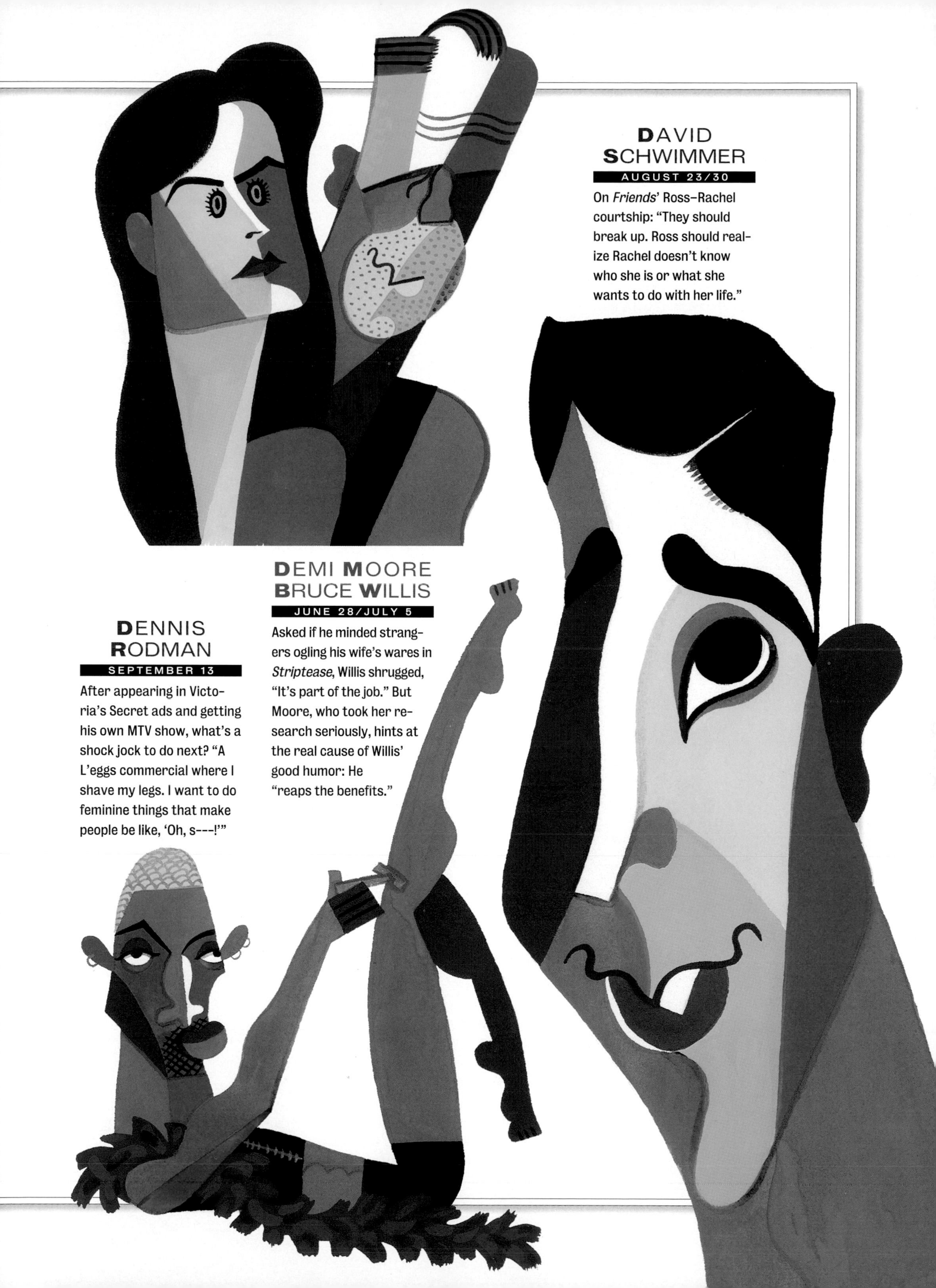

DAVID SCHWIMMER

AUGUST 23/30

On *Friends*' Ross–Rachel courtship: "They should break up. Ross should realize Rachel doesn't know who she is or what she wants to do with her life."

DEMI MOORE BRUCE WILLIS

JUNE 28/JULY 5

Asked if he minded strangers ogling his wife's wares in *Striptease*, Willis shrugged, "It's part of the job." But Moore, who took her research seriously, hints at the real cause of Willis' good humor: He "reaps the benefits."

DENNIS RODMAN

SEPTEMBER 13

After appearing in Victoria's Secret ads and getting his own MTV show, what's a shock jock to do next? "A L'eggs commercial where I shave my legs. I want to do feminine things that make people be like, 'Oh, s---!'"

STYLE

WHEN A PLATOON of wide-eyed supermodels invaded the stage at the 68th Annual Academy Awards, the year in fashion looked less than promising. But Hollywood couples like Brad 'n' Gwyneth and Demi 'n' Bruce helped to pick up the style pace. Collars turned up, and so did colors. Necklines plunged. Animal prints roared back (this *was* the year Cruella De Vil returned—as a fashion designer). Meanwhile, Bloomingdale's embraced entertainment, from chic (*Evita*) to street (*Rent*). And ethereal Jane Austen dresses took a place beside hard-edged Urban Decay nail polish. As if 1996 style weren't jumbled enough already. —*Degen Pener*

Into the deep with MTV's Jenny McCarthy

Taking The Plunge

IT WAS THE TREND that set off tremors among celebrity fashion plates: necklines, from designers like Donna Karan and Gucci, that plunged almost as deep as fault lines. Since the look exposes what can only be called undercleavage, Wonderbras weren't an option.

Sharon Stone

Jamie Lee Curtis

Christine Lahti

Daisy Fuentes

Sharon Lawrence

Halle Berry

TV host Giselle Fernandez

All the Hues That Fit

WHETHER IN jersey, satin, or shantung, stars were suddenly heading somewhere over the rainbow last spring. The awards circuit was flooded with brilliant gowns that spanned the color spectrum. And that made Roy G. Biv—the mnemonic for the red, orange, yellow, green, blue, indigo, and violet of the rainbow—a celebrity in his own right.

Hair Do's...

THE BEST HAIR went up, up, and away in 1996. From pixie cuts, upswept 'dos, and pulled-back falls for women to the new short, spiky "freestyle" for men, locks that stayed off the face were right on base.

Gillian Anderson pins her curls to the '40s

Annette Bening crops her way to the top

Brad Pitt gets on the up-and-up

Nicole Kidman enters the *Valley of the Dolls*

David Caruso's big, bad return

Navy Cross explains Moore's lock out

Sandra Bullock's a hit, but her hair's a flop

...And Hair Don'ts

BET THESE stars would love to wash themselves right out of this hair. Okay, Demi Moore doomed her dome for the movie *Navy Cross*, but the rest don't have that excuse—especially Fran Drescher, who got over-flower-powered at the Golden Globes.

Could fauna lurk in Drescher's flora too?

Winona Ryder's badly cast plastered 'do

A Panoply of Paltrow

HERE'S THE YEAR in fashion as brought to you by Gwyneth Paltrow. In 1996, all the designers wanted to dress the rising star, and sometimes it seemed as though each one did. No wonder Brad's girl won a VH1 Fashion Award for personal style last October. Appropriately, it wasn't her parents or her agent she thanked—it was her main fashion man, Calvin Klein.

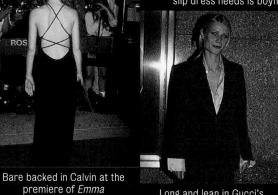

Leopard print. Bare midriff. Grungy sneakers.Three trends in one.

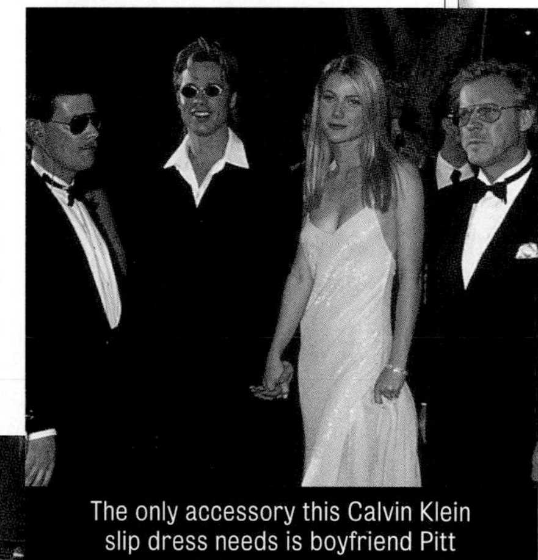

The only accessory this Calvin Klein slip dress needs is boyfriend Pitt

Pure Audrey Hepburn, by way of Calvin Klein. Award by VH1.

Bare backed in Calvin at the premiere of *Emma*

Long and lean in Gucci's velvet pantsuit

Angela Bassett's $6.5 million Oscar-night loaner from Harry Winston

Ashley Judd in her super-chic Onassis sunglasses

Jennifer Tilly nails the manic manicure

Celebrity Trendathon

SEVEN STARS, seven trends: diamonds, Jackie O. shades, wild nail polish, cross-dressing, clashing prints, gold dresses, and cutout gowns. But when Sharon Stone, fashion's eighth wonder of the world, turned up at the Oscars in a $22 Gap mock turtleneck, she created a craze herself.

Sharon Stone puts her hands together for cheap and casual chic

Something borrowed? Dennis Rodman steals RuPaul's look.

Elizabeth Hurley in peekaboo Versace

Geena Davis takes a gilt trip in Richard Tyler

A hit-and-mismatched Lea Thompson

Cruella De Vil wants to hush puppies

Style Stories

DON'T CRY for entertainment tie-ins. *Evita* and *101 Dalmatians*, plus Broadway's *Rent*, enthralled the fashion world. Spotted Hush Puppies were rushed into production, while Bloomingdale's sold fashions inspired by Eva Perón and East Village artists.

Rent's Daphne Rubin-Vega

Evita's a material girl, too

Animal Instinct

ANIMAL PRINTS WERE the cat's meow as runways began to feel like a scene from the Bible, namely Noah's Ark. Dolce & Gabbana's leopards, Versace's tigers, and Anna Sui's zebras—even Gucci's ponies—had celebrities crying "Oh, my!"

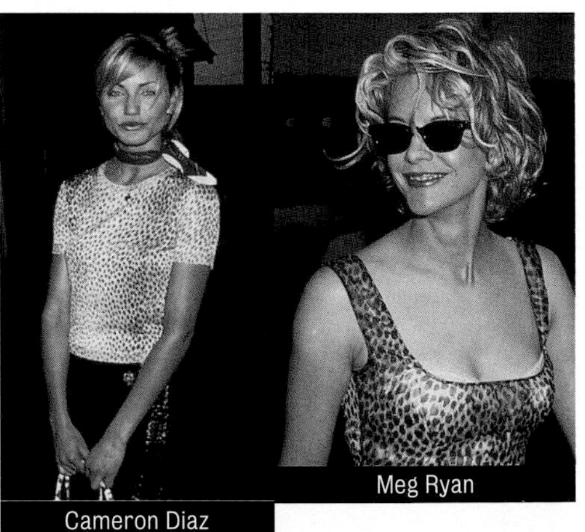

Meg Ryan

Cameron Diaz

Wide-Collar Workers

Brad Pitt spreads it on

Kevin Bacon stays alive with chest hair to spare

ACTORS PUT formal wear into a '70s tailspin. At the Golden Globes, Brad Pitt shucked black-tie for designer Richard Tyler's open-collar look. For the MTV Video Music Awards, Kevin Bacon looked ready to do the hustle.

A Waist to Go

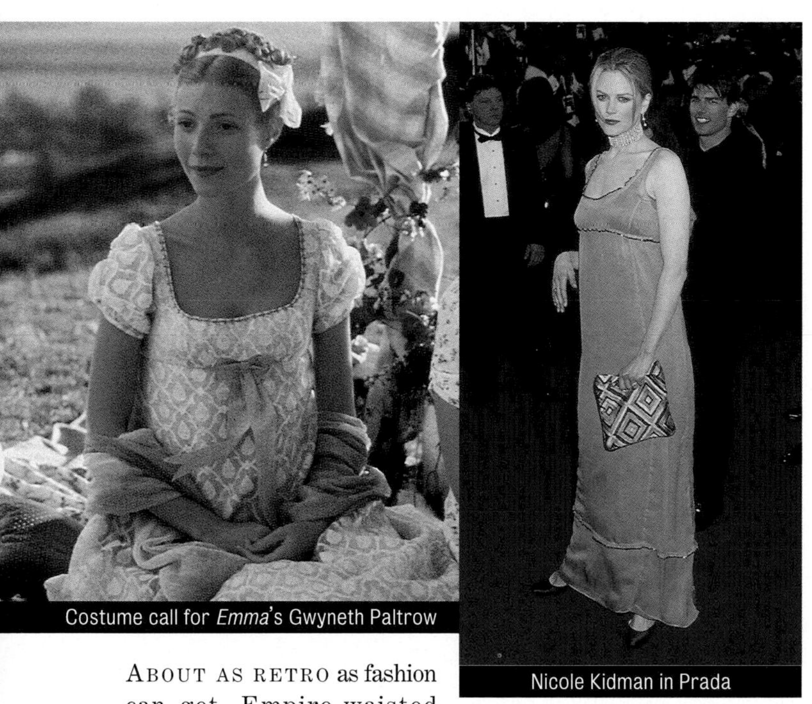

Costume call for *Emma*'s Gwyneth Paltrow

Nicole Kidman in Prada

ABOUT AS RETRO as fashion can get, Empire-waisted dresses made a comeback, thanks to Hollywood's obsession with Jane Austen. Adaptations of *Emma*, *Pride and Prejudice*, and *Sense and Sensibility* had designers John Galliano, Oscar de la Renta, and Prada hoisting up waistlines to just below the bosom.

This Year's Models

Moore and Willis for Karan

Bon Jovi for Versace

Roth for Prada

Matt LeBlanc for Saks

Portman poses for Isaac Mizrahi

POSING FOR fashion designers can lend stars a cool aura; it can also mean free clothes. Celebrities like Jon Bon Jovi (for Versace), Tim Roth (for Prada), and *Mars Attacks!*'s Natalie Portman (for Isaac Mizrahi) took the bait. Even Hollywood's highest-paid couple wasn't immune: Demi Moore and Bruce Willis shilled for Donna Karan.

HOT SHEET

BY JIM MULLEN

1 **KERRI STRUG** The tiny tumbler showed us what she was made of at the Olympics. Helium.

2 **PAMELA ANDERSON LEE** The talent-deprived *Baywatch* star managed to keep a high profile. Maybe she's had press implants, too.

3 ***STRIPTEASE*** Demi Moore flopped. So did the film.

4 ***THE RULES*** The best-seller on surefire ways to snag a man. Inheriting tons of money doesn't work anymore?

5 **MADONNA** Now that she's a mom, we can expect such future hits as "Because I Said So, That's Why" and "Don't Make Me Come In There."

6 **THE JACKIE O. AUCTION** People paid thousands more than the stuff was worth. It must have been the same crowd that sets CEO salaries.

7 **THE MACARENA** The dance craze of the summer. One small step for man, one giant leap for the hokey-pokey challenged.

8 **ELLEN** She may make television history. By being the first female in a leading role to play a blatant asexual.

9 **KELSEY GRAMMER/ROBERT DOWNEY JR.** The big money, the drinking, the drugs, the bad publicity—they might have a future in politics.

10 **MICHAEL JACKSON** He's going to be a daddy. And, as soon as he's old enough, the kid will get his father's nose.

13 ***ER*** BP 50 over 20! Vitals crashing! We're losing her! Clear! What happened to her? She accidentally bumped into George Clooney.

14 **JFK JR.** How did he keep the wedding of the year from the press? He didn't tell the FBI about it.

11 **DENNIS RODMAN** The press acts like it's never seen a parrot-headed, tattoo-covered, body-pierced, cross-dressing basketball star before.

12 **CIGARS** Very popular among people who have given up inhaling. Now what this country needs is a good five-cent gas mask.

15 **MIKE OVITZ** Why wasn't the world's most successful agent happy at Disney? Because they never let him wear the Michael Eisner costume.

16 **JENNY McCARTHY** The former Playmate is one of the most in-demand people in show business. She's worked her way all the way to a top.

17 **SPECIAL EFFECTS WIZARDS** The true stars of megahits *Independence Day* and *Twister*. And they can always make themselves an Oscar if they don't win one.

18 ***RENT*** The hit Broadway musical celebrates the life of starving artists. Lots of people stay poor now just because it's so with-it.

19 **CELEBRITY SWEATSHOPS** Kathie Lee Gifford and Michael Jordan were shocked. Why didn't the $5-a-day laborers have their agents and lawyers go over the contracts?

20 **ROSIE O'DONNELL** What other talk-show host knows all the words to "The Courtship of Eddie's Father" and eats Ring Dings? Besides Maury Povich, that is.

ILLUSTRATIONS BY
ERIC PALMA

SCENE

THE KEY TO the scene is to always be seen. And with so many festivals, awards shows, and premieres packing the calendar, it wasn't too hard to find someone to snap your mug. Cannes '96 turned into a showcase for camera-ready up-and-comers Liv Tyler and Ewan McGregor, while the indie snowfest Sundance became a see-and-ski staple for industry powerhouses. With big movies starring Tom Cruise, Robin Williams, and Demi Moore, it was hardly a mission impossible for party planners to haul out the photo ops. But the true starry, starry night kicked in when the gold statues were handed out. —*Jessica Shaw*

Best Actor Nicolas Cage and wife, Patricia Arquette

Strong Showing

OSCARS

NO HONORS for the girl or boy next door: 1996's best were a sociopath, a drunk, a prostitute, and a nun. Sorvino's acceptance speech honoring her father, Paul, and Reeve's touching appearance earned tears and applause. But it wasn't all drama: At post-Oscar bashes, the celebrations continued till close to dawn.

Best Actress Susan Sarandon shares the glow with a triumphant Christopher Reeve and his wife, Dana

Nominee Kate Winslet kisses up

Best Supporting Actress Mira Sorvino hefts her golden boy

Presenter Jim Carrey sizes up the future at the Governors Ball

Snow Business

SUNDANCE AT Robert Redford's snowbound indie film festival, top honors went to *The Spitfire Grill* and *Welcome to the Dollhouse*. There were no prizes for the steamy lesbian thriller *Bound*, but like many of the festival's hot tickets, it still generated plenty of sizzle.

Normal Life's Luke Perry grabs the frame

Drunks' Parker Posey takes a hit of java

Bound's Gina Gershon, Joe Pantoliano, and Jennifer Tilly

Mountain man Redford

Bar Belle

BARS THAT SMILE. That hair. That *bra*? Julia Roberts turned heads at New York City's biker bar and star hangout Hogs and Heifers. Too bad the public was more interested in her brassiere (which still hangs on the bar wall) than any of her recent movies.

Open Season

PREMIERES FOR SOME of 1996's biggest movie premieres, it was all about entourage. Will Smith brought his camouflaged crew to *Independence Day*, Demi Moore exposed the whole family for *Striptease*, and Robin Williams dragged some pals to *The Birdcage*.

The Birdcage's Robin Williams and friends give good face

Independence Day's Smith with son Trey and squeeze Jada Pinkett

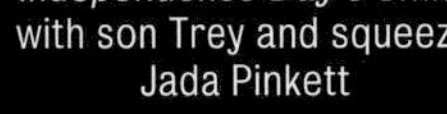

Striptease's Moore *en famille*

Mission: Impossible's Cruise with Nicole Kidman

Crash's Holly Hunter, James Spader, and Rosanna Arquette

American Buffalo's Dustin Hoffman

Herzigova basques in the limelight

French Twists

CANNES MODEL EVA Herzigova may have shown some skin, but the *étoile du jour* was Liv Tyler, whose movie *Stealing Beauty* debuted at the French festival. Top honors went to *Secrets & Lies* and *Breaking the Waves*, and David Cronenberg's controversial *Crash* won a special jury prize.

It Girl Tyler's best French impression

Top of the Pops

MTV THE NETWORK'S awards shows gave former video babe Alicia Silverstone top popcorn honors and Top 40 diva Alanis Morissette Best Female Video. But the music awards may be best remembered for the last public appearance of slain rapper Tupac Shakur.

Hard Rock Performance presenters Snoop Doggy Dogg and Shakur

Billy Corgan, Courtney Love, and James Hetfield

Shaquille O'Neal tops Silverstone

Fans got all turned out for Kiss

Road Skill

TOURS LOLLAPALOOZA'S summer love-in donned a full metal jacket with headline acts Metallica, Soundgarden, and Psychotica. But 1996's tours de force belonged to '60s throwbacks Phish and '70s comebacks Kiss.

Metallica madness in the pit

Psychotica's Pat Briggs rocks

Nominee Cybill Shepherd steps up

TV Nation

EMMYS SHORTLY BEFORE her sitcom coming-out rumors hit the fan, Ellen DeGeneres stepped out at the Emmys. The only L-words that night were the lime green gown on Julia Louis-Dreyfus, the *très chic* law student escorted by George Clooney, and the leather sling modeled by Matt LeBlanc.

David Schwimmer and LeBlanc hang out

Ellen DeGeneres and fan

Louis-Dreyfus' winning look

Hey, Macarena!

CRAZE FORGET THE hokey-pokey and the electric slide. The catchy Spanish song and dance that swept the country over the summer may have gotten a kick start on cruise ships and at resorts, but it became so popular that even Bill Clinton was seen busting a move. And look where it got him.

By Giorgio

STORES ITALIAN DESIGNERS Valentino, Versace, and Prada booted up New York with glittering parties celebrating new stores. But Giorgio Armani outdid them all, drawing everyone from Gwyneth Paltrow to Winona Ryder to Glenn Close.

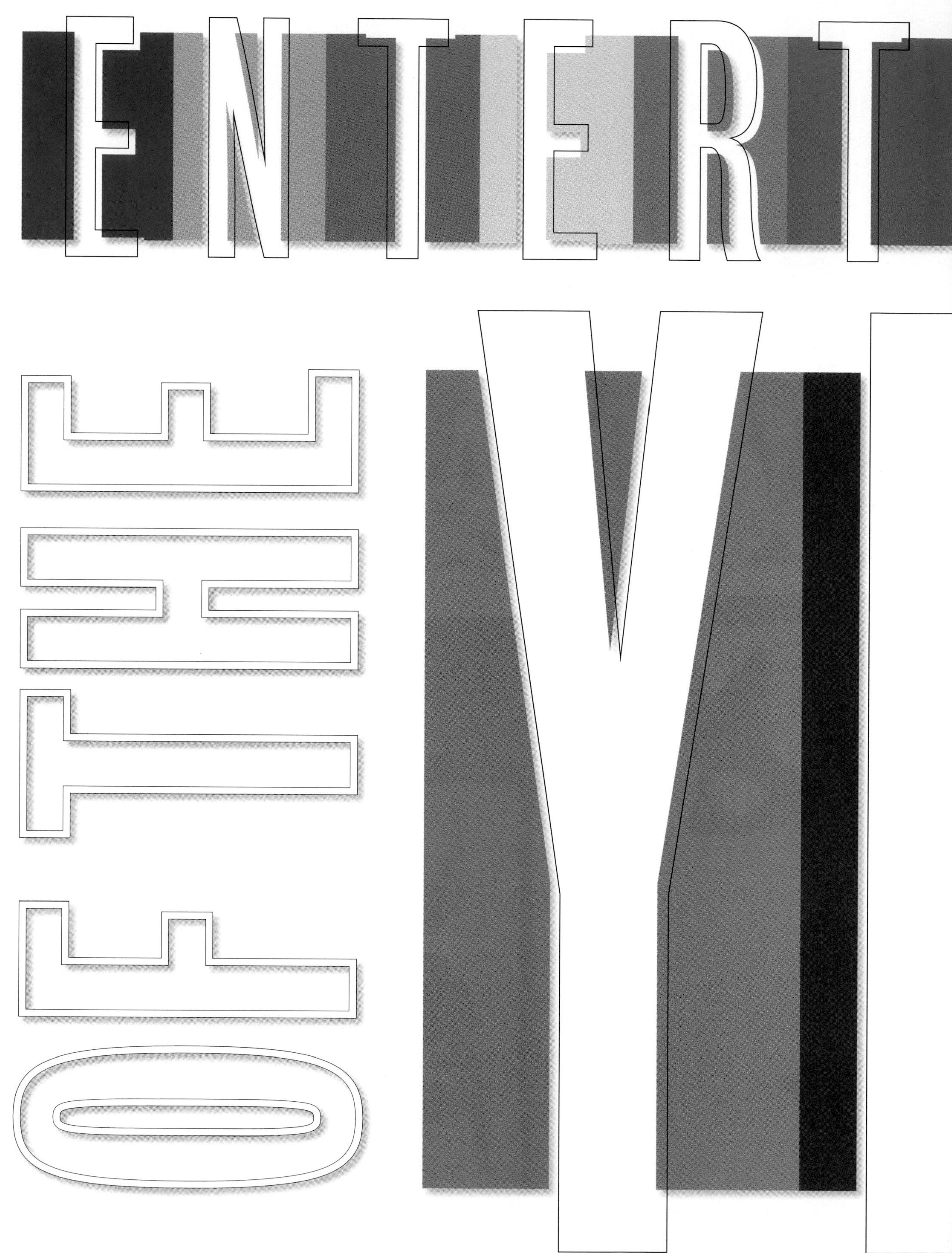
ENTERT
OF THE
Y

AINERS

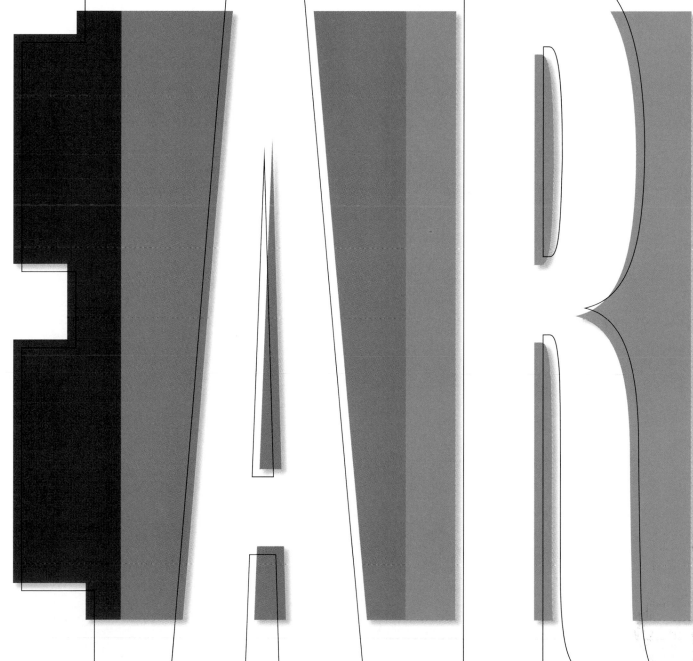

EAR

ROSIE

O'DONNELL

OK, we know, it may Regis and Kathie Lee made it kitschy. But only Rosie made it *cool* to watch daytime TV again. ◼ With her smart [illegible] charm, Rosie O'Donnell brought a sweet scent to a junk-heap genre. And during a year when nice was in and cranky was out (just ask Bob Dole), Rosie was the nicest of them all. She gushed unabashedly with genuine, infectious, and identifiable enthusiasm over celebrities ("I still have to pinch myself to know that I actually spoke to Elton John," she says), while winking the other way with a self-mocking sense of irony that preempted any possible uncoolness. ◼ She not only became Tom Cruise's No. 1 fan, but she actually proclaimed herself his stalker until he agreed to appear on the show. Cruise, like everyone else, got the joke. "I love Rosie," he says. "[illegible]

Nicole..." Even stars who haven't yet sat with her are fans: "Rosie makes you feel good," raves John Travolta. "She's like everybody's sister." At once sunny and street-smart, she's ambivalent about being dubbed the Queen of Nice. "In a way, it's a big detriment to me, because if I say anything mildly scathing, it's 'She's not nice, she's the Queen of Mean!' "

We'll reserve that title for whichever trash-talk host is in court this week. "I never had any interest in doing that kind of a show," says O'Donnell, slouching in a chair in her Rockefeller Center office, which is cluttered with playthings for her 17-month-old son, Parker. "I have limited tolerance for ignorance, so if somebody told me they slept with their sister's husband, I'd say, 'You're an idiot.' "

In her typically blunt fashion, the 34-year-old ex–stand-up claims her show is merely copying the celebrity-driven formula that kept Mike Douglas and Merv Griffin on the air for decades. Yet since those two hung up their mikes in the '80s, others have tried—and failed—to revive the format (whither Wil Shriner?). "When I first sent the idea out to studios, everyone was reluctant," O'Donnell recalls. "The line we kept getting was 'Variety is dead.'"

If it was, Rosie revived it: *The Rosie O'Donnell Show* premiered in June with the best numbers for any new daily talk show since *Oprah*, and it now consistently places in the top 20 among all syndicated shows. The inescapable conclusion: People *like* her.

She is not, however, too nice to butt heads with conventional wisdom; she took a break from a thriving movie career to star in *Grease!* on Broadway in 1994. "I stopped taking advice back when I was a VJ," she says, referring to her days on VH1. "Everyone told me not to do it, and I did it anyway. There's no map to get to success in this industry—you have to take a knife and hack your way through the jungle."

No showbiz success comes without some turmoil, and *Rosie* has been no exception. Executive producer Daniel Kellison (a *Late Show* vet) departed, and O'Donnell has jettisoned her sometimes-mediocre scripted monologues in favor of Regisesque ramblings. "When we had the rehearsal shows, I stood and tried to deliver a monologue like Johnny did, and it just is not my style," she says. "I don't really tell jokes. I tell stories." But like Johnny (and unlike Jay and Dave), she makes it look easy.

The nice queen also wears the crown of poster girl for women of a larger size (she's an 18). And don't expect an Oprah-like transformation any time soon. "I'm not the kind of person who'd get a cook and a trainer. If I do, call me up and remind me what I just said."

O'Donnell addressed that weighty issue again this year during a model-bashing monologue in the male-bonding movie *Beautiful Girls*. When she dismissed surgically enhanced centerfolds as "beauty freaks," says O'Donnell, who caught the flick with her sister at a New Jersey theater, "the women stood up and cheered. There was this huge uprising among these overweight, non-perfect women."

This year's other notable big-screen appearance, as an understanding nanny in *Harriet the Spy*, heightened her profile among kids, who have become some of her show's most avid fans. It's no surprise: With her giddy demeanor, a penchant for belting out goofy pop songs, and an insatiable taste for McDonald's Happy Meal doodads, O'Donnell often seems like an oversize kid herself. "Kids don't see a lot of adults being silly and playing with toys," she says. One of those toys, *Sesame Street*'s Tickle Me Elmo doll, became Christmas' most coveted item after making its debut on Rosie's show. "I don't take full credit," she says. "But I guess I take a little."

If Kmart execs see a sales increase this year, they can thank Rosie too: Her commercials with Penny Marshall—who directed O'Donnell's movie debut in the 1992 baseball comedy *A League of Their Own*—make shopping there seem almost hip (hey, we said *almost*). "I love anyone who can improv, and Rosie can improv," says Marshall. "Plus, she understands my mumbling, so she's a friend for life." But the ads did cause one problem for Rosie: "I was in Florida for Thanksgiving, and my VCR broke, so I went to the Wal-Mart around the block. It was in the paper: Rosie O'Donnell was at Wal-Mart—the traitor!"

Bad press doesn't bother her. She's prepared for the inevitable backlash: "I know it'll happen. ENTERTAINMENT WEEKLY will have me as Entertainer of the Year, and then you'll write: 'Entertainer of the Year? Gimme a break—look at her rear!' "

We'd never say that. It wouldn't be nice. —*Bruce Fretts, with reporting by Rebecca Ascher-Walsh, Tricia Laine, and Benjamin Svetkey*

M E L

GIBSON

MEL GIBSON has always been a package of classic proportions—a matinee idol's blue eyes, dark mane, and jutting jaw—but this past year he's proved there's more to him than wrapping. If other ticket-booth stalwarts like Harrison Ford and Tom Hanks provide us with an ideal mold for sturdy, decent, movie-star decorum, then Gibson tosses back the mold with a slight fracture in the porcelain. "They're regular guys, but Mel's a bit more of a time bomb," says actor Geoffrey Rush (*Shine*), who's known Gibson since their stage days back in Sydney, Australia, in the '70s. "There's something in there ticking away."

Indeed, 1996 was explosive for Gibson. He bookended the year with conquests creative and commercial, winning Best Picture and Best Director Oscars for *Braveheart*, and plundering the box office in the fall with *Ransom*. Not only did Gibson, 40, pass these milestones, he did so with the reckless ease that defines his big-screen appeal. He spent his downtime on the *Ransom* set cracking wise and playing Scrabble—this despite a bout of appendicitis *and* a potentially head-inflating attack of the Oscars in March.

2

Gibson has come off like a charismatic hybrid of Cary Grant and Beavis ever since his early outings in the *Mad Max* and *Lethal Weapon* series, but in 1996 he planted that roguish persona firmly in the pantheon of screen idols. —*Jeff Gordinier*

ALANIS MORISSETTE

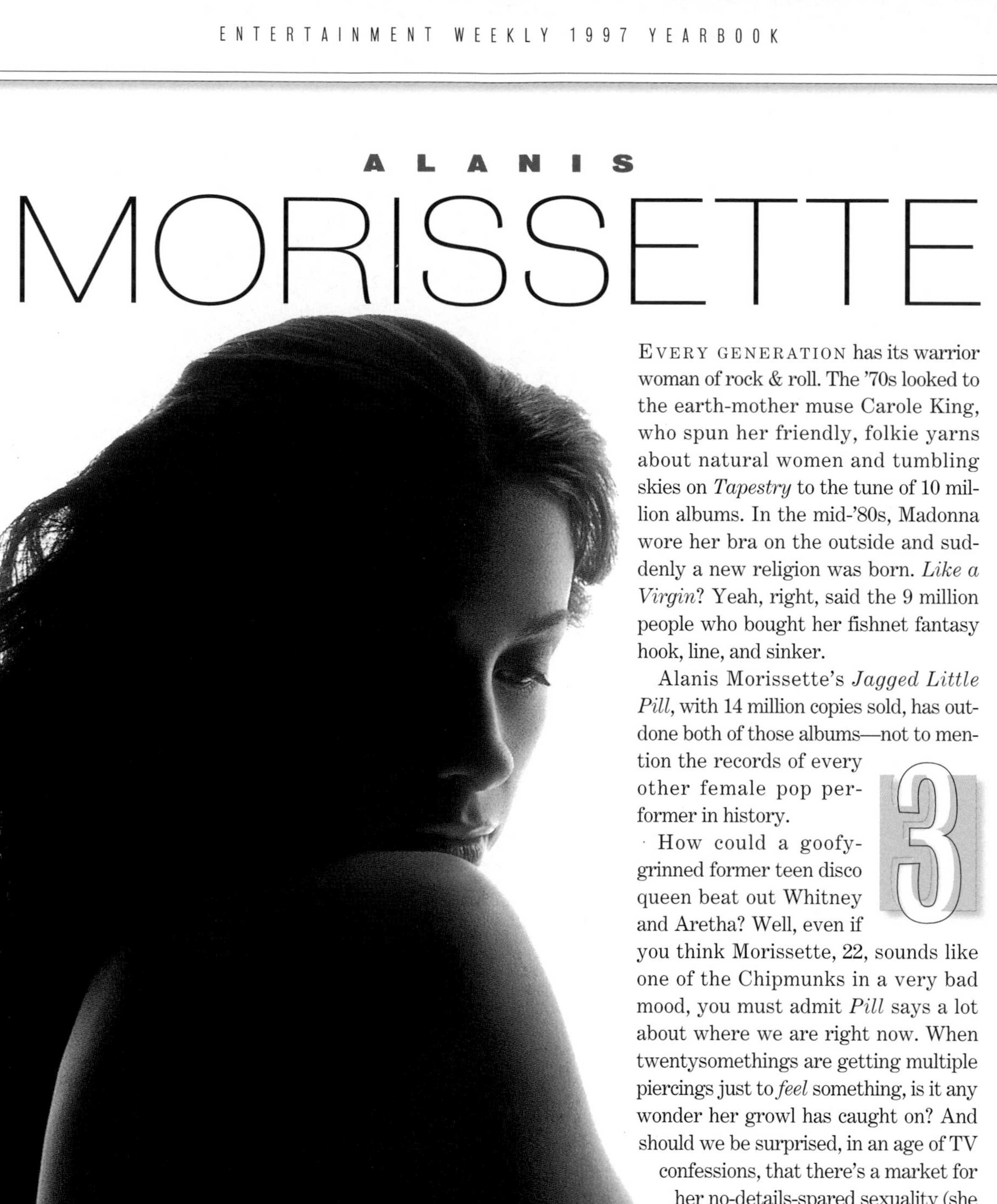

EVERY GENERATION has its warrior woman of rock & roll. The '70s looked to the earth-mother muse Carole King, who spun her friendly, folkie yarns about natural women and tumbling skies on *Tapestry* to the tune of 10 million albums. In the mid-'80s, Madonna wore her bra on the outside and suddenly a new religion was born. *Like a Virgin*? Yeah, right, said the 9 million people who bought her fishnet fantasy hook, line, and sinker.

Alanis Morissette's *Jagged Little Pill*, with 14 million copies sold, has outdone both of those albums—not to mention the records of every other female pop performer in history.

3

How could a goofy-grinned former teen disco queen beat out Whitney and Aretha? Well, even if you think Morissette, 22, sounds like one of the Chipmunks in a very bad mood, you must admit *Pill* says a lot about where we are right now. When twentysomethings are getting multiple piercings just to *feel* something, is it any wonder her growl has caught on? And should we be surprised, in an age of TV confessions, that there's a market for her no-details-spared sexuality (she did *what* in a movie theater?).

Morissette has her role models: She's got Carole's hippie dress code, Janis' tortured wailing, Mariah's diva-next-doorishness, and Madonna's in-your-face carnality. In fact, underneath it all, maybe Morissette is just an old-fashioned grrrl. Wouldn't *that* be ironic? *—David Hochman*

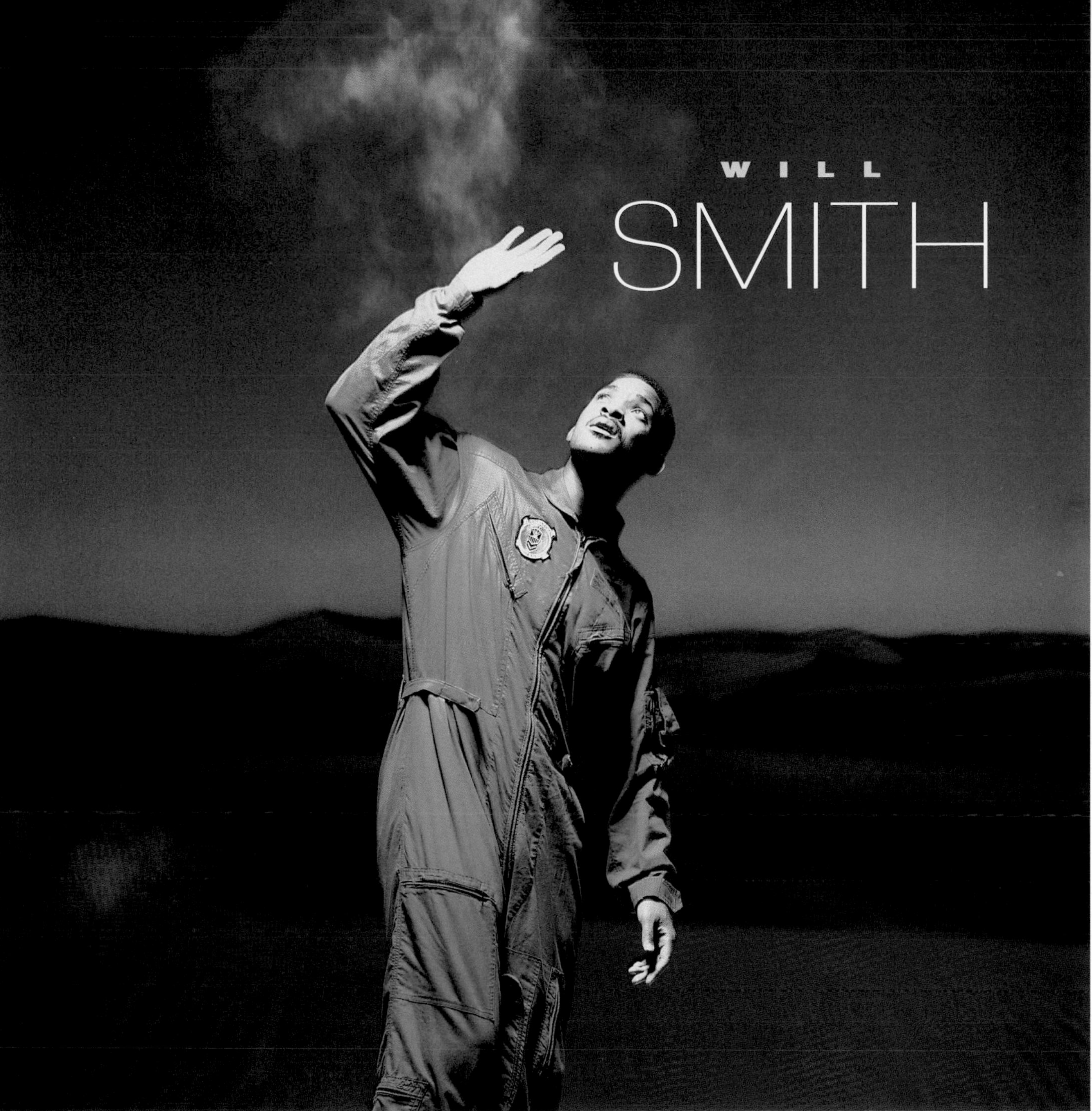

WILL SMITH

SUFFERING CONSTANT irritants like last summer's alien invasion, planet Earth seemed to be having a shortage of luck in 1996. No doubt because Will Smith, 28, hogged it all. With a casual puff of a cigar, a commitment to "whup E.T.'s ass," and a swift right hook, Smith distinguished himself in *Independence Day*, the year's highest-grossing movie, and went from being famous to being *famous*. "I was recognized from TV, but this is way beyond that," says the actor.

What really set Smith apart was that he arrived bearing a uniquely varied résumé. First, he was the rapper Fresh Prince; then he slid his way onto TV as a street-smart kid in *The Fresh Prince of Bel-Air*. When the show ended its run after six seasons, Smith proved his success wasn't a fluke. "The day before *Independence Day* opened, people on the street were like, 'Will, what's up?'" he says. "The day after, it was, 'Hey, Mr. Smith. How are you?' There's a *whole* different level of respect." (Fans may have also recognized his girlfriend Jada Pinkett from *The Nutty Professor* and *Set It Off*.)

4

All that heat feels a little alien to Smith. He's finished filming the sci-fi comedy *Men In Black* (due in summer '97) and is just trying to stay grounded. "Right now, I'm getting my golf stroke together," he says. And at the moment, he has no discernible handicap. —*Rebecca Ascher-Walsh*

5

GO AHEAD. Sneer at the hype, scoff at the latest tale of loutish misbehavior, block your ears to the umpteenth airing of "Wonderwall." There's still something about Oasis that manages to transform even the most lethargic listener into a blushing, knock-kneed teenybopper.

That sensation, once confined to the British Isles, swept the globe in '96. As the UK's fashion, film, and rock worlds buzzed with energy, a newly swingin' London found its cocky emblem in Oasis. The band brazenly cribbed from the Beatles, churned out sumptuous slabs of ear candy like "Champagne Supernova" and "Don't Look Back in Anger," sold 4 million copies of *(What's the Story) Morning Glory?* in the U.S. alone, and became the first British group since the heyday of new wave to mount a beachhead on Yankee shores.

Meanwhile, the five blokes in the band—hit spinner Noel Gallagher; his firebrand brother and singer Liam; guitarist Paul "Bonehead" Arthurs; bass player Paul McGuigan; and drummer Alan White—challenged the royal family as England's kings of controversy. And frankly, that's why we love them. American rock has sunk into a torpor since Kurt Cobain's death, but Oasis spent every minute of 1996 on the brink of detonation, the way rock stars are *supposed* to. *—JG*

OASIS

STEPHEN KING

6

A CRAZY COP and witchy wolves. A deified inmate and a magical mouse. They leapt with ease from the imagination of Stephen King, 49, and bolted onto the best-seller lists during a year of prolific output. First came his six-part serialized novel, *The Green Mile,* about a death-row facility in the 1930s South. *Mile* showed King at his best, weaving suspense, pathos, and the supernatural into a lovely rumination on aging and loneliness. With the six parts totaling more than 20 million copies in print, King jockeyed with *himself* for positions on best-seller lists.

"I got letters from people who'd never read anything of mine before, and that was cool," says the author, who followed *Mile* with the dual publication of Viking's *Desperation*—a gripping yarn of demon-battling Nevada tourists—and Dutton's *The Regulators,* its homely half-sister written under the pseudonym Richard Bachman (the ever-quirky King insisted that the novels be published simultaneously).

With 43 books behind him, King seemed to reintroduce himself to the world in 1996, and readers liked what they saw—the good, the bad, and the brilliant. "I write all kinds of stories," he says. "There's a lot of stuff I do that isn't necessarily horror. In a way, I'm fiction's best-kept secret." —*Jess Cagle*

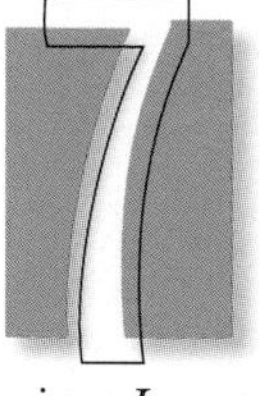

AT $20 MILLION per role, things were going just fine for Tom Cruise, who might well have remained rich and famous simply by relying on his smile, or stripping to his Skivvies and dancing for his supper. But last summer, in *Mission: Impossible*, the sweet-faced actor looked us dead in the eye and warned us not to underestimate him: "You haven't *seen* me mad," he growled. Actually, we'd never seen him so *adult*. After *Mission*—Cruise's maiden producing voyage—made a fearsome $180 million, the 34-year-old impressed us again by taking a lighter approach. As a down-and-out sports agent in *Jerry Maguire*, Cruise proved once and for all that there's more to him than cheekbones and charm. His next role, opposite wife Nicole Kidman, will be in *Eyes Wide Shut*, for director Stanley Kubrick.

If his turn as Jerry Maguire is remarkable for its cynicism and antiheroism, you'd be hard-pressed to find such character flaws in Cruise, who spent much of his downtime in 1996 rescuing people from dangerous situations and, as always, masterfully minding the media. "There's so much going on in my life all the time," he says. "The kids. The work. The traveling. Yeah, it does kinda seem like a lot." Admitting to being overwhelmed: How very grown-up of him. —*RAW*

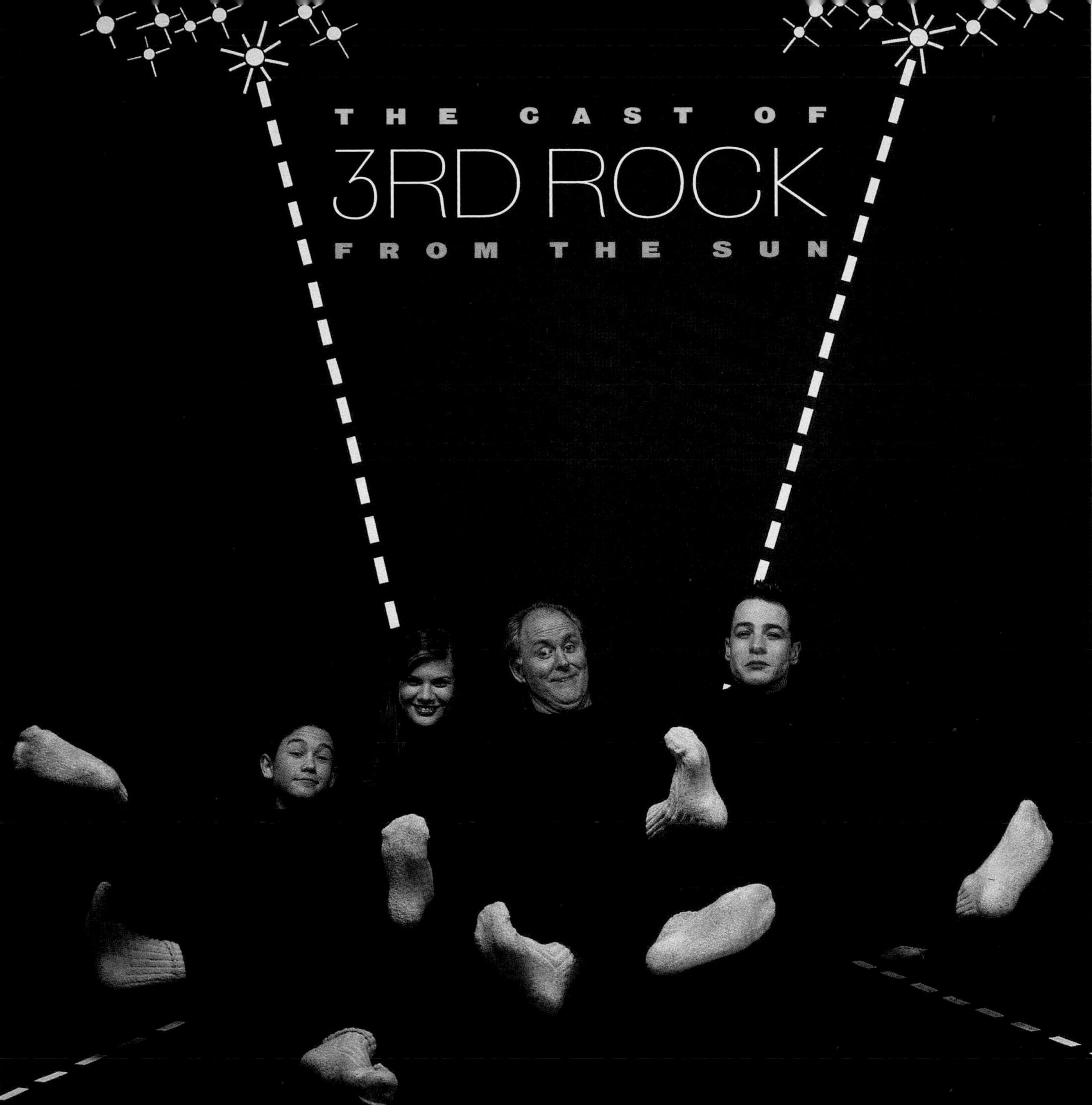

8

AS MORK, E.T., ALF, and the squawking green creatures from *Mars Attacks!* have proved, human behavior—always a knee-slapper—is never funnier than when being studied by aliens who don't have a clue about table manners. And these days there are no funnier, less inhibited extraterrestrials patrolling the airwaves than the crew from *3rd Rock From the Sun.* When mission leader Dick Solomon (John Lithgow, second from right) and his team touched down on NBC's earth in January 1996, assuming human forms and coagulating into a nuclear—if nutjob—family unit, the network had a breakout hit on its hands.

As high commander of the ensemble lunacy, the very tall Lithgow gets to pretzel himself into very strange situations, many of them involving his romance with earthling Dr. Mary Albright (wonderful Jane Curtin, back where she belongs). But his contortions are no odder than those of Amazonian first assistant Sally (Kristen Johnston, second from left); scientist-turned-teen Tommy (Joseph Gordon-Levitt, left); and universal oddball Harry (French Stewart, right), a squinty-eyed clown who'd be out of place on *any* planet. Every move they make is carefully worked out by a cast that enjoys making total fools of themselves. It's a dork's universe on *3rd Rock*—and it feels like home. —*Lisa Schwarzbaum*

JONATHAN LARSON

HIS DYING words have been heard around the world. Jonathan Larson's rock-opera blockbuster, *Rent*—completed shortly before his death of an aortic aneurysm on Jan. 25, 1996—had the critics rhapsodizing, the crowds lining up, the movie studios clamoring, and the theater world reeling. Inspired by Puccini's *La Bohème*, Larson, who was 35 when he died, recast the 19th-century tale of tormented outsiders with the 20th-century denizens of Manhattan's East Village—disenfranchised artists grappling with homelessness and AIDS. In doing so, he brought Broadway up-to-date, boldly marrying the modern urban zeitgeist to the hopeful, life-affirming traditions of the American musical.

An emigrant to Manhattan from White Plains, N.Y., Larson waited tables during the seven years it took to bring *Rent* to life. "He was lousy at sports," jokes his sister, Julie Larson McCollum. "So there was nothing else for him to do.... Very early on we were given a sense of social awareness, as well as a love for theater. I think Jonathan ultimately tried to combine the two."

With advance ticket sales of $6 million and projected earnings into the tens of millions, *Rent* has proved itself worthy of the hype.

9

"[Jonathan] was never afraid to say 'I'm going to change the face of musical theater,'" says *Rent* star Anthony Rapp. "That was something he took as a given." —*Kipp Cheng*

WINFREY

10

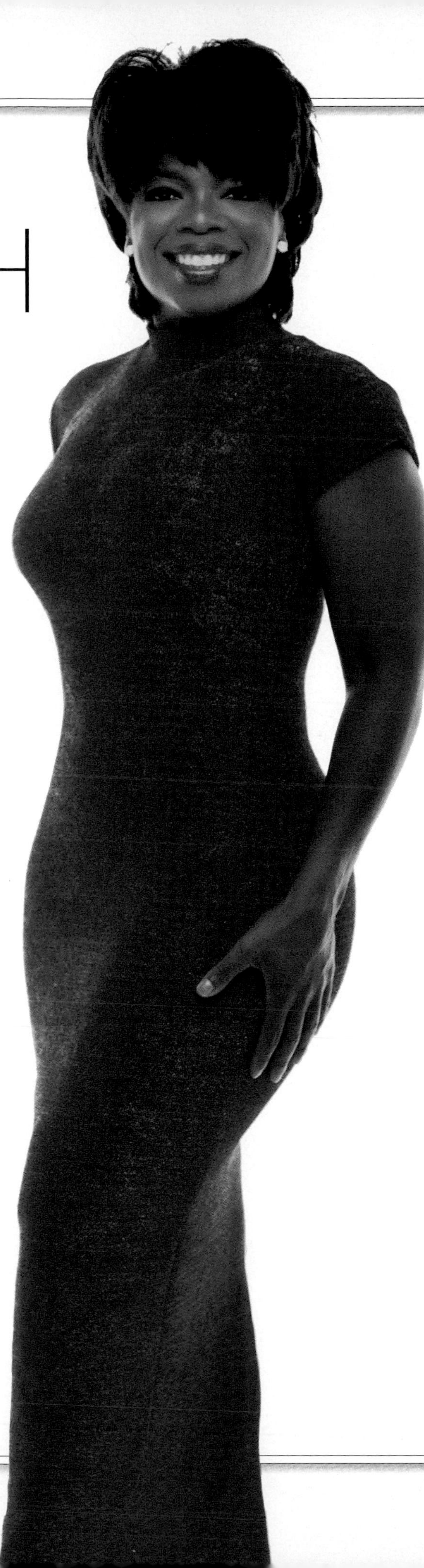

WHEN THEY WRITE the book on book publishing, they'll cover the giants of the industry: Gutenberg. Scribner. And of course, Oprah. At least if the past year was any indication. For 1996 was the year Oprah Winfrey, the Chicago-based chat show host, started her televised Book Club—and became the most powerful force in the business of literature.

The monthly club debuted in September—and offered immediate rewards for the first three lucky tomes (Jacquelyn Mitchard's *The Deep End of the Ocean*, Toni Morrison's *Song of Solomon*, and Jane Hamilton's *The Book of Ruth*). By December, the number of copies of the books in print had increased by 2.3 million, more than triple their pre-*Oprah* print runs.

Leave it to Winfrey, 42, to turn literary yakkety-yak into riveting TV. Formatted as a dinner with the author and four fans, the club offers a chatty approach that is girlfriend-to-girlfriend, full of teary how-this-book-changed-my-life tales. Still, it *is* about books. And as such, it's the latest brilliant example of Winfrey distancing herself from Dysfunction TV, a now-troubled genre she began dissing in 1994. She now embraces uplifting topics such as "Are We Too Rude?" The risk has paid off: After an initial dip, her '96 ratings rose again, to almost double those of her nearest competitor, *Live with Regis and Kathie Lee*. Now that's one for the books. —*A.J. Jacobs*

JOHN SAYLES

WHEN *LONE STAR*, a sprawling, intricate tale of murder, mystery, and incest set on the Tex-Mex border, was released last June, grateful audiences reacted as if they'd discovered the cinematic equivalent of a good read. The movie—its crowded cast ranges from Kris Kristofferson as a small-town sheriff to new hunk on the block Matthew McConaughey—had story to spare. *Novelistic*, critics called it. Writer, director, and sometime actor John Sayles, 46, enjoyed the biggest hit of his 18-year directorial career. Shot for just $5 million, the film grossed nearly $13 million by year's end.

In an era when last year's indie wunderkind is often this year's studio sellout, the self-reliant Sayles sets his own independent course. "John stands apart," says John Pierson, author of the indie-world survey, *Spike, Mike, Slackers & Dykes*. "He cuts a fantastic figure in the way he's handled his career."

But though he lives in upstate New York, with his companion and producing partner Maggie Renzi, Sayles refuses to cut himself off from Hollywood, where screenwriting assignments (like an *Apollo 13* gig) help pay for his own projects. "I'm not antagonistic toward Hollywood, but most of what I want to make isn't appropriate for a major studio," says Sayles, who is filming his next movie, *Men With Guns*, in Spanish in Mexico. How independent can you get?

—Gregg Kilday

HELEN
HUNT

ON A TEAM OF tornado-chasing daredevils in *Twister*, she was the kind of tough, game professional chick that scientists want along for the ride. In a marriage to a neurotic, joke-cracking New Yorker on NBC's *Mad About You*, she's the kind of upbeat, self-possessed wife who reassures neurotic, joke-cracking, would-be romantics that there's hope for the future. Helen

12

Hunt is proof that discipline and what high-school guidance counselors call a Good Attitude pay off: *Twister*'s half-billion-dollar worldwide gross turned the 33-year-old actress into a bankable movie player, and her first Emmy, as Best Actress in a Comedy Series, underscored her invaluable contribution to *Mad About You*'s success. "It's a collective sensibility," Hunt says of the show, which, in its fifth season, frequently wins against *Roseanne* in its Tuesday-night time slot.

More recently, Hunt has been scuttling from her *Mad* soundstage to the movie set of *Old Friends*, which she describes as a "complicated romantic comedy" from James L. Brooks, in which she costars with Jack Nicholson. But she feels no need to dump TV for the big screen: "I think of the TV show as a five- or six-year movie." And when the Buchman baby arrives—probably in time for May's ratings sweeps—"it will still be about the couple, and how to introduce a baby into their lives," she says. "Jamie will be full of opinions." And viewers will be full of affection. —*Lisa Schwarzbaum*

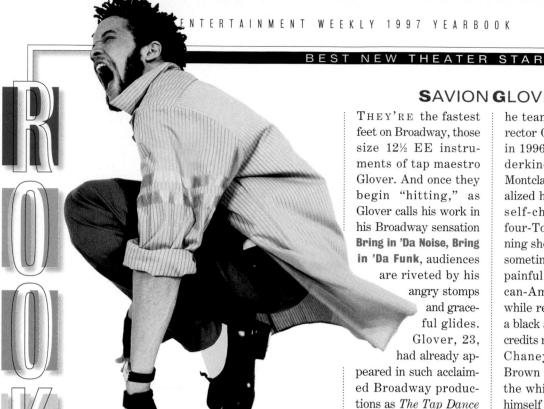

ROOKIES

BEST NEW THEATER STAR

SAVION GLOVER

THEY'RE the fastest feet on Broadway, those size 12½ EE instruments of tap maestro Glover. And once they begin "hitting," as Glover calls his work in his Broadway sensation **Bring in 'Da Noise, Bring in 'Da Funk**, audiences are riveted by his angry stomps and graceful glides. Glover, 23, had already appeared in such acclaimed Broadway productions as *The Tap Dance Kid* and *Jelly's Last Jam*, but it wasn't until he teamed up with director George C. Wolfe in 1996 that the wunderkind from Upper Montclair, N.J., fully realized his vision. In his self-choreographed, four-Tony-award-winning show, he teaches a sometimes funny, often painful lesson in African-American history while reclaiming tap as a black art form. Glover credits mentors like Lon Chaney and Buster Brown in the show, all the while establishing himself as the future of the genre. Now, *that's* a feat. —*Jessica Shaw*

JON FAVREAU

A DEBUT screenplay about a group of skirt-chasers leads to a $5 million studio payoff? Not bad! But for Favreau, 30, crafting his hilariously repetitive dialogue in **Swingers** just meant aping what he heard every day. He'll follow up by starring in and directing the Hasidic Western *The Marshal of Revelations*. "I didn't think I'd get any writing heat off this," says the once-struggling actor. "I was just giving myself a good role to play." —*Dave Karger*

BEST NEW SCREENWRITER

BEST NEW MOVIE ACTOR

EDWARD NORTON

NORTON may be even more of a mystery than the deceptively benign bumpkin he played with chilling brilliance in **Primal Fear**. As Aaron Stampler, the hick accused of murder, Norton, 27, fooled defense lawyer Richard Gere—and the audience. The press-shy Norton says his main goal is to find great character roles. "I tend to look at a part and wonder if 10 other young men can do it," he says. "I look for something I can bring a particular take to." The year's reluctant It Boy next brought his particular take to *The People vs. Larry Flynt*, in which he plays Flynt's attorney (on the set, Norton reportedly began a relationship with costar Courtney Love), and to Woody Allen's *Everyone Says I Love You*, in which he sings. Singing? Courtney Love? Clearly, the words *primal fear* are not in Norton's vocabulary. —*Dana Kennedy*

BEST NEW DIRECTORS

STANLEY TUCCI & CAMPBELL SCOTT

THANKS TO **Big Night**, the year's most delicious movie, our pasta and panini dreams got a lot more saucy. In telling the tale of two Italian émigré brothers trying to save their 1950s New Jersey restaurant, actor-directors Tucci and Scott used pathos and humor (plus some oregano and olive oil) to create one orgasmic, out-of-this-world objet d'overindulgence. "It's a secret recipe handed down to my mother from my father's mother's family," Tucci says of the film's girth-quaking timpano dish, a giant pasta pie shaped like a kettledrum, "but nobody listens." Actually, Hollywood *is* listening: Between them, Tucci and Scott have at least nine projects lined up. Still, Tucci thinks he might be in the wrong field. "Business at Italian restaurants is picking up wherever the movie is playing. The movie's doing fine, but I wish I had a piece of that action." *—David Hochman*

BEST NEW MOVIE ACTRESS

RENEE ZELLWEGER

SOMEONE forgot to teach Zellweger two rules of acting: Never star opposite kids or

Tom Cruise. Which is fine, since Zellweger, Cruise's love interest in **Jerry Maguire**, more than matched her leading man and her other costar (Jonathan Lipnicki, 6). "When I got called to read opposite Cruise, I was laughing," says the Texas native, whose experience was mostly limited to low-budget films like *The Return of the Texas Chainsaw Massacre*. "I thought, 'That's funny.' I was happily unemployed." If Zellweger, 27, would rather be idle, her future looks bleak: She's finished *Liar* with Tim Roth and is set to play a Hasidic Jew in *Price Below Rubies*. "I never thought about being famous," she says. "That's all mythical." Tell that to her costar. *—Rebecca Ascher-Walsh*

EWAN MCGREGOR

RARELY HAS an actor made a grimier entrée into stardom. As the chief junkie in **Trainspotting**, the much-hyped saga about a pack of smack fiends in Scotland, McGregor turned blue from an overdose, writhed on a sweaty cot, plunged into the bowels of a filthy latrine—and wooed the world in the process. "Some of the things he's doing are repellent," says director Danny Boyle, "and yet there's a charm that makes you feel deeply ambiguous about it. You're drawn to him." Like Tom Cruise, McGregor knows the

power of a killer grin. Whether he's leering into a windshield in *Trainspotting* or courting Gwyneth Paltrow from horseback in *Emma*, the 25-year-old Scot somehow manages to flash a puckish smile that makes you want to get into risky business with him. The grin'll come in handy; next, McGregor mans a morgue in *Nightwatch* and kidnaps Cameron Diaz in Boyle's *A Life Less Ordinary*. *—Jeff Gordinier*

BEST NEW IMPORT

CAREY LOWELL

YOU'D THINK IT would be tough joining the ensemble of **Law & Order**, a show that goes through cast members the way Jim Carrey goes through facial expressions. But Lowell, 31, is the new element in *L&O* that has people paying fresh attention to the seven-year-old drama. As assistant DA Jamie Ross, the former model and *Licence to Kill* Bond girl makes plea bargaining pleasing, managing to be grim, intelligent, and alluring at the same time. Lowell's a divorced single mom (she

was married to actor Griffin Dunne). So is Jamie, and, says the actress, "I don't know if I'm giving anything away, but Jamie's ex-husband, who's a defense attorney, might come into an episode. It's kind of a Marcia Clark custody thing—the mother's too busy working, and the husband will try to take the child away, with Jamie in the Marcia Clark position." Unlike Clark, however, Lowell has no trouble making a tough assignment fit like a glove. —*Ken Tucker*

BEST NEW TV ACTRESS

BEST NEW NOVELIST

JENNIFER BELLE

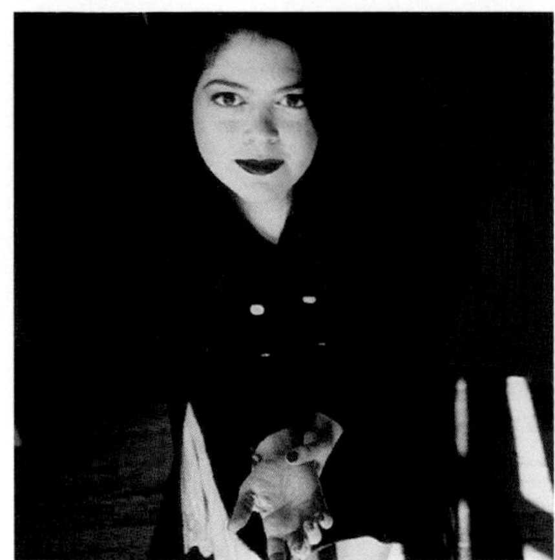

ASK HER how her debut novel, **Going Down**, has changed her life, and Belle, a sometime actress, starts imitating her answering machine: "Hi! This is Madonna. Call me! *Beeep.* This is New York Telephone. We need to talk about the $950 you owe us. *Beeeep.*" Belle, 28, claims she's more broke than ever, despite a movie deal. "They haven't *paid* me yet," she insists. Yet her sad-clown story of an NYU student's foray into the world's oldest profession earned praise from the likes of Jay McInerney and Tama Janowitz. And oh, yes, from Madonna, who ousted many "safer" contenders for the film rights because Belle is such a huge fan. "I mean, how safe can you really be in Hollywood?" Belle deadpans. She's never played it safe before—why start now? —*Alexandra Jacobs*

BEST NEW TV ACTOR

RAY ROMANO

"I'M A SKEPTIC at heart, and pessimistic all the time," says Romano, star of CBS' **Everybody Loves Raymond**. Take his reaction to the standing ovation he got after a recent taping: "They were getting up to leave anyway." As fans of the put-upon comic know, Romano, 39, is prime time's most appealing new stand-up sitcom star. In *Raymond* he basically plays himself: a mensch with three kids, a sharp wife (on camera, Patricia Heaton; off camera, Anna), tough parents, and a droopy brother. Ratings success has proved elusive. It didn't help that *Raymond* premiered against ABC's hit *Sabrina, the Teenage Witch*. "My daughter watched *Sabrina*," he says. "I had a zero share in my own house." The news that CBS has ordered five new episodes brought *some* cheer to his household. "My wife went right to the mall," says Romano. "She's spending syndication money already." —*Bret Watson*

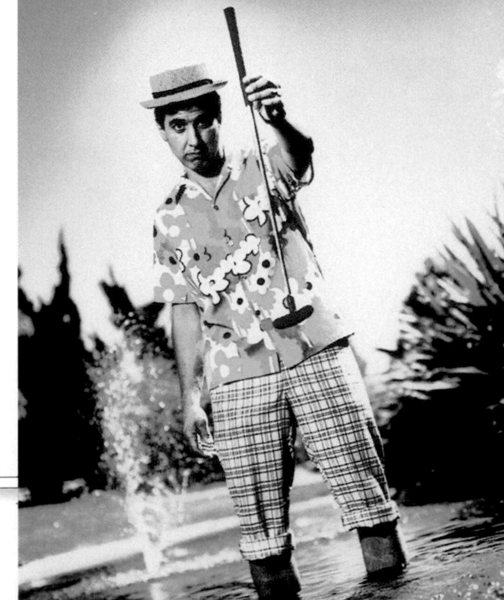

BEST NEW BAND

THE FUGEES

CONSIDER us killed. Adding little more than a canny beat and some reggae flavor, the Fugees redefined "Killing Me Softly" for a new generation—and that was just the passageway into the crossover smash **The Score**. Imagine Arrested Development with a sense of humor, or Snoop with a conscience, and you approach the ground the Fugees found between tired "positive" rap and hardcore nihilism. With the looks and pipes for a solo career, Lauryn Hill gets such deep-dish support from her two Haitian-American cohorts, no reasonable fan could wish her spun off. Though the Fugees were technically not frosh, the more than 4 million scanned for *Score* initiates a gritty, celebratory subgenre we'll call "post-gangsta." In 1996 the Fugees—and rap itself—seemed brand-new. *—Chris Willman*

SHIRLEY MANSON

SHIRLEY MANSON grew up in the Calvinist confines of Scotland. Maybe that explains why some of her utterances betray such an *austere* approach to the pleasures of love. "I can't use what I can't abuse," the scarlet-haired chanteuse from Garbage purrs in "Vow." "I came to cut you up, I came to knock you down, I came around to tear your little world apart." In 1996, the little world had no choice but to surrender. Her band's debut, **Garbage**, went platinum, spitting out a slew of bewitching hit singles ("Stupid Girl," "Only Happy When It Rains") and turning the pale Manson into an object of flushed adoration. If rock is dominated by screamers and strummers, Manson, 30, stands out because she is neither; she prefers to slice to your heart with a velveteen sneer. As she puts it in "Queer," "You learn to love the pain you feel." *Ouch. —JG*

BEST NEW FEMALE SINGER

TONY RICH

IS TONY RICH *the man*, or what? In 1996 the 25-year-old singer-songwriter-producer's debut album, **Words**, went platinum; the melancholy "Nobody Knows" became a lite-radio staple; and the critical kudos kept coming. Best of all, it was on Rich's terms: *Words* was exactly the record he wanted to make, its music a seductive R&B variant tailor-made to appeal to people who normally give R&B a wide berth. Yes, success has its rewards—like all those new friends. "I was having lunch with Sheryl Crow last week, and Eric Clapton stopped by," says Rich nonchalantly. "I told him, 'Listen, I need a *bad* guitar player for my new album.'" (The guitarist took a rain check but roped Rich into singing backup on a song for *his* next album.) Rich's sophomore effort is due in late '97, but he doesn't relish the thought of losing his newcomer status. "You only get one shot at being a 'Best New Artist.'" *—Tom Sinclair*

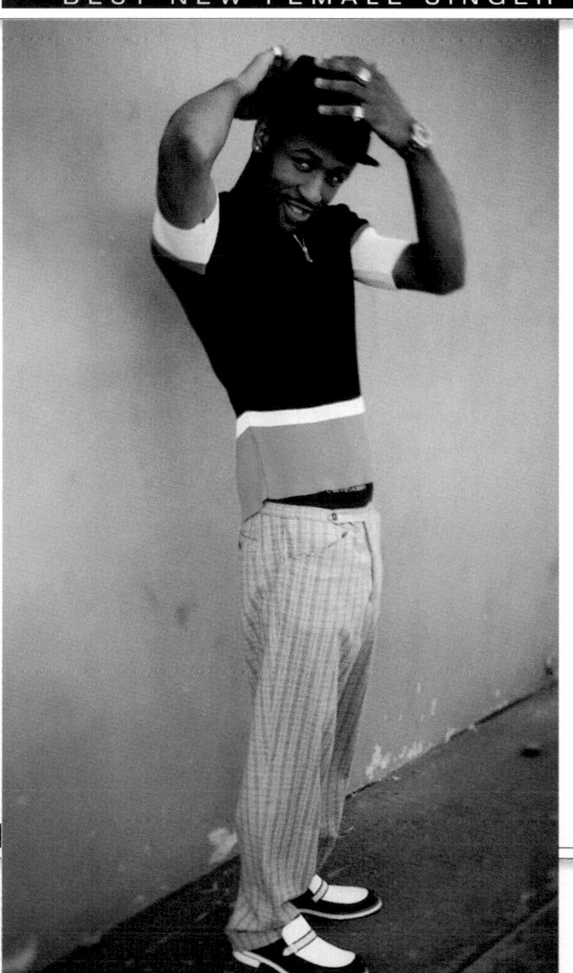

BEST NEW MALE SINGER

THE
YE
REV

AR IN

IEWS

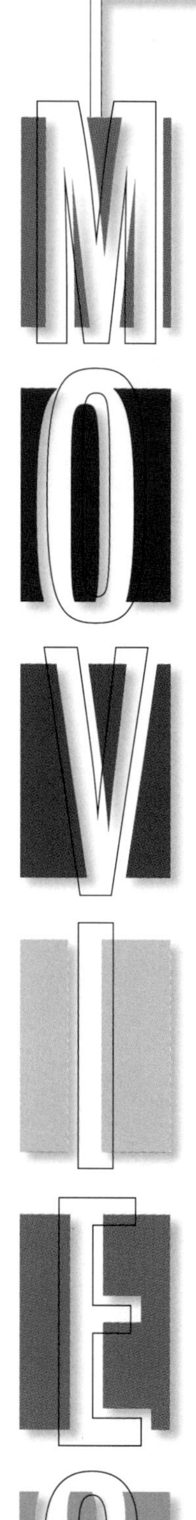

BREAKING THE

WAVES

SOME MOVIES ARE like fairy tales—they don't just tell stories, they cast spells—and Lars von Trier's lyrically transfixing epic works that kind of magic. The moment we meet Bess, who enters into a marriage of erotic and spiritual bliss, becomes crazed with grief when her husband goes away, and is reunited with him through an act of God that would test Job, von Trier dips us into rivers of emotion. The film's eerie power derives from the way it combines portents and miracles with a dazzlingly "secular" documentary surface. Emily Watson, in a fearless, bewitching performance, is as spontaneous as a child at play, yet there's a grave enchantment to the way her trust is transmuted into open-eyed self-sacrifice. Years from now, I think *Breaking the Waves* will be remembered as the first great movie to tap the passions of the millennium—a yearning for transcendence that's a whisper away from doom. **BY OWEN GLEIBERMAN**

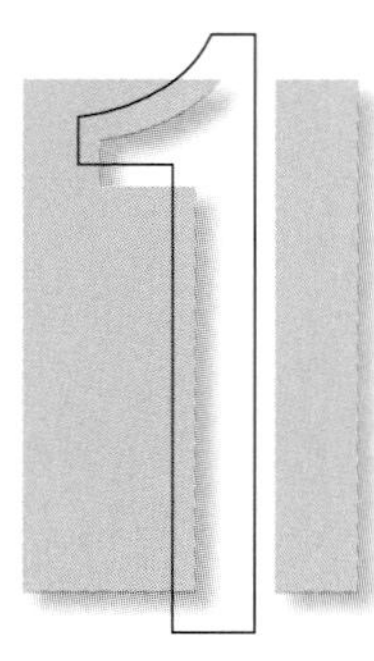

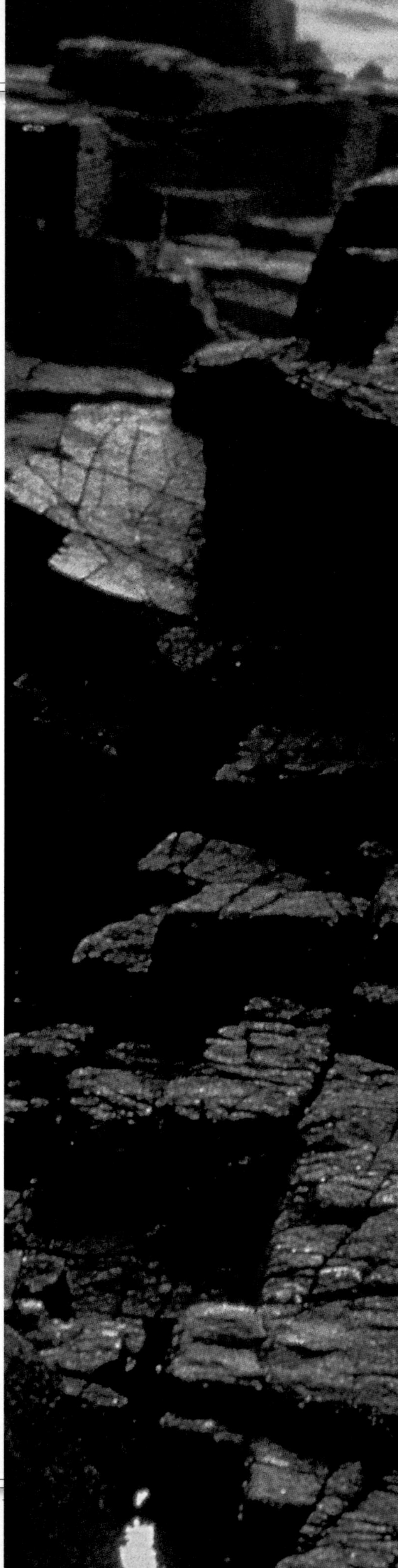

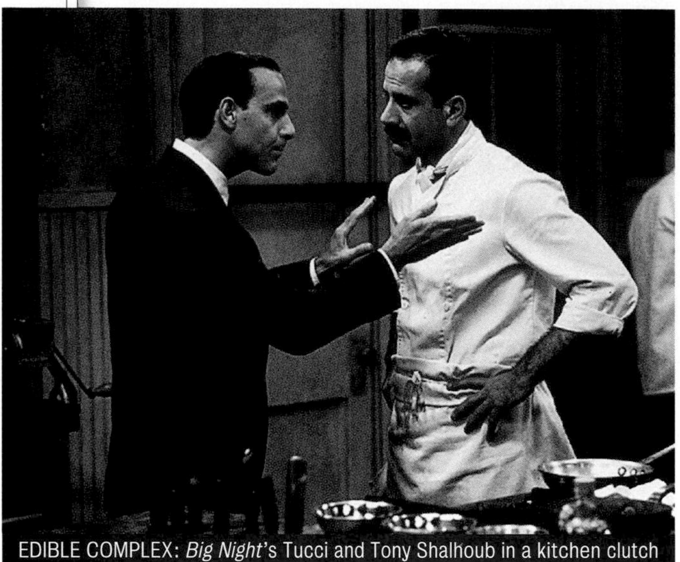
EDIBLE COMPLEX: *Big Night*'s Tucci and Tony Shalhoub in a kitchen clutch

BIG NIGHT

2 The most ecstatic scene of the year consists of a man cooking an omelette. The camera doesn't even move: It just sits there on Stanley Tucci, who plays the owner of an Italian restaurant in 1950s New Jersey, as he gives birth to a meal. Codirected by Tucci, the exquisitely deft *Big Night* transcends the usual food-porn "deliciousness" (*Like Water for Chocolate*). The movie is about many things: the love of brothers, the ache of exile, the quest for the perfect risotto. Mostly, it's about the way that food, the universal art form, connects us to each other and to ourselves.

TRAINSPOTTING

3 Danny Boyle's rudely cathartic rock-and-drug joyride was underrated by its heroin-chic hype. In an era of glib moralizing, it was liberating to see a movie that understands the pleasures—and the perils—of addiction. Yet *Trainspotting*'s music-video zing, its mad scatological humor, and its celebration of smack's death-trip allure wouldn't have meant much if it didn't offer a hero as soulful as Ewan McGregor's Renton, a Junkie Without a Cause who dives headfirst into addiction in order to come out the other side.

THE CRUCIBLE

4 Director Nicholas Hytner transforms Arthur Miller's popular classic into an adrenaline-fueled rocket engine of a movie. Hytner doesn't just liberate the play from the stage. He makes Miller's parable of lust, guilt, hysteria, and doublethink take on an immediacy it never had before. Far from just dramatizing the Salem witch-hunts (or the treachery of McCarthyism), Miller lays bare the calculus of totalitarian psychology. And the cast endows his dialogue with a flesh and blood that leaves you thrilled, shattered, cleansed.

WITCH WAY OUT: Winona Ryder

SCOTS ON THE ROCKS: (From left) Jonny Lee Miller, McGregor, Kevin McKidd, and Ewen Bremner make tracks in *Trainspotting*

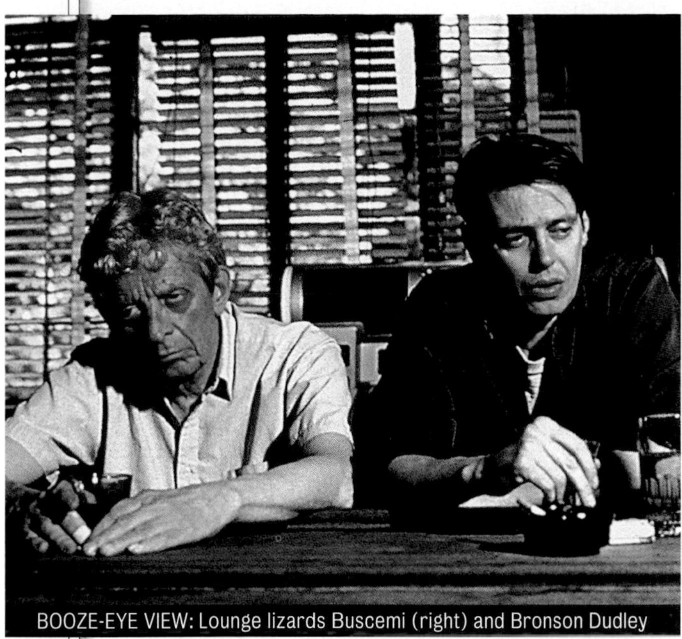
BOOZE-EYE VIEW: Lounge lizards Buscemi (right) and Bronson Dudley

TREES LOUNGE

5 It's no surprise to see that Steve Buscemi, making his debut as a writer-director, digs with raffish gusto into the role of Tommy, a wheedling barfly who spends his days trading quips at a dank Long Island saloon. The surprise is that Buscemi also turns out to be a major filmmaker. An ebullient portrait of the modern blue-collar blues, *Trees Lounge* has an inspired ensemble cast (standouts: Chloe Sevigny and Daniel Baldwin), and Buscemi orchestrates their performances with the kind of lifelike flow and dark-comedy-of-the-soul frankness a director like *Secrets & Lies*' Mike Leigh gets far more credit for only because he lets the seams show.

I SHOT ANDY WARHOL

6 In 1968, Valerie Solanas walked into Andy Warhol's office and pumped three bullets into his chest. Was she a paranoid fantasist, high on hate? Or a crackpot visionary testing the waters of feminist rage before it was fashionable? The beauty of Mary Harron's film is that it understands that Solanas was both. Lili Taylor plays Valerie as a scowling, ratlike crank who is nevertheless so blithe, so outrageously rational about her own "philosophy," that you can't help but like her. And Harron's re-creation of the Warhol Factory proves she's the rare filmmaker who can turn pop history into art precisely because she respects the truth of what happened.

SHOT IN THE DARK: Taylor as Solanas

TWISTER

7 This $242 million blockbuster is also the most underrated movie of the year. Director Jan De Bont gets the scary, dreamlike spectacle of tornadoes right up there on screen. The wonder isn't so much in their destructive power as in the fact that they're natural phenomena that seem supernatural—indeed, they seem like *beings*. De Bont, a wizard of roiling kinesthetic excitement, directs with the fluidity and grandeur of Steven Spielberg in his great '70s films, staging the tornadoes as impossibly vast spectral-meteorological events. The love-triangle plot is dopey, but the performances of Helen Hunt and Bill Paxton aren't. They make the characters feel romantically bound—to each other, and to the audience—through their desire to gaze, with tremulous awe, upon one twister after another.

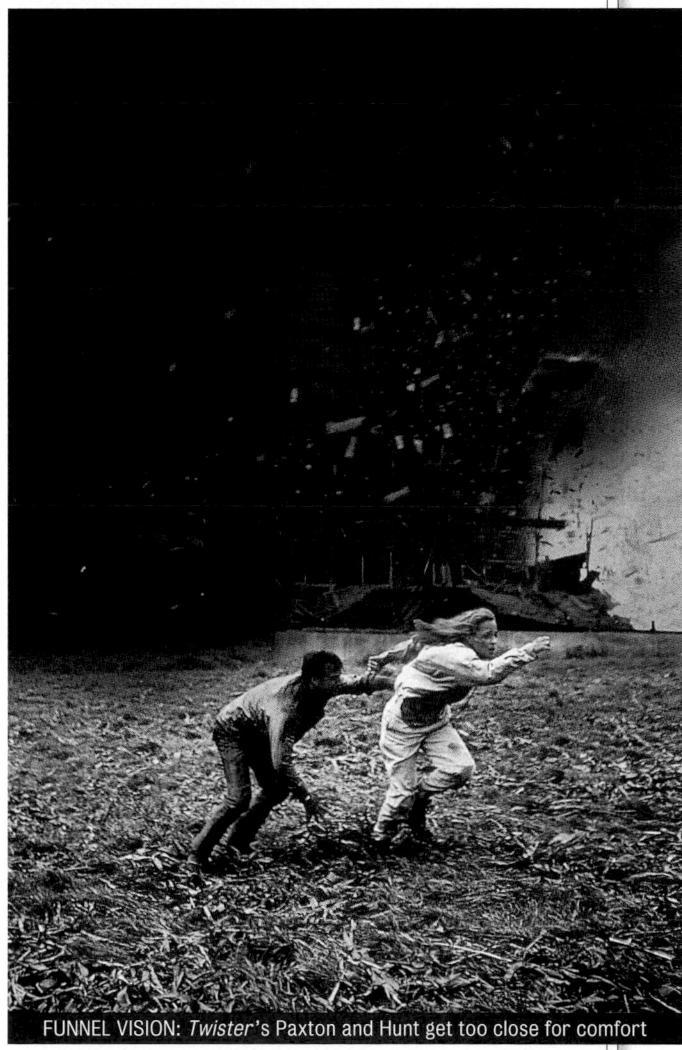
FUNNEL VISION: *Twister*'s Paxton and Hunt get too close for comfort

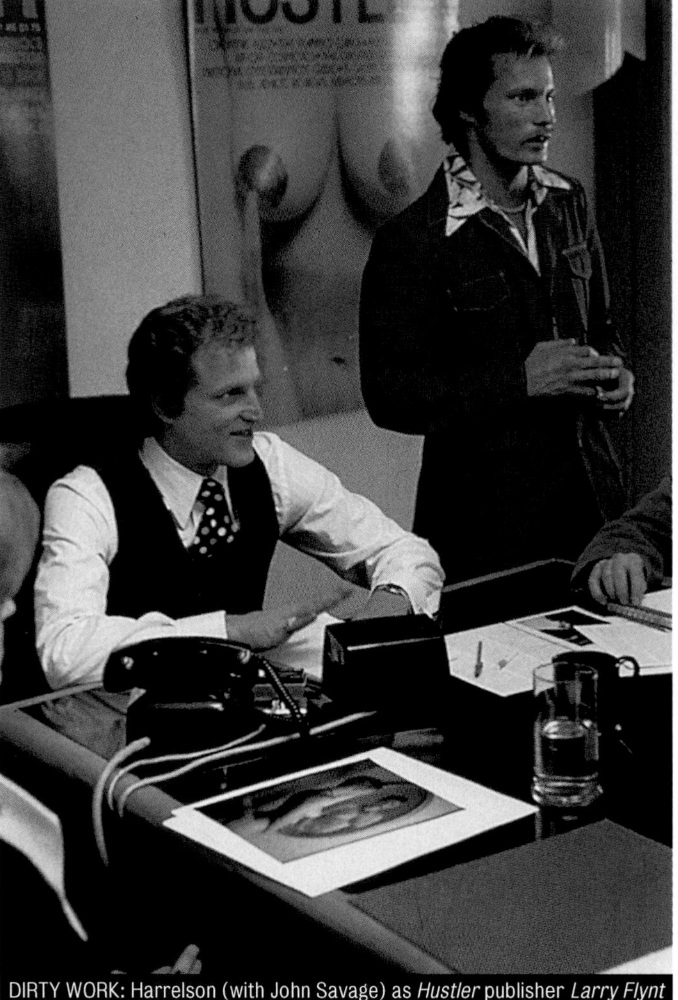

DIRTY WORK: Harrelson (with John Savage) as *Hustler* publisher *Larry Flynt*

SWINGERS

8 A bracingly witty look at desperate young dudes on the L.A. martini-and-swing-bar circuit. The movie understands that these days, the real romantic comedy takes place *before* boy meets girl. Just beneath their babbly debates about how to make all the right moves, you can hear the characters tying themselves in knots trying to be Alpha Males and Nice Guys at the same time. Screenwriter and costar Jon Favreau turns his neuroses into antsy, jostling hilarity, spawning the catchphrase of the year ("You're *money*!"), and Vince Vaughn, as his glam-jerk sidekick, already has the charisma of a star.

THE PEOPLE VS. LARRY FLYNT

9 When Larry Flynt created *Hustler* magazine in the mid-'70s, he pushed past the boundaries of what a mainstream skin publication could show, and that's exactly what got him in trouble with the law. The inspiring joke of Milos Forman's richly funny and exuberant docudrama is that the scuzzier Flynt's magazine became, the more it turned him into a hero, a renegade crusader for the First Amendment. Woody Harrelson's audacious performance takes off after Flynt is shot and paralyzed: Doped up and enraged, his voice a nerve-damaged mumble, Flynt suddenly has nothing to lose—and so he takes on the courts, Jerry Falwell, the world, becoming the whacked-out Lenny Bruce of porn. And Courtney Love, as Flynt's drug-addled party-girl wife, demonstrates that she has the force and instinctive humor of a major actress.

TIN CUP

10 The most radiant example of movie-star magic this year. As washed-up golf pro Roy McAvoy, Kevin Costner shakes off his scowl and embraces the joy of seediness. Roy has to play the game on his own terms, even if it means losing, and Costner, face crinkling up with pleasure, digs so far into the character's ornery grace that he seems to be rediscovering what it means to be a star. Ron Shelton's leisurely fable doesn't have quite the romantic chemistry of his 1988 *Bull Durham*, but it's an even niftier sports movie, with a climax that defies prediction even as it satisfies your every cornball wish.

CUP RUNNETH OVER: Golfer Costner romances psychologist Rene Russo

A SECOND OPINION

IN LISA SCHWARZBAUM'S roster of the year's best films, the Coens' cracked-crystal *Fargo* goes farthest

A WINTER'S TALE: *Fargo*'s unflappable sheriff Frances McDormand

FARGO

1 Lots of snow. A very pregnant police chief. A wood chipper. Yah, sure, it's heaven, Coen brothers-style. The gonzo-gothic vision of Joel and Ethan has never been more focused, more beautifully structured, or, in its twisted way, more compassionate than in this startling American original.

BIG NIGHT

2 Food movies have goodwill built into them—what's not to like about watching happy people with good appetites? But this beaut, starring, cowritten, and codirected by Stanley Tucci, is graced with a bigness of spirit that touches the heart as well as the taste buds.

WELCOME TO THE DOLLHOUSE

3 Filmmaker Todd Solondz, working with the breathtakingly game young actress Heather Matarazzo, nails the agony of junior high school geekitude, gawky-girl division, in a story that teeters almost recklessly between being brutally funny and just plain brutal.

THE CRUCIBLE

4 Director Nicholas Hytner makes an expansive movie out of a stage-bound setting. He's helped by some of the best performances of the year, particularly by Joan Allen. But it takes more than good stars to create a production that so powerfully weaves themes of integrity, sexual hysteria, and hypocrisy; it takes inspired movie artistry.

TRAINSPOTTING

5 The grimmest of subjects—heroin addiction among dead-end Edinburgh kids—turned into audacious, funny, artsy...*fun*. Is this, as Martha Stewart would say, a Good Thing? Your call. Is this a brilliant bit of moviemaking? My call: Yup.

TIN CUP

6 Ron Shelton's triumph of adult Hollywood moviemaking: a relaxed, romantic sports comedy by, for, and about middle-aged folks who have lost a few and therefore savor the joy of winning all the more.

LONE STAR

7 John Sayles' deeply satisfying Western/mystery is filled with the kind of richly shaded characters and intricate plot twists that are listed in the dictionary under *Saylesian*. But who knew a Sayles production could be so sexy?

ANGELS & INSECTS

8 Belinda and Philip Haas' fascinating, idiosyncratic adaptation of A. S. Byatt's novella about casual decadence in Victorian England starts out stately and gets fabulously weirder. It's fabulously dirty, too, and you can't take your eyes off the bugs, the coupling bodies—or Kristin Scott Thomas.

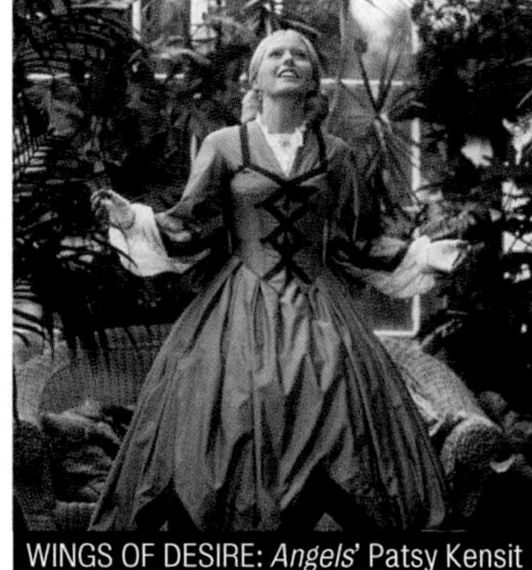

WINGS OF DESIRE: *Angels*' Patsy Kensit

THE TRUTH ABOUT CATS & DOGS

9 Two words: Janeane Garofalo. She's our favorite insecure heroine, she's the girlfriend you want or the girl you want to be, and she turns this smart romantic comedy into pure bliss. Uma Thurman's in it too, and cute Brit Ben Chaplin as the guy who wisely chooses depth (that's our Janeane) over gloss.

MA SAISON PREFEREE

10 André Téchiné's pensive film about the complicated bonds of family feels artless and uncomposed. That's a good thing. In fact, this delicately perceptive study, starring Catherine Deneuve and the *magnifique* Daniel Auteuil, is a gift for moviegoers who know how to pay attention.

THE WORST

MULHOLLAND FALLS

1 In this brain-dead knockoff of *Chinatown*, Nick Nolte leads a crew of detectives who seem less concerned with getting to the bottom of a nuclear-radiation scandal than with parading around like showroom dummies in their stick pins and perfectly unsmudged hats.

FALLS GUYS: Nolte's team

ANTONIA'S LINE

2 How do you fight the patriarchy? In Marleen Gorris' insufferable art-house crowd-pleaser, the answer is simple: You form a matriarchy. And you make sure that everyone in it is sweet and proud and just a bit kooky. Beneath its feminist pieties, *Antonia's Line* is the most cloying vision of communal eccentricity since *King of Hearts*.

ERASER, THE ROCK, & BROKEN ARROW

3 If you were looking to numb yourself into oblivion, which of these movies would you choose? Which has the most derivative plot, the most incoherent action, the most mindlessly "kinetic" MTV editing, the biggest pileup of stupid, explosive clichés? Personally, I couldn't decide. All three qualify as the Slam-Bang, Punch-Your-Face, Blow-Your-Socks-Off, Roller-Coaster Action Knockout of the Year.

THERE'S THE RUBOUT: *Eraser*

HEAVY

4 It should have been called *Slow*. In a remote woodland diner, a fat chef stands around making pizzas and gawking at sexy new waitress Liv Tyler. Mostly, he just stands there. Staring. For minutes. On end.

ALL WET: *Heavy*'s Tyler

EVITA

5 Was Eva Perón a power vixen or a saint? We can hardly tell from Alan Parker's bombastic musical, a series of sluggish, dissociated production numbers. Madonna erases her own charisma, receding into the murk of Andrew Lloyd Webber's luridly dated kitsch. *—OG*

CRITICS' CHOICES

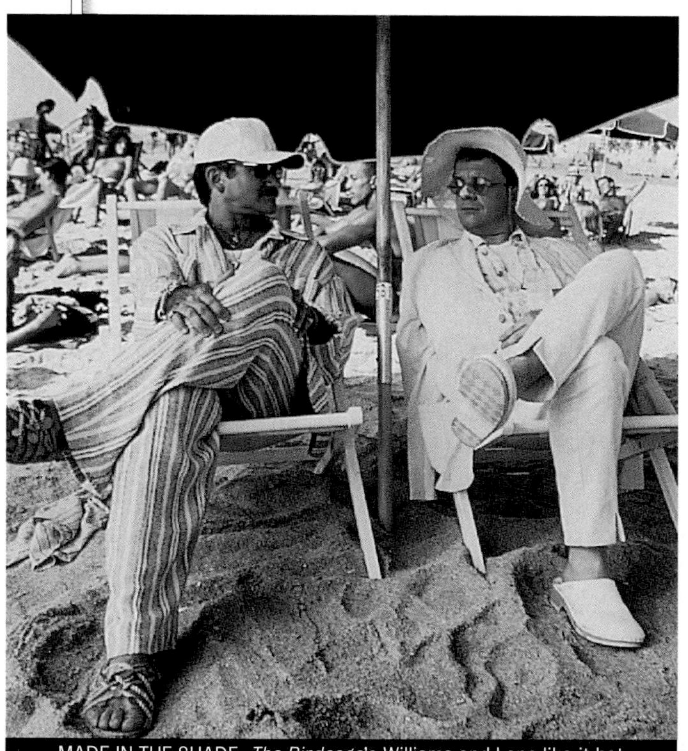
MADE IN THE SHADE: *The Birdcage*'s Williams and Lane like it hot

HEIDI FLEISS: HOLLYWOOD MADAM

(Unrated) An amazing new documentary about the Beverly Hills physician's daughter who became a madam to the stars. The director, Nick Broomfield, takes us through every back-alley detour of his investigation, the wrong turns as well as the right ones. It's a technique ideally suited to a movie about life in the exploitation Babylon, since the people Broomfield talks to are, for the most part, pathological liars. **A** *(#314, Feb. 16) —OG*

THE BIRDCAGE

(R) Enchantingly witty. In this remake of the 1978 French farce *La Cage aux Folles*, Albert (Nathan Lane), a middle-aged drag queen, headlines at the South Beach nightclub owned by his longtime lover, Armand (Robin Williams). When Armand's son announces his engagement to the daughter of a right-wing senator (Gene Hackman), the couple host a dinner party in which they attempt to pass themselves off as "normal" heterosexuals. The beauty of *The Birdcage* is that its jokes and its message are one

GETTING OVER THE HUMP: Disney's *Hunchback* turns Quasimodo's plight into a tuneful quest for self-acceptance

and the same. These characters couldn't change themselves if they tried. **A–** *(#318, March 15) —OG*

THE YOUNG POISONER'S HANDBOOK

(Unrated) It's like a Charles Addams cartoon directed by Alfred Hitchcock. Based on the early-1960s case of Graham Young, a teenager from the London suburbs who became obsessed with poisoning people, Benjamin Ross' film seduces the audience into viewing the most appalling acts with smirky, jaundiced detachment. As Graham, Hugh O'Conor, with his big, dark, unblinking eyes (he looks like a handsome owl), almost convinces you that homicide is a reasonable extension of adolescent rebelliousness. **A–** *(#320, March 29) —OG*

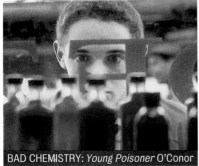

BAD CHEMISTRY: *Young Poisoner* O'Conor

FLIRTING WITH DISASTER

(R) From the twisted mind of filmmaker David O. Russell comes an ingratiatingly antic ensemble comedy. Ben Stiller stars as Mel, a mildly neurotic guy raised by adoptive parents (Mary Tyler Moore and George Segal, a terrific Punch-and-Judy match), who sets out to find his biological parents. The top-drawer cast includes Patricia Arquette as Mel's wife, Téa Leoni as a deadpan social worker, and Lily Tomlin and Alan Alda as Mel's birth parents, still hippies after all these years. *Flirting* is a little too weighed down with stage business to soar. But episode for episode, it's one of the ha-ha funniest movies currently around. **B** *(#321, April 5) —LS*

PARENT TRAP: *Disaster*'s Arquette, Stiller

THE HUNCHBACK OF NOTRE DAME

(G) Beautiful and transporting—the best of Disney's "serious" animated features in the multiplex era. Quasimodo has been recast as a teenage lonely-boy version of Charles Laughton's grotesque creature. As he becomes the protector of Esmeralda, the aqua-eyed Gypsy beauty (who has the voice—and face—of Demi Moore), we share his romantic longing with bittersweet rue. The movie has a rich visual grandeur; Notre Dame itself suggests a fortress made of gingerbread. And the Alan Menken–Stephen Schwartz score has been woven into the action as seamless recitative, creating a true folk-pop

operetta. Will children grasp the nuances? So strong is the storytelling that they'll feel the film's elemental passions. They'll understand that Quasimodo's most telling quest isn't, finally, to win the love of Esmeralda—it's to emerge from his cathedral prison and discover that there's a place for him too on those beautiful Parisian streets. **A** *(#332, June 21)* —*OG*

OUTFOXED: *The Frighteners*

THE FRIGHTENERS

(R) A smart, subtle movie disguised as a dumb, noisy one. After his wife dies in a car accident, Frank (Michael J. Fox) can see spirits risen from the grave. Lonely and cynical, he works a con with a trio of comical ghosts as a "psychic investigator." Shaken out of complacency by Lucy (Trini Alvarado), whose husband is killed by a murderous spirit, Frank tries some real psychic detecting. Directed by Peter Jackson (*Heavenly Creatures*), this is that rare horror film that gets better as it proceeds. **B+** *(#337, July 26)* —*KT*

COURAGE UNDER FIRE

(R) Lieut. Col. Nathaniel Serling (Denzel Washington) returns from the Gulf War and investigates the case of a medevac pilot (Meg Ryan) killed in action.

FLY-BY KNIGHTS: *ID4*'s pilots Smith and Harry Connick Jr. watch the skies

Serling interviews each of the men under her command, and, in a series of vivid battle flashbacks, we see different versions of the events. The film takes its urgency from the undercurrents of desperation in Washington's haunted, nearly implosive performance. **B+** *(#337, July 26)* —*OG*

INDEPENDENCE DAY

(PG-13) Techno-horny and hokey, corny and adorable: This big-ass sci-fi thriller about hostile outer-

FIRE IN THE BELLY: Gulf War hero Ryan (with Matt Damon) displays *Courage* as a posthumous Medal of Honor recipient

MOLL RAT: *Bound*'s Tilly makes a killing as a mobster's girl gone bad

space aliens who invade the earth, inspiring all of humanity to fight back, is the first futuristic disaster movie that's cute as a button. And, as such, it's intrinsically American, of-the-moment fun. The story may be light as Wonder bread, but the script, larded with references to popular culture, is witty. And, as a snappy Marine fighter pilot who at one point slugs a particularly ornery extraterrestrial who has hit the Arizona sand, the hip and fabulously likable Will Smith lofts us to heights of satisfied giddiness. **B+** *(#335, July 12) —LS*

BASQUIAT

(R) A teasingly unresolved docudrama about Jean-Michel Basquiat, the rock star of the '80s art scene. In the title role, Jeffrey Wright is spacey in a seductive, monosyllabic way, as if he were swimming around in feelings he didn't have the words for. The scenes of Basquiat's rise are juicy inside glimpses of the New York art world, with David Bowie ripely overplaying Andy Warhol's drop-dead murmurings. By the end, though, we realize director Julian Schnabel has reconfigured *Basquiat* as a kind of ghostly myth, and that we've never completely seen the man behind it. **B+** *(#340, Aug. 16) —OG*

THAT THING YOU DO!

(PG-13) In Tom Hanks' lovingly crafted fable, the Wonders rise to fame on the strength of one Beatlesque single. Yet they aren't really stars (they're the cogs of the moment), and the fact that they don't realize it lends a sly irony to everything we're seeing. **A-** *(#347, Oct. 4) —OG*

BOUND

(R) A clever if trendy caper featuring Coen brothers-style gore, Scorsese-style Mob double-crossings, and Joe Eszterhas-style lesbians. *Schwing!* Gina Gershon plays a provocatively grime-covered ex-con and apartment handy gal; Jennifer Tilly is the velvety mobster's moll who loves her. As the women hatch a plan to make off with $2 million in Mafia greenbacks, filmmakers Larry and Andy Wachowski pile on the film noir references, producing an inventive updated take on the genre. **B+** *(#348, Oct. 11) —LS*

MICHAEL COLLINS

(R) A serious historical film drained of serious history. Director-writer Neil Jordan tells the tale of Collins, a key figure in what became the Irish Re-

GETTING HIS IRISH UP: Neeson leads the way as IRA rebel *Michael Collins*

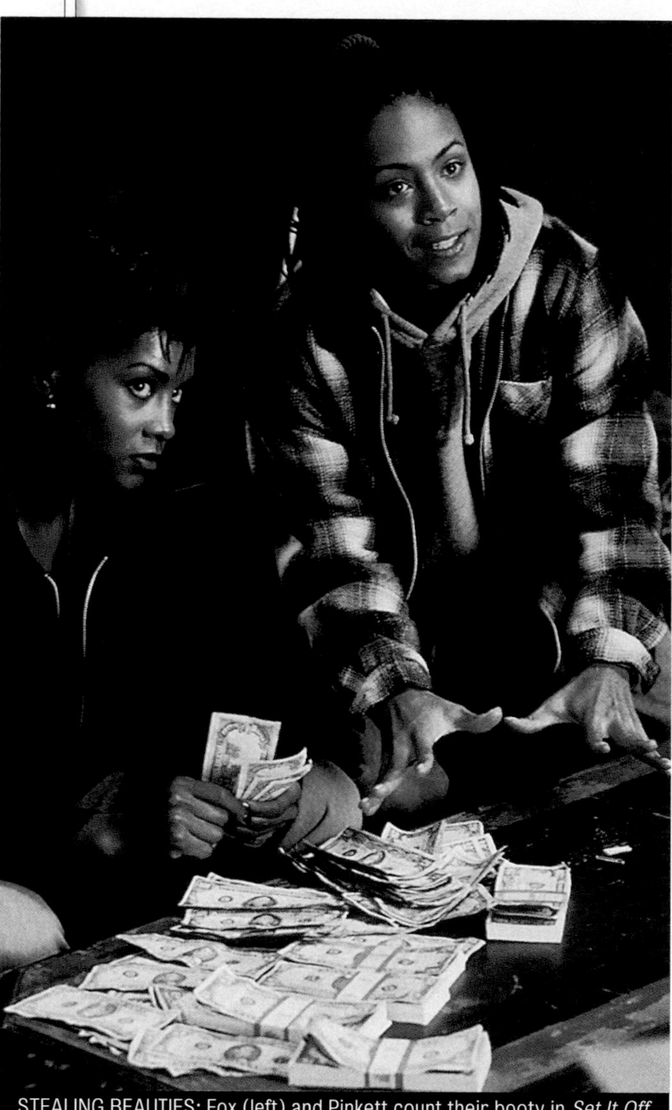
STEALING BEAUTIES: Fox (left) and Pinkett count their booty in *Set It Off*

publican Army in the early part of this century, and gets a classic performance out of Liam Neeson. As the reluctant rebel-turned-statesman, Neeson combines the earnest intensity he radiated in *Schindler's List* with the two-fisted swagger he brought to *Rob Roy*. Julia Roberts provides the love interest; she's charming, but the romantic triangle between her, Neeson, and Aidan Quinn (as Collins' best friend) is hokey and contrived. **B+** *(#350, Oct. 25) —KT*

NICO ICON

(Unrated) An entrancingly lurid documentary about Nico, the zombie chanteuse of the late '60s. We first see her intoning songs with the Velvet Underground in her druggy, lugubrious, Berlin-is-burning-and-I-don't-care monotone, and then as an X ray of her former self—gloomy and ravaged, strung out on smack, traveling from one club to the next to perform her listless cabaret doom rock. The queasy dance of before-and-after images lends the film a voyeuristic intrigue. Yet Nico herself remains aloof to the point of unknowability, a *Vogue* cover rotting away before our eyes. **A-** *(#312, Feb. 2) —OG*

SET IT OFF

(R) There are echoes of *Boyz N the Hood* and *Thelma & Louise* in this girl-pack story about four housing-project girlfriends who decide to rob banks, but that doesn't account for the very particular dark and loose qualities of this fresh work. The story doesn't always hang together, but the foursome—Jada Pinkett, Vivica Fox, Kimberly Elise, and the astonishing Queen Latifah—are tight. And as reality closes in on their fantasy world, the film swings off on a powerful, tragic trajectory. **B+** *(#352, Nov. 8) —LS*

VELVET FOG: *Nico*'s iconoclast

SHINE

(PG-13) A moving biographical drama from Australia's Scott Hicks about fellow countryman David Helfgott, a child prodigy of a pianist whose career was shattered by a breakdown when he was in his 20s. A lyrical style from Hicks and strong performances from Noah Taylor and Geoffrey Rush (as David younger and older) and Armin Mueller-Stahl (as the pianist's overwhelming immigrant father) make this a powerful piece of work. The rest of the luster comes from the shine we reflect back onto a movie about one man's resurrection from the institutionalized dead. **B+** *(#355, Nov. 29) —LS*

BLUE NOTES: *Shine*'s troubled pianist Taylor (right, with John Gielgud)

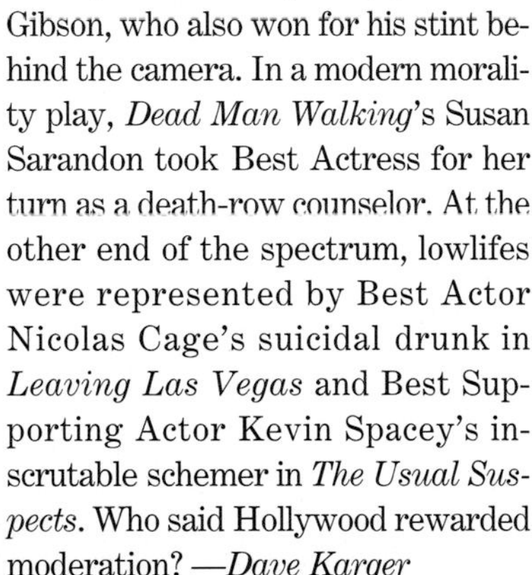

BEST PICTURE: *Braveheart*

BEST ACTOR: Nicolas Cage (*Leaving Las Vegas*)

BEST ACTRESS: Susan Sarandon (*Dead Man Walking*)

BEST SUPPORTING ACTRESS: Mira Sorvino (*Mighty Aphrodite*)

OSCAR WINNERS

ANOTHER YEAR, another night of extremes at the Oscars, as the gold man continued his tradition of honoring human triumphs and despair. From the uplifting camp came Best Picture *Braveheart*, which had the earmarks of an Oscar fave: a crowd-pleasing historical epic directed by the popular Mel Gibson, who also won for his stint behind the camera. In a modern morality play, *Dead Man Walking*'s Susan Sarandon took Best Actress for her turn as a death-row counselor. At the other end of the spectrum, lowlifes were represented by Best Actor Nicolas Cage's suicidal drunk in *Leaving Las Vegas* and Best Supporting Actor Kevin Spacey's inscrutable schemer in *The Usual Suspects*. Who said Hollywood rewarded moderation? *—Dave Karger*

BEST SUPPORTING ACTOR: Kevin Spacey (*The Usual Suspects*)

BEST DIRECTOR: Mel Gibson (*Braveheart*)

MOVIES

CHART-TOPPERS

THERE *ARE* other movie stars out there besides Tom Cruise, Robin Williams, John Travolta, and Arnold Schwarzenegger. But you might not know it from looking at a list of 1996's top movies, eight of which came from that quartet of usual suspects: Cruise (the top grosser, with a total 1996 take of $263.9 million), Williams ($182.6 million), Travolta ($175.1 million), and Schwarzenegger ($158.5 million). Although the fab four were already proven all-stars when they made their '96 films, the No. 1 movie went to the bench for its stars, launching Will Smith and Bill Pullman to the A list with the sci-fi smash *Independence Day*. Likewise, *Twister* introduced the world to the windswept charms of Bill Paxton, Helen Hunt, *and* a flying cow. *—D. Karger*

TOP 25		YEAR-END GROSS
1	**INDEPENDENCE DAY** *20th Century Fox*, Bill Pullman	$306.2
2	**TWISTER** *Warner Bros.*, Bill Paxton	241.7
3	**MISSION: IMPOSSIBLE** *Paramount*, Tom Cruise	180.9
4	**THE ROCK** *Hollywood*, Nicolas Cage	134.1
5	**RANSOM** *Touchstone*, Mel Gibson	129.1
6	**THE NUTTY PROFESSOR** *Universal*, Eddie Murphy	128.8
7	**THE BIRDCAGE** *United Artists*, Robin Williams	124.0
8	**101 DALMATIANS** *Walt Disney*, Glenn Close	121.8
9	**A TIME TO KILL** *Warner*, Samuel L. Jackson	108.7
10	**THE FIRST WIVES CLUB** *Paramount*, Goldie Hawn	104.6
11	**PHENOMENON** *Touchstone*, John Travolta	104.5
12	**ERASER** *Warner*, Arnold Schwarzenegger	101.3
13	**THE HUNCHBACK OF NOTRE DAME** *Disney*, Animated	100.1
14	**STAR TREK: FIRST CONTACT** *Paramount*, Patrick Stewart	89.1
15	**SPACE JAM** *Warner*, Michael Jordan	85.4
16	**JERRY MAGUIRE** *TriStar*, Tom Cruise	83.0
17	**BROKEN ARROW** *Fox*, John Travolta	70.6
18	**THE CABLE GUY** *Columbia*, Jim Carrey	60.1
19	**COURAGE UNDER FIRE** *Fox*, Denzel Washington	59.0
20	**JACK** *Hollywood*, Robin Williams	58.6
21	**JINGLE ALL THE WAY** *Fox*, Arnold Schwarzenegger	57.2
22	**EXECUTIVE DECISION** *Warner*, Kurt Russell	56.7
23	**PRIMAL FEAR** *Paramount*, Richard Gere	56.1
24	**BEAVIS AND BUTT-HEAD DO AMERICA** *Paramount*, Animated	54.1
25	**TIN CUP** *Warner*, Kevin Costner	53.9

DATA SOURCE: EXHIBITOR RELATIONS INC.

TELEVISION

NYPD BLUE

1

(ABC) TV's most varied, humane, and exciting drama took more chances in 1996 than a hit show needs to and became a richer series for the effort. A key to exec producer David Milch's work this season is his idea that once you have a character people care about, that creation can do questionable, even bad things, and viewers won't just accept the behavior but will feel that badness in their bones. I'm thinking not only of the racism embedded in Andy Sipowicz (Dennis Franz) but of the increasing complexity of Bobby Simone (Jimmy Smits). Whether slapping around that creep Henry (Willie Garson) or unable to resist little-boy selfishness with girlfriend Diane (Kim Delaney), Smits somehow managed to make every flicker in Bobby's mind register on his stoic face. **BY KEN TUCKER**

FEDERAL CASE: As a paranormal-obsessed agent on the extraordinary *X-Files*, Duchovny's Fox Mulder gets all wrapped up in his work

THE X-FILES

2 *(Fox)* The concept most alien to this show—displays of simple human emotions—is what kept *The X-Files* fresh and intriguing this season. David Duchovny's Fox Mulder and Gillian Anderson's Dana Scully now give off a united glow that says to the world, "We're right, you're wrong, back off." There's no denying that *The X-Files* is more uneven these days—that episode where Mulder was remembering past lives was more heartburn commercial than X-File—but this is one series in which such erraticness is less a sign of creative exhaustion than of an admirably heedless faith in flaky flukiness.

THE LARRY SANDERS SHOW

3 *(HBO)* Garry Shandling is television's purest artist, quietly yet aggressively laboring over an unmatched portrait of show-business egotism. Very often, *Larry Sanders* is so funny I have to choke back a guffaw lest I miss the next punchline. And I can't think of another sitcom that repays taping and repeated viewing as well. Representing a final flourish of '90s irony, it's both a deconstruction of talk shows that's now even better than David Letterman's and an analysis of the sitcom that is funnier than any other sitcom.

NEWSRADIO

4 *(NBC)* Former *Sanders* collaborator Paul Simms has managed something Shandling has opted not to try: an iconoclastic sitcom that nonetheless adheres to the strictures of network TV. Dave Foley, as the radio station's put-upon news director, is probably the subtlest actor in sitcoms, whereas Phil Hartman and Andy Dick thrive on reckless excess.

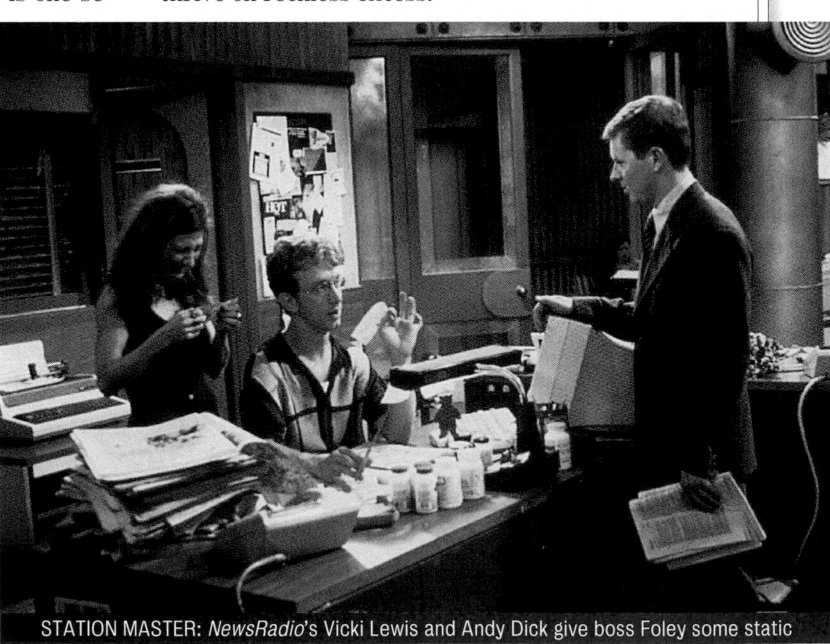

STATION MASTER: *NewsRadio*'s Vicki Lewis and Andy Dick give boss Foley some static

THE SIMPSONS

5 *(Fox)* Unappreciated now because the media celebrated Bart-mania years ago, *The Simpsons* continues to be the most reliable satire on network TV. The season opener, in which Homer and family left Springfield to work and live in a happy-faced, fascist corporate community, was such a dead-on critique of the Disney empire, I swear I could almost hear Rupert Murdoch chuckling.

FRIENDS

6 *(NBC)* Overexposure has led to a widespread underrating of this still excellently written, hilariously performed show. True, Lisa Kudrow's Phoebe seems stuck in a dumb-chick rut, and David Schwimmer's Ross is becoming dismayingly sappy. But Matt LeBlanc's Joey and Courteney Cox's Monica have flourished anew, while Jennifer Aniston's Rachel and Matthew Per-

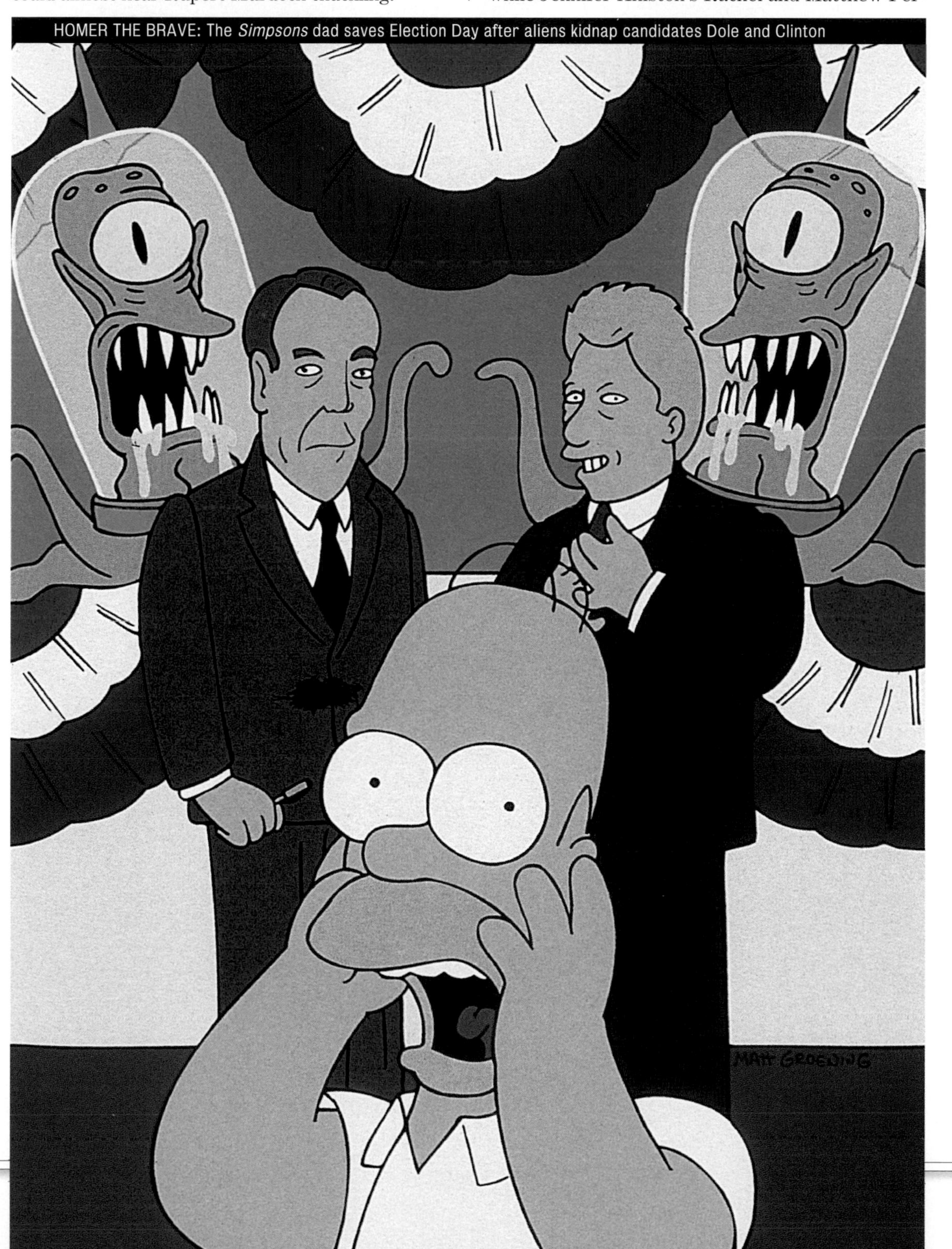

HOMER THE BRAVE: The *Simpsons* dad saves Election Day after aliens kidnap candidates Dole and Clinton

GRIPPING DRAMA: *Murder One*'s star lawyer LaPaglia, center, courts McCormack, left, and welcomes new associate DB Woodside

ry's Chandler are steadily becoming comic creations of remarkable intricacy. Think I'm exaggerating? Look at this show with an open mind and try not to be beguiled.

MURDER ONE

7 *(ABC)* By the end of last season, Daniel Benzali had become known in my house as "the boring bald guy." But that debut run of *One* also pulled off the show's then-central conceit—keeping you engaged in a single trial over 21 episodes. This season, Anthony LaPaglia replaced Benzali and offered a hero who was prickly and arrogant in a more engaging way. *The Waltons'* Ralph Waite has been a marvelous skunk of a baddie, and Missy Crider's work as a hapless murder defendant who also happened to be, as one character puts it, "a major hottie," gave *One* a fresh jolt of energy. Add to this the budding office romance between LaPaglia and Mary McCormack, and you've got a law show that behaves like a good nighttime soap. But so few viewers are watching that this vote is probably for a lost cause: big mistake, America.

PROFIT

8 *(FOX)* In the year's stupidest programming move, Fox canceled this strikingly original series after a scant four episodes. You probably don't remember, but *Profit* was a wittily bleak show about corporate shark and high-functioning sociopath Jim Profit (the magnificently oily Adrian Pasdar), who'd been raised in a cardboard box and parented by an always-turned-on TV set. Less a bitter dig at big business than a fulmination against all media culture, *Profit* was the funniest scary drama of the year.

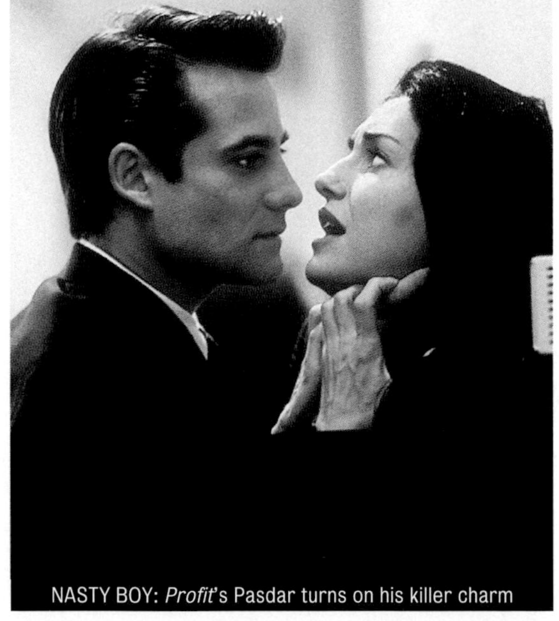

NASTY BOY: *Profit*'s Pasdar turns on his killer charm

A SECOND OPINION

Critic BRUCE FRETTS airs his own views on the best of 1996's television comedy, drama, soap, and chat

NEWSRADIO

1 *(NBC)* The falling-down funniest show on TV features one of the finest comic ensembles in prime-time history. Forget the Friends—it's Dave Foley and company who should be household names. Lost in Wednesday's 14-sitcom morass, *NewsRadio* deserves a spot on NBC's Thursday lineup. *This* is Must See TV.

HOMICIDE: LIFE ON THE STREET

2 *(NBC)* The blazingly original drama has only gotten better and still finds fresh ways to subvert cop-show clichés. Detective Pembleton's stroke has allowed Andre Braugher to exhibit new vulnerability, and Michelle Forbes' Julianna Cox has become *Homicide*'s strongest female character yet.

THE LARRY SANDERS SHOW

3 *(HBO)* New episodes didn't arrive until November—but it was worth the wait. Highlights have included David Duchovny's fearless flirtation with Larry (the great Garry Shandling), and soulless sidekick Hank Kingsley (Jeffrey Tambor) reclaiming his Judaism in an episode so remarkable it inspired a *New York Times* op-ed piece.

NYPD BLUE

4 *(ABC)* The plots aren't quite as inventive as *Homicide*'s, but the tangy dialogue and textured characters (especially Dennis Franz and Kim Delaney's recovering-alcoholic cops) more than make up for the sometimes-predictable cases. And no other series deals with racial issues more honestly.

FINE WHINE: *Sanders*' Rip Torn, left, and Shandling improve with age

WEDDING BELLES: *Savannah*'s beauties

FRASIER

5 *(NBC)* Just how indestructible is this sitcom? While Kelsey Grammer was in rehab, David Hyde Pierce's Niles took over the starring role for an episode, and the show didn't miss a beat. That's a sure sign of a perfectly constructed farce.

CRACKER

6 *(A&E)* It's an old joke: the shrink who's crazier than his patients. Yet Robbie Coltrane takes it to tragic new depths as a forensic psychologist with his own gargantuan demons in this blistering British mystery series.

THE ROSIE O'DONNELL SHOW

7 *(Syn.)* Daytime's newest queen seems as comfortable talking with the Duchess of York as with her doorman. But she's her own best guest—a one-woman *Regis & Kathie Lee.*

EVERYBODY LOVES RAYMOND

8 *(CBS)* Even with three adorable moppets in the cast, Ray Romano's smart family sitcom avoids *Full House*'s cutesy pitfalls. If CBS really wanted to have a "Big Comedy Monday," it'd move *Raymond* there.

MOESHA

9 *(UPN)* In the black-sitcom ghetto of UPN and The WB, only Brandy Norwood's joyous teen show stands out. Appealing actors, clever scripts, bright direction—so why are you watching *Mad About You* instead?

SAVANNAH

10 *(The WB)* The best-acted soap on prime-time TV, Aaron Spelling's Southern serial is as delectable as a Georgia peach. Its ridiculously low ratings are the pits.

SITTING UP IN MY ROOM: Norwood, left, as the bouncy teen Moesha, shares a heart-to-heart talk with Kellie Williams' Charisse

SEINFELD

9 *(NBC)* Last season's concluding episode, in which George's fiancée, Susan, died a ridiculous death (poisoned by the glue on cheap wedding-invite envelopes), was widely decried for its coldheartedness. I laughed at the episode *and* at the protests—what, from writer-cocreator Larry David you expected *warmth*? So far, the David-less new season has been uneven but agreeably wacky. High point thus far: Michael Richards' Kramer accidentally entering the corporate world and having his entire business career rise and fall in the space of 30 minutes.

MOESHA

10 *(UPN)* There's no current sitcom star with ebullience equal to Brandy Norwood's; as Moesha, she's prime time's most engaging teenager. Beyond that, *Moesha* is a consistent pleasure, with punchlines that deploy hip-hop cadences with a cleverness beyond mere laugh making. Plus Countess Vaughn, as Moesha's eye-fluttering, hip-wiggling best friend, Kim, deserves a best supporting actress Emmy. As he proved with the brief, terrific *South Central* (1994), producer-creator Ralph Farquhar knows how to bring African-American life to television without disguising or cheapening it.

THE WORST

BAD SPORTS: *Arli$$* strikes out

ARLI$$

1 *(HBO)* A lot of current sitcoms contain no laughs, but the arid *Arli$$* isn't just mirthless, it's the year's most pathetic rip-off. It thieves attitude and atmosphere from *The Larry Sanders Show*, rendering its unfunniness not merely sad but infuriating.

MR. RHODES

2 *(NBC)* Even if this show about a hepcat teacher didn't star the charmless, barber-deprived Tom Rhodes, its ceaseless procession of ignorant yet cool students would make the show's "education is good" message merely depressing.

DARK SKIES

3 *(NBC)* The second-worst copycat, this time an insufferably pretentious *X-Files* variation. The ongoing theme—alien invasions in the time of the Kennedy administration—manages to be boring, trite, and tasteless all at the same time.

THE JEFF FOXWORTHY SHOW

4 *(NBC)* The redneck routines that brought Foxworthy fame were pleasant and innocuous, but in retooling the comic's flop ABC sitcom, the NBC version turns his material into marathons of joke-free vulgarity.

X-RAIDED: *Baywatch's Nightmare*

BAYWATCH NIGHTS

5 *(Syn.)* All-powerful producer and bathing-suit wearer David Hasselhoff has turned *Nights* into *The X-Files* with *Plan 9 From Outer Space* F/X. The results are dumb, sure, but also lacking in *Baywatch*'s blithe goofiness. Besides, how can they do an *X-Files* rip and not include at least one episode about the alien forms occupying Donna D'Errico's maillot?

BEST KIDS SERIES

SABRINA, THE TEENAGE WITCH

1 *(ABC)* Perky yet worldly Melissa Joan Hart made a successful transition from *Clarissa Explains It All* to the title role here, and she's the main reason *Sabrina* has become the strongest show in ABC's "TGIF" kid's-programming lineup.

RUGRATS

2 *(Nickelodeon)* The cable channel's most popular cartoon gives us a baby's-eye view of the world. Featuring a raucous group of tykes, *Rugrats* remains a show that parents and children can enjoy for its insight as much as for its giddy humor.

BRAND SPANKING NEW DOUG

3 *(ABC)* It's not as if the old, reliable *Doug* wasn't pretty terrific. But in making the move from Nickelodeon to ABC, this well-drawn cartoon about a polite young man lost none of its charm while, one hopes, increasing the number of youthful minds it soothes.

LIGHT FANTASTIC: Superman fights the forces of darkness

SUPERMAN

4 *(The WB)* From the folks who gave us the beautifully dark *Batman* cartoon series comes a luminously bright *Superman*, with the voice of Dana Delany giving Lois Lane special tartness.

ARTHUR

5 *(PBS)* Marc Brown's children's books about a bespectacled aardvark came to TV with their quiet thoughtfulness intact, no small feat in a medium where most good things are coarsened.

BEST DOCUMENTARIES

CINEMA EUROPE: THE OTHER HOLLYWOOD

1 *(TCM)* A history of European movies in a mere six hours, this archival project by producers David Gill and Kevin Brownlow proves you can bring an academic approach to television without being terribly stuffy.

AMERICAN MASTERS: NICHOLS AND MAY—TAKE TWO

2 *(PBS)* Lenny Bruce, Lenny Schmoose—Mike Nichols and Elaine May were the real geniuses of stage comedy in the early '60s, as proved by this fine assemblage of the team's most intricate, penetrating routines.

MUHAMMAD ALI: THE WHOLE STORY

3 *(TNT)* Truth in titling: This TNT production did indeed tell the whole story, spending almost as much time detailing the boxer's conversion to Islam as it did his fisticuffs career, which is as it should be. A portrait that gave Ali his due as an athlete who also has influenced world culture.

RAW FOOTAGE

4 *(Independent Film Channel)* Host Alec Baldwin's interview with the filmmakers who made the Ollie North documentary, *A Perfect Candidate*, was the year's most insightful chat—informed, curious, and provocative. Baldwin's enthusiasm for the independent film was both infectious and instructive, giving us a real sense of how movies get made and argued over by filmmakers and their subjects.

A KNOCKOUT: TNT's *Ali*

FRONTLINE: SECRET DAUGHTER

5 *(PBS) Frontline* producer June Cross' look at her own life as the daughter of a white mother and African-American father (her stepfather is *F Troop*'s Larry Storch) was bravely self-revealing yet never egocentric—Cross' thoughtful and thought-provoking quest to understand her parents rendered them this film's complex stars.

BEST DAYTIME TELEVISION

THE ROSIE O'DONNELL SHOW

ROSIE PICTURE: With Clooney, Lucci

1 *(Syn.)* An instant hit, O'Donnell has proved she can maintain her enthusiasm—she's no movie star doing television for a lark. Unafraid to be giddy or hard-nosed when the occasion demands, she's succeeded by relating to viewers as pals.

THE OPRAH WINFREY SHOW

2 *(Syn.)* Whether touting real literature or teasing a mega-celeb like Streisand, Winfrey always seems warm and informed. She makes her own celebrity seem like a license to share a boundless curiosity that ends up sparking millions of viewers.

FOX AFTER BREAKFAST

3 *(Fox)* The low-rated talk show set in a real New York City apartment is both silly and savvy—fluff with bite. But now less sharp, with the recent departure of bright cohost Laurie Hibberd and that fuzz-bag puppet, Bob. Can stalwart human host Tom Bergeron maintain the air of funny smarts?

QUINCY, M.E. RERUNS

4 *(A&E)* This 1976–83 Jack Klugman series, which airs in the afternoon, is comfortingly dated and blissfully unconvincing (compare grouchy but soft Quincy to the tough medical examiners on *Homicide*), yet lulling as well-crafted camp. Look at the thumbs on Jack—these are not the hands of a doctor.

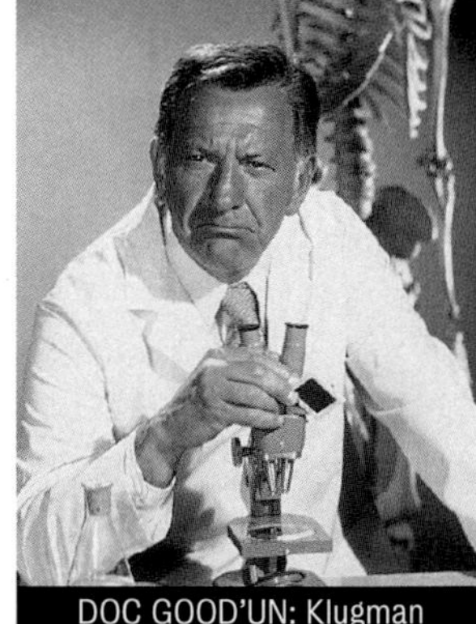
DOC GOOD'UN: Klugman

LIVE WITH REGIS & KATHIE LEE

5 *(Syn.)* Philbin is still good and cranky, Gifford is still frighteningly self-absorbed, especially while weathering her child-labor controversy; they remain a more fascinating couple than any you'll find on a daytime soap.

OUTSTANDING DRAMA: *ER*

LEAD ACTOR, DRAMA: Dennis Franz (*NYPD Blue*)

EMMY WINNERS

NOBODY WAS A LOSER at this year's Emmy Awards—at least, no major network was. NBC's *Frasier*, *Seinfeld*, *Mad About You*, and *3rd Rock From the Sun* dominated the comedy categories (with the exception of Supporting Actor, which went to a much-deserving Rip Torn for HBO's *The Larry Sanders Show*). The Peacock's top-rated *ER* also won Outstanding Drama, although the docs didn't take home any other awards. CBS' canceled shows *Picket Fences* and *Christy* took three of the four dramatic acting honors, and Dennis Franz snatched up Lead Actor for ABC's *NYPD Blue*. Even Fox snagged five Emmys for its sci-fi hit, *The X-Files*. Guess the truth really *is* out there. —*Kristen Baldwin*

LEAD ACTRESS, DRAMA: Kathy Baker (*Picket Fences*)

OUTSTANDING COMEDY: *Frasier*

LEAD ACTOR, COMEDY: John Lithgow (*3rd Rock From the Sun*)

LEAD ACTRESS, COMEDY: Helen Hunt (*Mad About You*)

TELEVISION

CHART-TOPPERS

ON COMEDY CENTRAL they joked that Must See TV sounds vaguely fascist. It also happens to be accurate. In the 1995–96 season, NBC's redoubtable Thursday night became even more of a ratings juggernaut, boasting no fewer than six of the season's top eight shows. And the most must-see of them all was *ER*—the first drama to claim the No. 1 spot since 1984–85's *Dynasty*. NBC could also crow about its surprise mid-season hit, *3rd Rock From the Sun* (22nd). At a resurgent CBS, the venerable newsmagazine *60 Minutes* finished in the top 10 for a record 19 years in a row, and *Touched by an Angel* ascended from 81st the previous season to a heavenly 23rd. But, signaling trouble for ABC, *Home Improvement* dropped from first to fifth, *Roseanne* fell from 9th to 19th, and *Ellen* plunged from 13th to 44th. —*A.J. Jacobs*

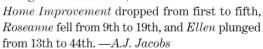

	TOP 25	VIEWERS, IN MILLIONS
1	ER NBC	32.0
2	SEINFELD NBC	31.6
3	FRIENDS NBC	28.0
4	CAROLINE IN THE CITY NBC	25.9
5	HOME IMPROVEMENT ABC	25.1
6	THE SINGLE GUY NBC	24.8
7	NFL MONDAY NIGHT FOOTBALL ABC	23.8
8	BOSTON COMMON NBC	23.3
9	NYPD BLUE ABC	19.8
	60 MINUTES CBS	19.8
11	20/20 ABC	19.6
12	FRASIER NBC	19.4
	WALKER, TEXAS RANGER CBS	19.4
14	GRACE UNDER FIRE ABC	19.2
15	COACH ABC	19.1
16	AMERICA'S FUNNIEST HOME VIDEOS ABC	18.8
17	NBC SUNDAY NIGHT MOVIE NBC	18.5
18	NBC MONDAY NIGHT MOVIE NBC	18.2
19	ROSEANNE ABC	18.1
20	CHAMPS ABC	17.9
	THE NANNY CBS	17.9
22	3RD ROCK FROM THE SUN NBC	17.8
23	TOUCHED BY AN ANGEL CBS	17.1
24	MURPHY BROWN CBS	17.0
25	LOIS & CLARK ABC	16.9

SOURCE: NIELSEN MEDIA RESEARCH; SEPT. 18, 1995–MAY 22, 1996

British
UK

ALMOST ANYTHING

BRITISH

1

FOR THE FIRST time since Boy George sprang for eyeliner, the British pop scene came astonishingly *alive* in 1996. They may be schooled in U.K. rock, but there's nothing quaint about the sardonic fop-rock of Pulp or the brawny songcraft of Oasis. The carousing high jinks of Pulp's Jarvis Cocker and Oasis' Liam Gallagher were also refreshing after years of fame-shy American alt-rockers. The British Reinvasion didn't end there, as proven by the space-age club beats known as jungle, trip-hop, and drums-and-bass—all featured on the soundtrack to *Trainspotting.* To sample more of the music that will be heard on that bridge to the 21st century, dive into the work of DJ-mixers like L.T.J. Bukem and Tricky. Together, this consortium of musicians and remixers creates music whose very chaos—synthesizer washes atop sandpaper-scratch rhythms—evokes our everyday clatter. London's calling, and once again, we're happy to take the call. **BY DAVID BROWNE**

'WALKING' TALL: Everything But the Girl spin dreamy dance tunes

WALKING WOUNDED

2 *Everything But the Girl* (Atlantic, album) An idea so simple, it's amazing no one thought of it before: adapt the burbling beats of the new U.K. pop to melodies with Bacharachesque elegance. It worked on these new-wave-cabaret veterans' 1995 hit remix of "Missing," and the experiment continues on this under-your-skin masterpiece. In the songs of Tracey Thorn and Ben Watt, the pangs and pains of teen-style infatuation linger long after they should: Thorn's forlorn voice is like a prolonged sigh. Percolating around her, the trip-hop beats deepen the melancholy; they're like the cautious beating of a lovesick heart. EBTG not only uncovered a new genre—dance music for the head—but discovered themselves as well.

CALIFORNIA LOVE

3 *2Pac (Featuring Dr. Dre)* (Death Row/Interscope, single) Rap's late lost soul and its most formidable producer proclaim the death and rebirth of gangsta. With its techno-reggae sway and slurping voice-box hook, this throwdown takes gangsta funk to a new level. No "bitches" here, either: The song's depiction of the West Coast as one big party is a player's form of civic pride. If possible, buy the British import—the sample of Joe Cocker's "Woman to Woman" (not cleared for the U.S.) is, along with that Nissan ad using Van Halen's version of "You Really Got Me," the year's most inventive recycling of classic rock.

TOUGH 'LOVE': The late Tupac

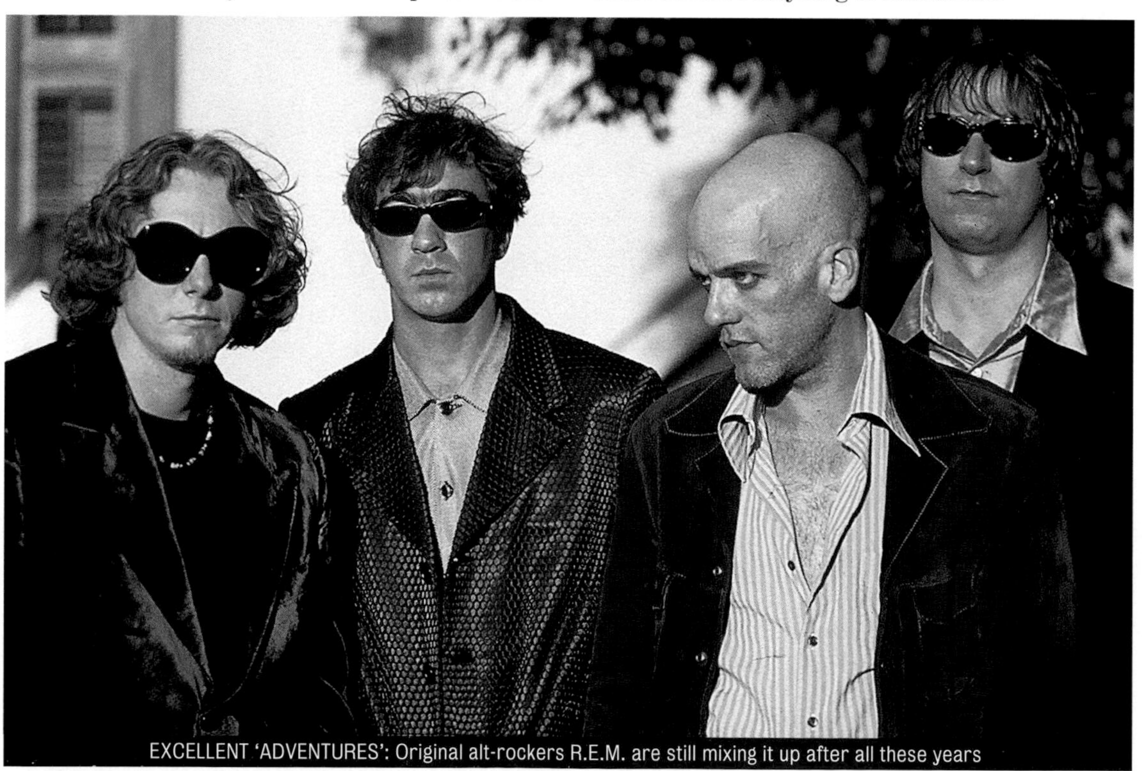
EXCELLENT 'ADVENTURES': Original alt-rockers R.E.M. are still mixing it up after all these years

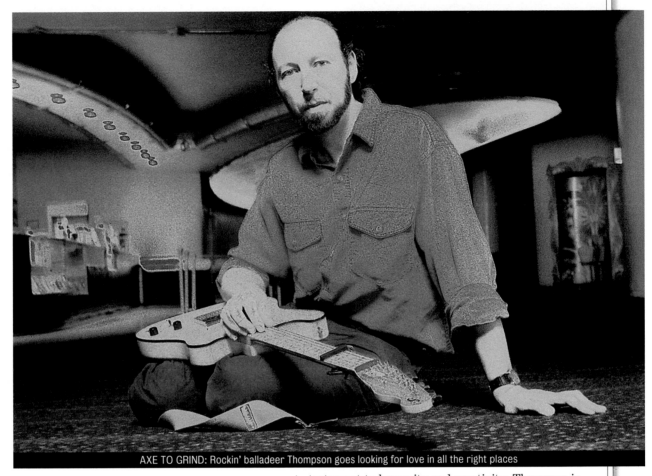

AXE TO GRIND: Rockin' balladeer Thompson goes looking for love in all the right places

NEW ADVENTURES IN HI-FI

4 *R.E.M.* (Warner Bros., album) They're elder statesmen with multi-million-dollar record deals, but that doesn't mean R.E.M. have fossilized. A throwback to the days when albums were sprawling let's-try-*this* mixes of mood and styles, the record swings from noise-fueled grinders to new twists on the band's autumn-leaves folk rock. And every so often, Michael Stipe abandons his usual ellipticism to reveal an actual hurt, angry human, which gives the music the extra emotional kick it needs.

YOU? ME? US?

5 *Richard Thompson* (Capitol, album) In the ever-pungent songs of this guitar hero and raconteur, the mating game can be dark, comical, or both simultaneously. On this rich double disc, Thompson succumbs to the "razor dance" of romantic friction; in lighter moments, he sneaks into his lover's room to size up photos of her exes. The Celtic metal is jagged and scarred, the deserted-moor ballads filled with sharp narrative detail. A testament to longevity and creativity, Thompson is now officially the British Neil Young.

C'MON N' RIDE IT (THE TRAIN)

6 *Quad City DJ's* (Big Beat/Atlantic, single) That enticing command, that pumping piano, that locomotive *whoo-whoo!* hook, that comical double entendre—summer (or any time of year) was intended for an irresistible groove like this, courtesy of the producers of "Whoot, There It Is." The corresponding dance is nearly as dumb as the Macarena, but that's no reason not to get on board.

TAKING A 'RIDE': Quad City DJ's get into the groove

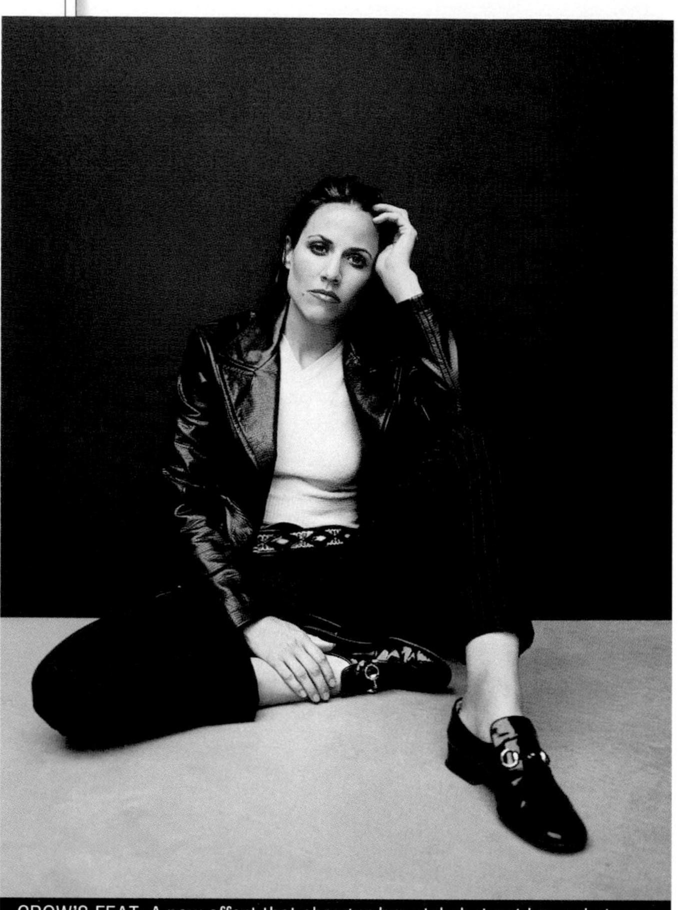
CROW'S FEAT: A new effort that changes her style but not her substance

SHERYL CROW

7 *Sheryl Crow* (A&M, album) Crow deglamorized herself for her second album, but she thankfully didn't raze the pool-hall funkiness or studio craft of its predecessor. Playing streetwise urchin one moment, concerned liberal the next, Crow remains an enigma, albeit a tuneful one. The variety of sounds and roles could simply mean she's using music to find her identity—which, when you think of it, is what many of us do every day.

MOTHER MOTHER

8 *Tracy Bonham* (Island, video) Remember when a stunning music video could flesh out an undistinguished song? On record, "Mother Mother" is a mocking letter home, wailed in post-Alanis screamer-songwriter fashion. It's the video, directed by Jake Scott, that brings Bonham's sentiments brilliantly to life. On a TV in her family living room, Bonham lip-synchs her sarcastic "everything's fine" lyrics. Oblivious to her daughter on the tube, Mom (played by Bonham's actual mother) cleans and dusts. Photographed in one continuous take, the video is a model of simplicity and execution, and it personifies rock's role as the voice of yet another disaffected generation. Call it video punk-rock.

STORE IN A COOL PLACE

9 *Able Tasmans* (Flying Nun, album) Before they disbanded, these merry New Zealand alterna-bohemians recorded this stunner: interlocking male-female harmonies wedded to winsome love songs and rocky melodies that conjure stormy, lonely evenings. A left-field surprise that reminds you that stirring music can come anytime, from any place.

WORDS

10 *The Tony Rich Project* (LaFace/Arista, album) Although the explosion of smooth-groove R&B singers is heartening, too many are interested in re-creating the past rather than shaping the future. Rich has no such problem. His debut is as seductively melodic as old-school soul ("Nobody Knows" is the "Tracks of My Tears" of the '90s). Yet, from its taut syncopations to its Babyface-with-muscle harmonies, it gently argues that sensitive-guy R&B needn't be stuck in the '70s.

POPULAR

11 *Nada Surf* (Elektra, single) His voice growing more unhinged with each verse, singer-guitarist Matthew Caws recites a litany of teen-popularity truisms over unrelenting, hypnotic grunge-drone. If *Revenge of the Nerds* were ever turned into a musical, this should be the opening number.

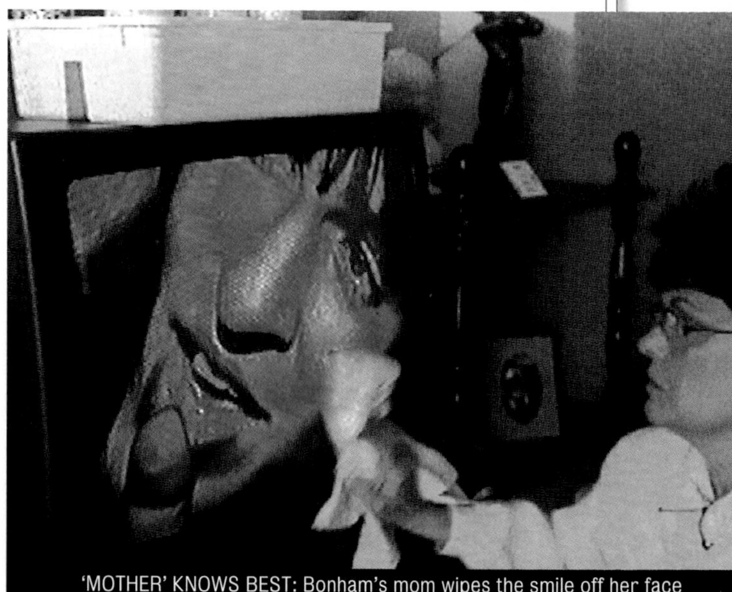
'MOTHER' KNOWS BEST: Bonham's mom wipes the smile off her face

THE WORST

FALLING INTO YOU

1 *Celine Dion* (550 Music/Epic) A nuance-impaired French Canadian belting American power ballads with the occasional washed-out reggae twist. This can't be why the term *world music* was invented.

EVIL EMPIRE

2 *Rage Against the Machine* (Epic) Screaming that war is bad and corporations worse—and other over-obvious truths of life in the '90s—Zack De La Rocha makes you yearn for the comparative subtleties of Peter, Paul, and Mary. At least they lectured us with hummable melodies. All Rage have is their tired rap-metal, which is no longer, ahem, revolutionary.

'EMPIRE' STRIKES OUT: Impotent Rage

LIVE FROM THE FALL

3 *Blues Traveler* (A&M) They could have built on the improved chops and writing of their previous albums, but *noooo*. These two bloated concert discs, stuffed with interminable harmonica and guitar solos, feel longer than all the dates on the H.O.R.D.E. tour combined.

'FALL' FROM GRACE: No better Blues

THE DON KILLUMINATI/ THE 7 DAY THEORY

4 *Makaveli* (Death Row/Interscope) If Tupac Shakur hadn't actually died in a hail of bullets in Las Vegas, then this exploitative, hastily completed finale would have finished the job. A shoddy postscript to a frustrating, but often promising, career.

NO CODE

5 *Pearl Jam* (Epic) No coherence or sense of direction, either—but plenty of garbled spirituality and woozy grunge.—*DB*

GONE AGAIN

12 *Patti Smith* (Arista, album) The influential and frequently overrated priestess returns, this time to mourn the deaths of family (including her husband, Fred "Sonic" Smith) and close friends. In tragic irony, the result is her most focused work—death becomes her. From the garage-band thrash of the title song through folkish numbers that have the feel of Appalachian death ballads, Smith makes up for the unexpected mawkishness with ravaged nobility and genuinely poetic insight.

UNPLUGGED

13 *Kiss* (Mercury, album) If you thought the magic lay only in the makeup, this acoustic performance—recorded shortly before the band's full-scale summer revival tour—sets the record straight. Both the anthems ("Do You Love Me," "Plaster Caster") and the obscurities ("A World Without Heroes") are revealed for the hooky, undeniable songs they are, and the reunion tracks featuring the original quartet, which close out the record, are a hoot. Added plus: It's the most worthwhile "Unplugged" in ages.

POETIC JUSTICE: Rock's high priestess lays her ghosts to rest

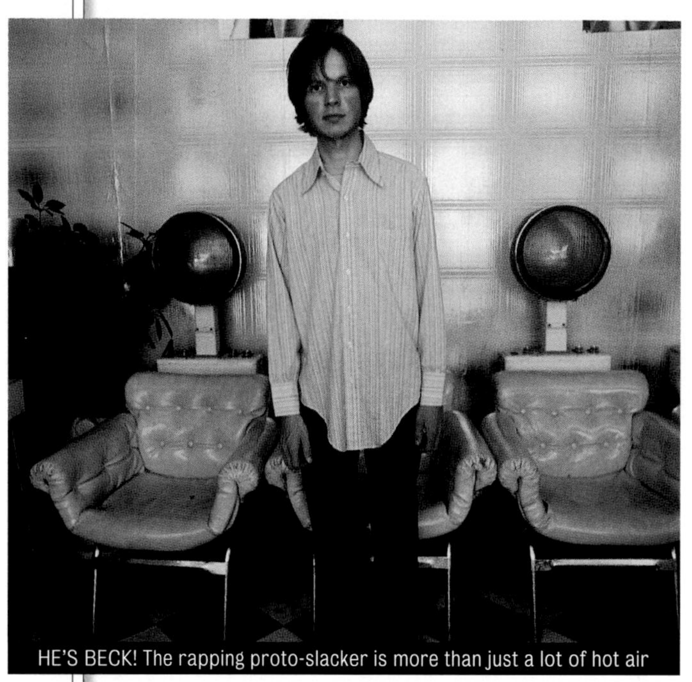
HE'S BECK! The rapping proto-slacker is more than just a lot of hot air

A COMMON DISASTER

14 *Cowboy Junkies* (Geffen, single) Amazing what a little friction can do, especially when applied to these Prozac country-rockers. This quietly ear-grabbing record isn't merely the best single of their decade-long career (listen to Margo Timmins' voice swoop along with the power chords on the chorus). For these nostalgists, it's also downright modern. Only in the '90s could a love song sport the refrain "Won't you share a common disaster?"

ODELAY

15 *Beck* (DGC, album) Despite a disturbing reliance on cutesy sound effects over original melodies, alt-rock's jive-talkin' white boy continues to play that funky music. Who knows what to make of lines like "Got a devil's haircut in my mind"—much less his high-speed Cuisinart of rap, folk, psychedelia, and whatever else grabs his attention. But digesting Beck's method and sonic madness is half the fun.

BEST COUNTRY/FOLK

I FEEL ALRIGHT

1 *Steve Earle* (Warner Bros.) Country's baddest boy rebounds from jail and heroin addiction with a rocking album that owes much to his semi-acoustic Guitar Town sound. Whether he's playing it tender (the almost sentimental "Valentine's Day") or tough ("Billy and Bonnie"), Earle keeps his usual bravado in check, although he still has a flipped finger at the ready.

STRIKING EARLE: He's *Alright*

BLUE CLEAR SKY

2 *George Strait* (MCA) On this perfect modern country album, Strait proves that he feels equally at home on both sides of the rural/urban divide, finding as much inspiration in the music of Frank Sinatra as in that of Hank Williams. A wooden Indian in concert, Strait is still the master of complex country emotion on record.

THE WAY I SHOULD

3 *Iris DeMent* (Warner Bros.) Iris DeMent's third album takes a giant leap, leaving her trademark personal meditations for angry songs about social issues. A broader musical framework also fleshes out her country-folk hybrid. This record is essentially a tribute to Merle Haggard, whom DeMent has credited for spurring her political consciousness, and who collaborated on *The Way I Should*'s most transcendent ballad, "This Kind of Happy."

ANOTHER RIVER

4 *Harley Allen* (Mercury) Departing from his bluegrass roots, Allen crafts a startlingly pure album that eschews Nashville formula and goes straight to the heart of great romantic storytelling. From the modern mythology of "The Waving Girl" to the age-old lesson of "Between the Devil and Me," Allen injects country with a much-needed dose of good old-fashioned anxiety.

A FEW SMALL REPAIRS

5 *Shawn Colvin* (Columbia) Proving that divorce can be a powerful artistic motivator, Colvin turns her private disappointment into a powerful portrait of middle-aged angst and depression. Sifting through such songs as "Sunny Came Home," in which a troubled woman casually sets her house on fire, unearths something unexpected in Colvin's personal rubble—the best album of her career. —*Alanna Nash*

'SMALL' WONDER: Colvin

BEST JAZZ

SOUND MUSEUM HIDDEN MAN SOUND MUSEUM HIDDEN WOMAN

1 *Ornette Coleman* (Harmolodic/Verve) Forget the high concept: two simultaneously released albums of the same band performing the same 13 compositions. Ignore the history: This is Coleman's first work with a conventional piano-based quartet in some 35 years. These companion albums are matching sets of brilliant, maturely playful music. Perhaps Coleman, like the scientific eggheads he emulates, has always been right: You don't need to understand chaos theory to appreciate its result—boundlessly varying, natural beauty.

'SOUND' MUSIC: Coleman

COMPOSER

2 *Cedar Walton* (Astor Place) In a milieu in which riffs and decades-old chord patterns qualify as compositions, Walton has slowly built a body of fully developed works with the sophistication and intricacy of chamber music. Don't blame him if he remains best known as a pianist; few musicians play anyone's music with Walton's insight and sensitivity.

THE BLUES CHRONICLES: TALES OF LIFE

3 *Gary Bartz* (Atlantic) A masterly exploration of the blues, its rich variety of forms, and its mercurial history, by 1996's Saxophonist Most Worthy of a Major Rediscovery. With a hypnotic guest turn by vocalist Jon Hendricks.

SILVER CITY: A CELEBRATION OF 25 YEARS ON MILESTONE

4 *Sonny Rollins* (Milestone) If Rollins' contemporary recordings have become increasingly reflective, this compilation of the saxophone mammoth's prime material reveals an artistic life worth reflecting on: Twenty-five years of profound tumult.

THE CARNEGIE HALL JAZZ BAND

5 (Blue Note) Recorded in unedited takes with two microphones, the debut CD by Carnegie Hall's official jazz ensemble (led by trumpeter Jon Faddis) sounds not merely "live" but *alive*. That vitality makes this crack 17-piece band unique in institutionalized jazz. —*David Hajdu*

MUSIC

CHART-TOPPERS

WITH DUE apologies to James Brown: It's a woman's, woman's, woman's world. Or so you would conclude from the year's top sellers: Female or female-fronted acts claim all five top spots, and six of the top 10. Sensitive hellcat Alanis Morissette's 1995 *Jagged Little Pill* was swallowed by another 7 million-plus buyers on its way to becoming the biggest female debut album ever. For a more traditional spoonful of sugar, America had French Canadian good girl Celine Dion, whose *Falling Into You* became the year's first surprise smash. The Lauryn Hill-led Fugees bucked the trend of high-debuting, fast-fading hip-hop albums by hanging at the top for months. By year's end, the big news was No Doubt's late starter *Tragic Kingdom* (which finished at No. 19). Gwen Stefani: Just a girl, or just a millionairess? —*CW*

	TOP 15 ALBUMS	WEEKS ON CHART*
1	**JAGGED LITTLE PILL** Alanis Morissette	75
2	**DAYDREAM** Mariah Carey	59
3	**FALLING INTO YOU** Celine Dion	36
4	**WAITING TO EXHALE** Soundtrack	46
5	**THE SCORE** Fugees	40
6	**THE WOMAN IN ME** Shania Twain	90
7	**FRESH HORSES** Garth Brooks	52
8	**ANTHOLOGY 1** The Beatles	29
9	**CRACKED REAR VIEW** Hootie & the Blowfish	123
10	**MELLON COLLIE AND THE INFINITE SADNESS** The Smashing Pumpkins	56
11	**SIXTEEN STONE** Bush	97
12	**ALL EYEZ ON ME** 2Pac	40
13	**(WHAT'S THE STORY) MORNING GLORY?** Oasis	59
14	**LOAD** Metallica	24
15	**THE GREATEST HITS COLLECTION** Alan Jackson	56

	TOP 10 SINGLES	
1	**MACARENA** Los Del Rio	50
2	**ONE SWEET DAY** Mariah Carey/Boyz II Men	27
3	**BECAUSE YOU LOVED ME** Celine Dion	33
4	**NOBODY KNOWS** The Tony Rich Project	47
5	**ALWAYS BE MY BABY** Mariah Carey	32
6	**GIVE ME ONE REASON** Tracy Chapman	35
7	**THA CROSSROADS** Bone Thugs-N-Harmony	20
8	**I LOVE YOU ALWAYS FOREVER** Donna Lewis	24
9	**YOU'RE MAKIN' ME HIGH/LET IT FLOW** Toni Braxton	26
10	**TWISTED** Keith Sweat	24

SOURCE: *BILLBOARD*; RANKED BY SALES FROM DEC. 2, 1995–NOV. 30, 1996.
*CHART DEBUT THROUGH NOV. 30, 1996.

BOOKS

INTO THE WILD

Jon Krakauer *(Villard, $22)* Transcending the materialism of everyday life was a hot book topic in 1996, but the sobering story of Chris McCandless outdoes them all. The 24-year-old walked into the Alaskan bush with hardly more than a bag of rice, boots, and a small-caliber rifle. Four months later, moose hunters discovered his remains

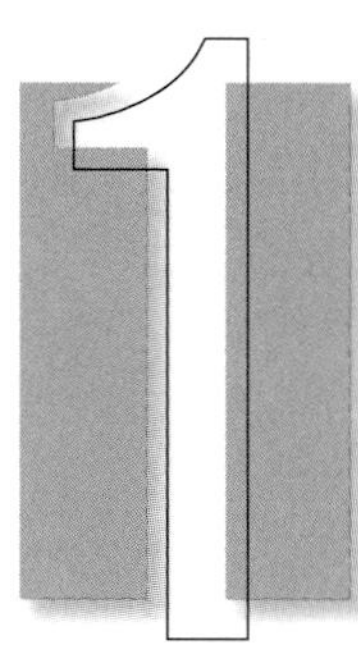

in the blue sleeping bag his mother had sewn from a kit. Apparently, he had died of starvation. Ending all communication with his frantic family, he'd embarked on a cross-country trek—inspired by the writings of Thoreau and Tolstoy—in which he discarded possessions with joyful abandon. Using McCandless' frequent journal entries, photos, and the postcards he sent to those who took him in or gave him work, Krakauer retraces the last two years of the backapcker's life with a tracker's zeal. Nonfiction, perhaps, but a mystery of the highest order.

EDITED BY ALEXANDRA JACOBS

ANGELA'S ASHES

2 Frank McCourt *(Scribner, $23)* The affecting story of the author's squalid upbringing. The eldest of seven children, only four of whom lived past infancy, McCourt was raised in Limerick, Ireland, on the eve of World War II by an alcoholic father and a "pious, defeated" mother. A rare non-celebrity memoir to hit best-seller lists and one that's also a page-turner, perhaps because it taps the universal hope that love and strength can rise out of misery.

THE SPARROW

3 Mary Doria Russell *(Villard, $23)* It's December 2059, and the survivor of a Jesuit space exploration has returned to Earth a mental wreck. Why? His interrogation by superiors alternates with flashbacks to the mission's genesis, growth, and collapse, bouncing readers from pure adventure to tangles of culture and politics. A hopeful sign that science fiction might reclaim its heritage as a literature with boundless capacity to kindle wonder.

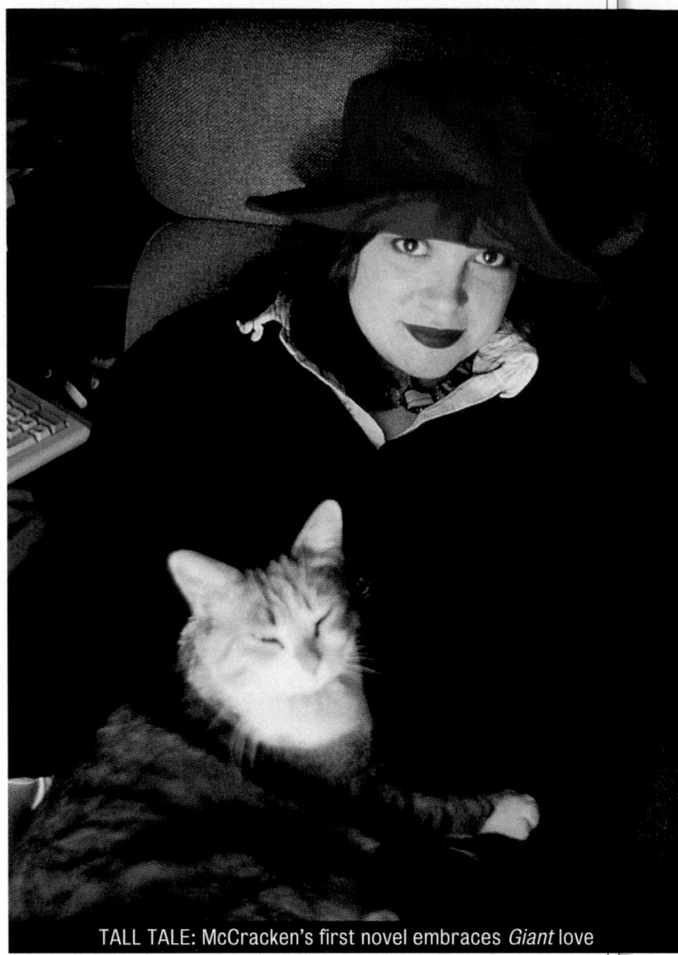

TALL TALE: McCracken's first novel embraces *Giant* love

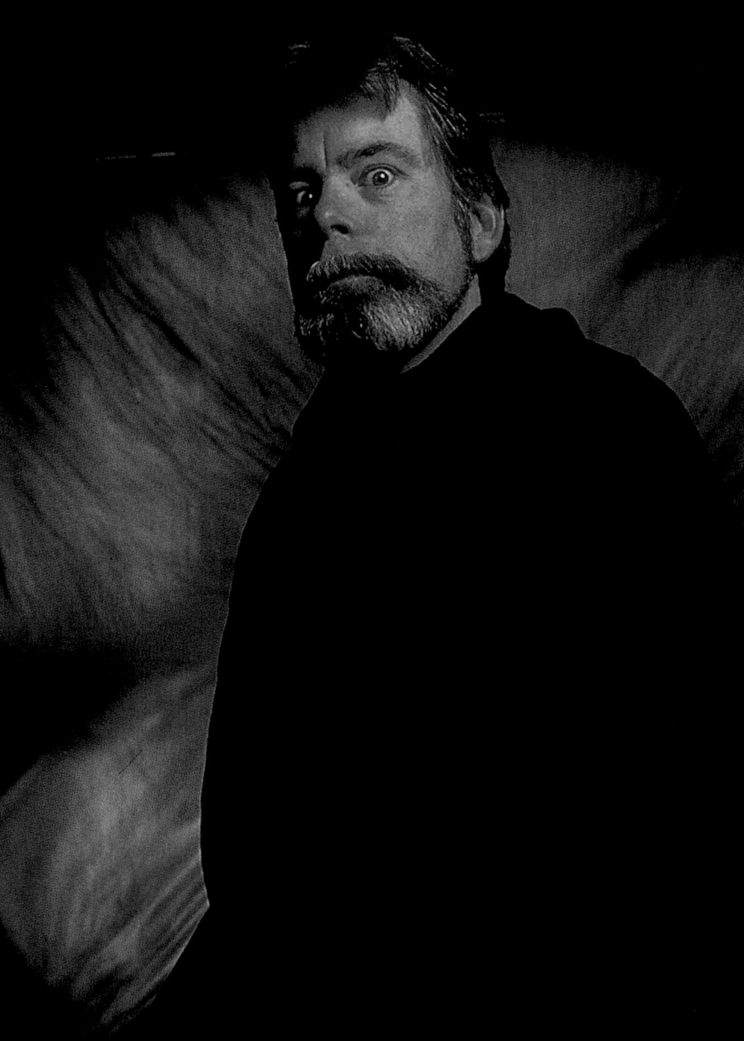

SERIAL THRILLER: King delivered one of his 1996 novels on the installment plan

THE GREEN MILE

4 Stephen King *(Signet, $18.94, boxed set)* Just when many in the book world were beginning to look anxiously ahead to the 21st century, King delivered a suspense story the old-fashioned way, via serialized installments. A clever marketing gimmick? Sure. But the publishing sensation of the year also happens to be the prolific shock master's best fiction in years, a richly narrated Depression-era prison novel that's as hauntingly touching as it is just plain haunted.

THE GIANT'S HOUSE

5 Elizabeth McCracken *(Dial, $19.95)* Despite its plot—a small-town librarian falls for a boy giant—this is a curl-up-by-the-fire first novel. Nominated for a National Book Award, it describes a "fundamentally sad" woman who, in the 1950s, befriends an 11-year-old who grows up to become the

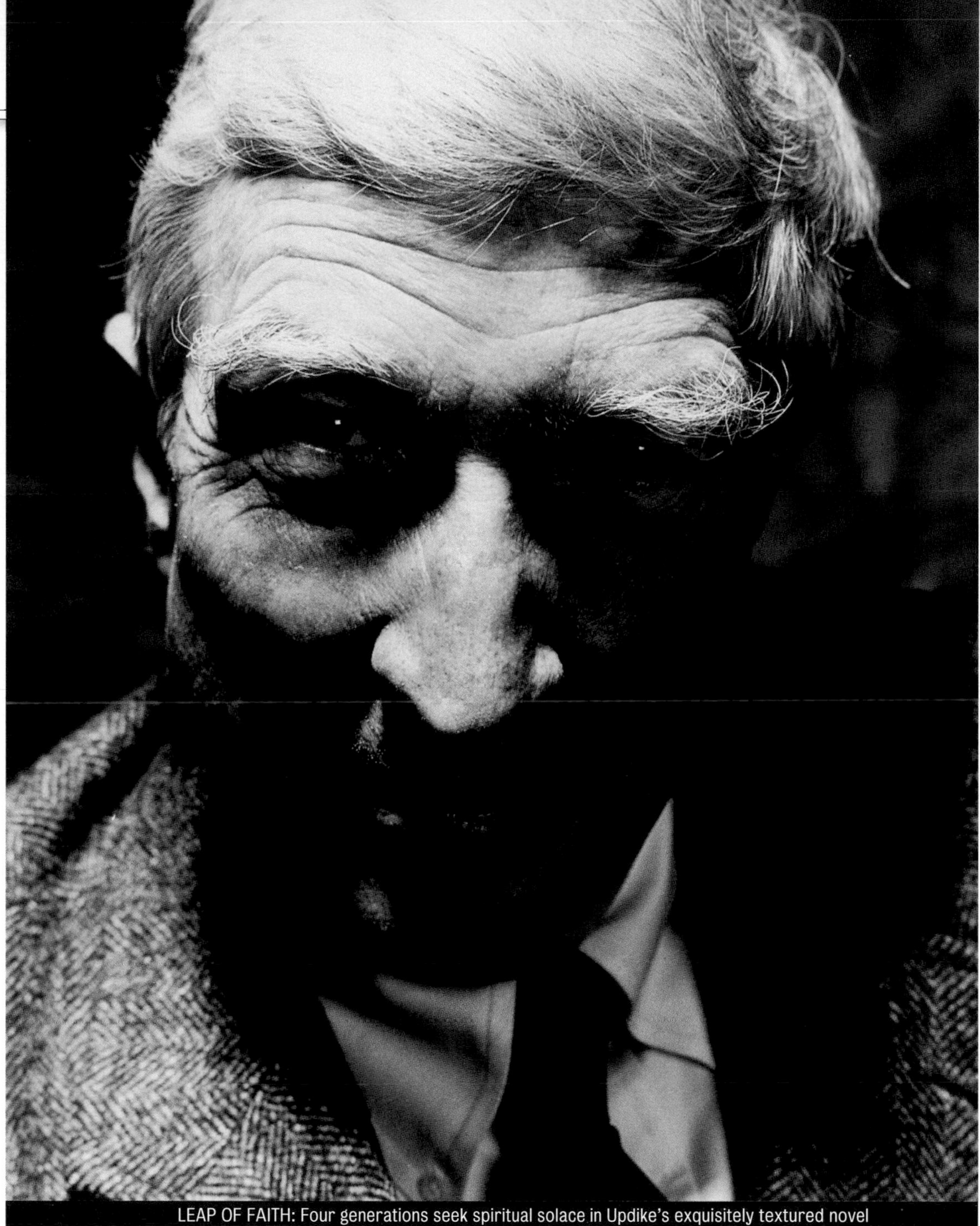

LEAP OF FAITH: Four generations seek spiritual solace in Updike's exquisitely textured novel

world's tallest man. Taking him under her wing after his mother dies, she conflates maternal and romantic impulses and finds herself in love with him. Warm, well written, and brimming with surprises.

ORSON WELLES: THE ROAD TO XANADU

6 Simon Callow *(Viking, $32.95)* Luckily for the biographer, Welles' glorious, mercurial life and sad, slow public decline are both marvelously well documented and teasingly contradictory (thanks in part to the actor-director's own prodigious gifts for stretching the truth). This helps Callow—himself an actor—produce a splendid, definitive work that traces the protean talent from his childhood to the release of *Citizen Kane*, using the tone of an admiring mentor who brooks no nonsense. A second volume will follow.

IN THE BEAUTY OF THE LILIES

7 John Updike *(Knopf, $25.95)* In 1910, a Presbyterian minister realizes that he no longer believes in God; meanwhile, D.W. Griffith is filming his latest Mary Pickford picture across town. What follows is a long, beautifully textured novel that somehow wends its way to the Branch Davidian standoff in Waco, Tex., four gen-

EYE SPY: George—inspired by her creation, investigator Thomas Lynley—gets into character for her eighth novel, *In the Presence of the Enemy*

erations later. An exploration of mass culture, religious faith, and family, by arguably our greatest living writer.

IN THE PRESENCE OF THE ENEMY

8 Elizabeth George *(Bantam, $23.95)* George is a writer who respects murder. There's only one in this wrenching mystery, and it occurs discreetly, between chapters. But the brutal pointlessness of the crime resonates solemnly throughout the novel, which pits two of England's most Machiavellian institutions—Parliament and Fleet Street—against each other over a 10-year-old girl's kidnapping. The eighth and best in her ever-gratifying series featuring Scotland Yard's cultured investigator, Thomas Lynley.

THE ARCHITECT OF DESIRE

9 Suzannah Lessard *(Dial, $24.95)* The author's famous—and infamous—ancestor, architect Stanford White, was killed by the husband of one of his sexual conquests in 1906. A thrilling story in itself, but Lessard delves deeper, using a hybrid format—part social history, part personal memoir—to tie together her family's strong and strange history, including her own sexual abuse and that of her sisters.

HIT & RUN

10 Nancy Griffin and Kim Masters *(Simon & Schuster, $25)* There's nothing even remotely fawning about this evisceration of the arrogant spendthrift Hollywood executives Peter Guber and Jon Peters. In describing how Sony lost $3.2 billion by hiring the two, Griffin and Masters correct the impression that *entertainment journalism* is an oxymoron. Meticulously researched though it is, the book is most engrossing when read as a collective psychobiography of Hollywood suits.

OBJECT OF *DESIRE*: Stanford White

THE WORST

ASK *ALICE*: Homes' tome

THE END OF ALICE

1 A.M. Homes *(Scribner, $22)* The much-hyped, highly self-conscious story of the creepy correspondence between a shoe salesman–turned–child killer and a female college sophomore who's ferociously attracted to a pubescent boy. An attempted tour de force that lands smack on its face.

LEADING WITH MY CHIN

2 Jay Leno, with Bill Zehme *(HarperCollins, $22)* This is the kind of amiable, toothless pastiche we've come to expect from TV comics over the past few years. But it's a colossal opportunity wasted, containing none of the difficult facts surrounding Leno's firing of the late Helen Kushnick or the battle to inherit Johnny Carson's throne at NBC.

THE TENTH INSIGHT

3 James Redfield *(Warner, $19.95)* The angel-ridden sequel to mega-best-seller *The Celestine Prophecy* falls short of even the comic-book novelistic standard set by its predecessor. Feel-good metaphysical goop.

SERVANT OF THE BONES

4 Anne Rice *(Knopf, $25.95)* This much can be said about Rice's long, often inpenetrable latest: It's not about vampires, but rather a spirit named Azriel who arrives on this plane and accosts an archaeology student so he can tell Azriel's awful history. And tell it he does—for 24 mind-numbing chapters. "Perhaps the story is chaos," Azriel muses at one point. Couldn't say it better ourselves.

THE HOTTEST STATE

5 Ethan Hawke *(Little, Brown, $19.95)* The affably intense Hawke (*Reality Bites*) has fashioned a thin, predictable novel about an actor named William who falls in love with a young woman named Sarah. Safe to say this coltish effort would never have gotten onto a major publisher's racetrack were it not for Hawke's celebrity.

SAD *STATE*: Hawke never flies

BEST COFFEE-TABLE BOOKS

THE LOOK OF THE CENTURY

1 Michael Tambini *(DK Publishing, $39.95)* As we screech toward the millennium, expect an explosion of retrospectives. This one could be a prototype—its survey of the design of everyday things (cars, wallpaper) is elegant, authoritative, and uncluttered by nostalgia. Pop culture at its most basic.

THE WEDDING

2 Photographs by Nick Waplington *(Aperture, $40)* Anyone who was fascinated by Mike Leigh's movie *Secrets & Lies* will take special interest in this intimate document, which chronicles the blending of two British working-class families, one black, one white. Waplington spent 10 years shooting his friends, and it shows: Nothing is posed, nothing seems voyeuristic in this breathtaking book.

SKYSCRAPERS

3 Judith Dupré *(Black Dog & Leventhal, $22.98)* It's gotta go on your coffee table, because there's no way it's going to fit on your shelves. A long, tall (18½ inches) book about long, tall buildings from Melbourne to Manhattan, as dramatically designed as the famous edifices themselves. There's also a good introductory interview with 90-year-old architect Philip Johnson. A surefire guest grabber.

THE LOST ARTWORK OF HOLLYWOOD

4 Fred E. Basten *(Watson Guptill, $40)* In a way, the title is a misnomer, since the wonderful drawings and movie posters culled from the teens through the '40s weren't so much lost as ignored. Painstaking ungimmicky renditions of classic stars such as Rita Hayworth showcase our early reverence for the motion picture.

PICTURE PERFECT: Hollywood's images

DOWN IN THE GARDEN

5 Anne Geddes *(Cedco, $49.95)* The hippest, funniest, least sanctimonious of a recent spate of baby books. Geddes transforms infants and toddlers into colorful potted marigolds, caterpillars, and pea pods, with the help of artful props, infinite patience, and (we assume) a pacifier or two.

BEST FOOD BOOKS

JUST DESSERTS: Ruffle cake

BAKING WITH JULIA

1 Dorie Greenspan *(Morrow, $40)* A daunting prospect, but still irresistible—isn't it? You won't get Julia Child's legendary trill or her broad, enthusiastic gestures in this book, which is based on her PBS series, but you will get a (decidedly not crash) course on baking everything from fancy cakes to "homey pies and tarts."

LOUISIANA REAL & RUSTIC

2 Emeril Lagasse with Marcelle Bienvenu *(Morrow, $25)* The New Orleans author can claim the top-rated show on the TV Food Network (*The Essence of Emeril*), in part because of a wham-bang yet Big Easy style that's as hot as his recipes. But substance wins out over style in these examples of Louisiana's melting-pot cuisine. (Jambalaya, anyone?)

GONE FISHIN': Cajun style

STEVEN JENKINS CHEESE PRIMER

3 Steven Jenkins *(Workman, $16.95)* Think cheese comes in a plastic squeeze bottle or in thin cellophane-wrapped squares? The author once thought so, too. Now one of the most respected cheesemongers in America, Jenkins has set out to enlighten the unenlightened, with a guide that tells—in opinionated, lively prose—how to choose, serve, and enjoy. Bye-bye Cheez Whiz, bonjour Chabichou.

PATRICIA WELLS AT HOME IN PROVENCE

4 Patricia Wells *(Scribner, $40)* Proof positive that cookbooks can be the best—and cheapest—way to "visit" another country. Just about every recipe is a winner, from artichoke soup to lavender-honey ice cream. Includes photos of the author's enviable stone farmhouse in the south of France and instructions for pantry stocking.

VERY CHERRY: Confiture

DEAN & DELUCA COOKBOOK

5 David Rosengarten, with Joel Dean and Giorgio DeLuca *(Random House, $24)* The founders of the eponymous gourmet shop have collaborated with foodie Rosengarten to produce this delicious self-tribute. It was in part thanks to them, after all, that America now knows such delicacies as infused oils and quail eggs. And they're as expert at chicken soup as bouillabaisse.

BEST SLEEPERS

AUDREY HEPBURN'S NECK

Audrey Hepburn's Neck
by Alan Brown
A NOVEL

1 Alan Brown *(Pocket Books, $21)* Toshi is a Japanese man in love with all things American, particularly women, particularly Audrey Hepburn. Raised in a fishing village, the young hero flees for Tokyo, where he works as a cartoonist and has a disastrous affair with his American teacher. Hollywood big shot Wayne Wang (*The Joy Luck Club*) has optioned this witty first novel.

BLUE ITALIAN

2 Rita Ciresi *(Ecco Press, $22)* Wisecracking social worker Rosa Salvatore believes that her husband, Gary, is having an affair: How else to explain his flagging interest in sex? That he actually has cancer is the tragic irony with which Ciresi opens her debut novel. Intimate flashbacks, biting humor, tactile prose, and a three-hankie finale are all contained in this vibrant tableau of marriage's imperfections and redemptions.

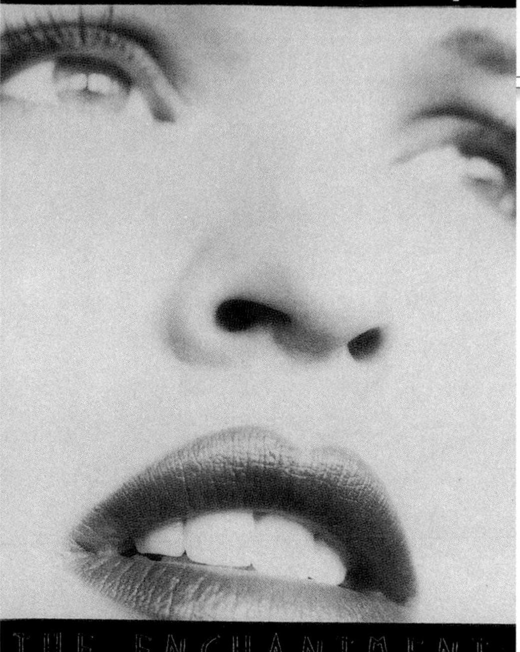

DROWN

3 Junot Díaz *(Riverhead Books, $21.95)* Díaz's stories focus on his Dominican Republic birthplace and the poor community in New Jersey where he was raised, exploring the emotional ambiguities (abandonment, trying to fit in) that arise when families change homelands. Although each stands on its own, the exquisitely crafted stories enhance and illuminate one another to create a sum far greater than its parts.

THE ENCHANTMENT OF LILY DAHL

4 Siri Hustvedt *(Holt, $23)* The title character is a small-town waitress who dreams of launching an acting career in New York City. Her quiet world is disturbed when she hears of an inert—possibly dead—Lily look-alike being spotted around town. With its dark plot and spirited, indomitable protagonist, this novel works as ghost tale, romance, and coming-of-age story. Exquisitely subtle and controlled fiction.

EMERALD CITY

5 Jennifer Egan *(Doubleday, $22.50)* Egan is a literary chameleon who can confidently set her stories in China and Kenya and Bora Bora, as well as write convincingly from a male point of view. Most impressive is her ability to put an exotic spin on the mundane—a walk through Manhattan, for example, in the title story. A wonderful discovery; an Ann Beattie for the '90s.

CHART-TOPPERS

THE BIGGEST STORY in books in 1996 was one of clever marketing. Stephen King used Dickensian tactics to take us down *The Green Mile*, releasing six slot-grabbing installments, much to the, um, horror of competitors. Anonymous (eventually revealed to be political columnist Joe Klein) penned a roman à clef about the Clinton campaign, *Primary Colors*, that created a sales-spiking national guessing game. And the written word's self-appointed publicist—talk-show empress Oprah Winfrey—sent a *Simple Abundance* of books straight to bestsellerdom. But the volume to which she gave the biggest boost was her own diet and fitness book. It figures. —*AJ*

25 BEST-SELLERS	
1	**THE RUNAWAY JURY** John Grisham
2	**MEN ARE FROM MARS, WOMEN ARE FROM VENUS** John Gray
3	**THE RAINMAKER** John Grisham
4	**SNOW FALLING ON CEDARS** David Guterson
5	**PRIMARY COLORS** Anonymous
6	**CHICKEN SOUP FOR THE SOUL** Jack Canfield and Mark Hansen
7	**THE DILBERT PRINCIPLE** Scott Adams
8	**THE ZONE** Barry Sears, Ph.D., with Bill Lawren
9	**EXECUTIVE ORDERS** Tom Clancy
10	**THE GREEN MILE, PART I** Stephen King
11	**MAKE THE CONNECTION** Bob Greene and Oprah Winfrey
12	**THE 7 HABITS OF HIGHLY EFFECTIVE PEOPLE** Stephen R. Covey
13	**THE GREEN MILE, PART 2** Stephen King
14	**SIMPLE ABUNDANCE** Sarah Ban Breathnach
15	**FALLING UP** Shel Silverstein
16	**IN CONTEMPT** Christopher A. Darden, with Jess Walter
17	**THE GREEN MILE, PART 3** Stephen King
18	**THE CELESTINE PROPHECY** James Redfield
19	**THE HORSE WHISPERER** Nicholas Evans
20	**BAD AS I WANNA BE** Dennis Rodman with Tim Keown
21	**DR. ATKINS' NEW DIET REVOLUTION** Dr. Robert C. Atkins
22	**THE TENTH INSIGHT** James Redfield
23	**THE RULES: TIME-TESTED SECRETS TO CAPTURING THE HEART OF MR. RIGHT** Ellen Fein, Sherrie Schneider
24	**THE GREEN MILE, PART 4** Stephen King
25	**THE LOST WORLD** Michael Crichton

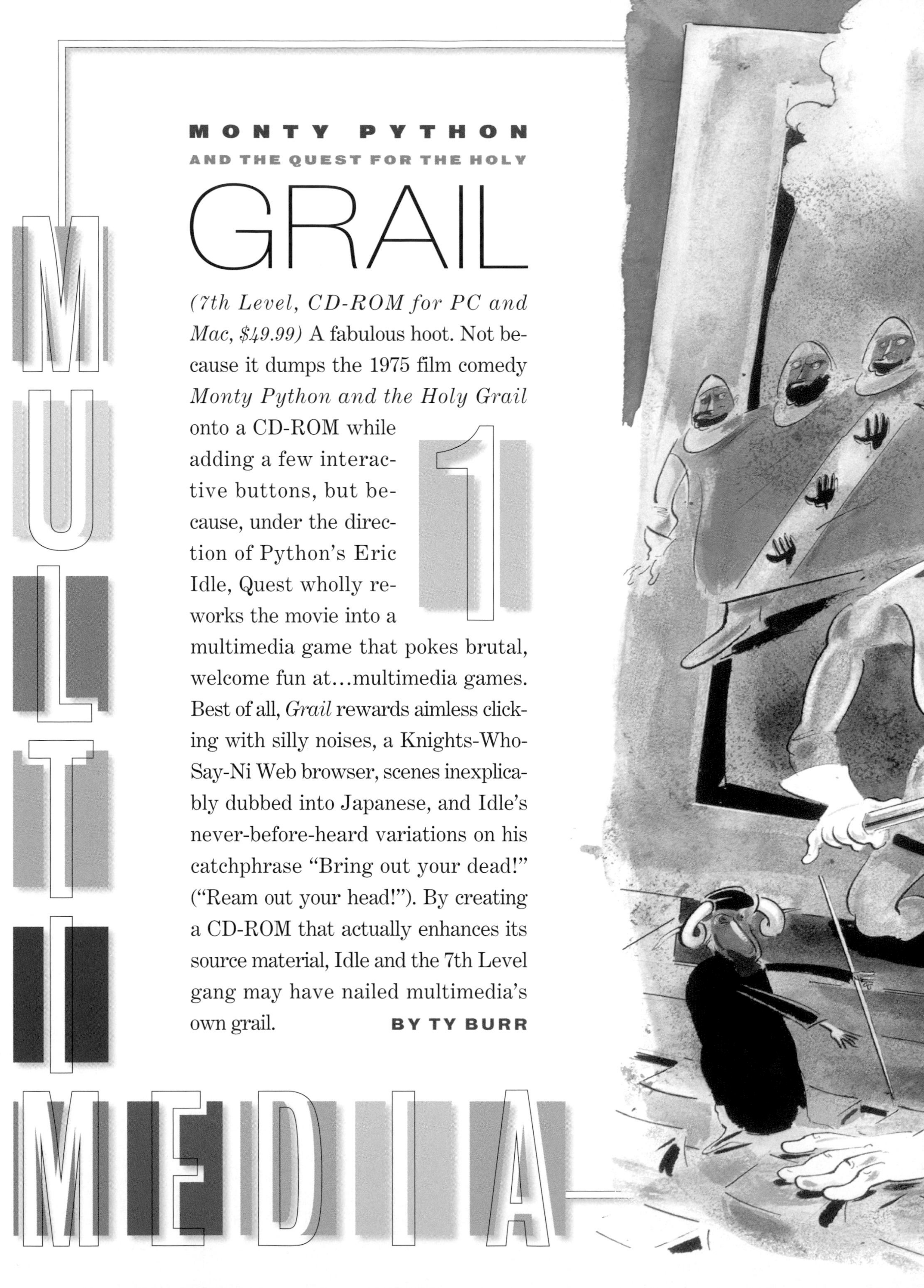

MULTI MEDIA

1

MONTY PYTHON

AND THE QUEST FOR THE HOLY

GRAIL

(7th Level, CD-ROM for PC and Mac, $49.99) A fabulous hoot. Not because it dumps the 1975 film comedy *Monty Python and the Holy Grail* onto a CD-ROM while adding a few interactive buttons, but because, under the direction of Python's Eric Idle, Quest wholly reworks the movie into a multimedia game that pokes brutal, welcome fun at...multimedia games. Best of all, *Grail* rewards aimless clicking with silly noises, a Knights-Who-Say-Ni Web browser, scenes inexplicably dubbed into Japanese, and Idle's never-before-heard variations on his catchphrase "Bring out your dead!" ("Ream out your head!"). By creating a CD-ROM that actually enhances its source material, Idle and the 7th Level gang may have nailed multimedia's own grail. **BY TY BURR**

WELCOME TO THE DALI-HOUSE: Surreal technicolor graphics straight from your creepiest nightmares in *9*

NINTENDO 64

2 *($199.99 for the game console, $59.95–$69.95 each game)* Even if you consider videogames one step up from splatter films on culture's Road to Hell, you may well be hypnotized by the fluidly immersive, alternate-world visuals of Nintendo's revolutionary new 64-bit game system. Here's a thought: In addition to game designers, why not set some artists and writers loose in this new medium?

GUYANA

3 *(www.word.com/place/guyana)* A trip diary/art installation hosted by the webzine *Word*, *Guyana* points to a whole new era of Web-based storytelling. Three American artists took a six-week boat trip up the Amazon basin, recording in their journals how their expectations of Eden came up hard against the realities of Third World development. A website of external travel, inner disenchantment, and end-of-the-world beauty.

MICROSOFT NETWORK

4 *(www.msn.com)* Whether you worship, scorn, love, or loathe Mr. Bill, there's no denying that Microsoft's recently relaunched online service raises the stakes for the entire World Wide Web. With elegant animation and soft-rock background music on nearly every screen, MSN is one lively surf—and its inaugural content isn't half bad either.

BAD MOJO

5 *(Pulse, CD-ROM for PC and Mac, $49.95)* *Myst* for slumlords, *Mojo* turns you into a cockroach and sends you scampering around in an effort to get human. If Kafka had played this, Gregor Samsa might never have made it out of bed.

ADA 'WEB

6 *(www.adaweb.com)* Is the Web a comfortable home for art? Can the Web *be* art? Yes and yes, say the fertile minds behind this far-thinking virtual gallery. Revelatory graphic design leads you to playful interactive exhibits, expanding your head and the medium in equal measure.

QUAKE

7 *(id software, CD-ROM for PC, $50)* With greater visual depth than forerunner *Doom* and a creepy-crawly score courtesy of Trent Reznor, *Quake* delivers the most carnage you can revel in without having to deal with jail time. No wonder bored office workers across the country love it.

SWITCHBOARD

8 *(www.switchboard.com)* The most prosaic, useful, and scary website imaginable, *Switchboard* is nothing more than the country's phone books in one zippy online database. Once you get past the novelty value—go ahead, look up your prom date—you'll notice how handy the thing is.

ONLINE GAMING

9 IT'S EVEN money that 1997's big Internet story is going to be the explosion of networked gaming communities available via the Web. Meridian59 (*www.meridian.3do.com*) has already seen a number of virtual weddings; Mplayer (*www.mplayer.com*) enables you to play *Quake* with strangers while taunting them via a voice hookup; Castle Infinity (*www.castleinfinity.com*) is an online playpen for kids. Games are mere bait—it's the visual community that's something new.

THE CDA APPEAL

10 WHEN THE Communications Decency Act was enacted last February, the cybercommunity despaired: The law threatened to dumb down the Internet by imposing broadcast-TV censorship standards on an entirely new medium. Fortunately, clearer minds prevailed—in particular, those of three judges who ruled the CDA unconstitutional. Expect the Supreme Court to weigh in next; meanwhile, expect filtering software to address parents' concerns more constructively than the CDA.

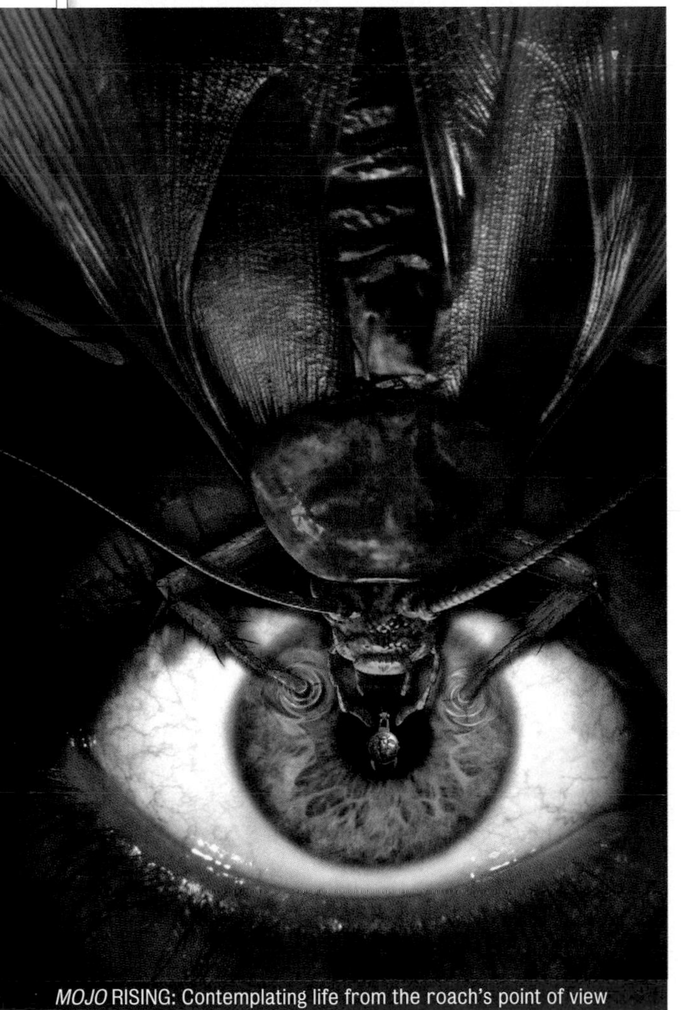

MOJO RISING: Contemplating life from the roach's point of view

QUAKE BATTLE 'N' ROLL: Demonic pleasures

INTERNET EXPLORER 3.0

11 1996 WAS the "Year of the Browser Wars," with early fave Netscape sent reeling by Microsoft's aggressive release of its own window on the Web. Netscape's worst problem was that IE 3.0 was so *good*.

NOIR: A SHADOWY THRILLER

12 *(Cyberdreams, CD-ROM for PC, $45)* After hordes of lame sci-fi/detective disc thrillers, it's nice to come across one that goes back to the cheapo values (moral *and* production) of the old 1940s films noir themselves. Six cases to crack on two CDs, all in glorious, cheesy black and white.

ELECTRIC MINDS

13 *(www.minds.com)* You can pop into AOL's chat rooms and have fifty 16-year-old boys demand "M or F?" Or you can log on to cybervisionary Howard Rheingold's electronic salon and have—heaven forfend—substantive discussions.

9

14 *(Tribeca Interactive/GT Interactive, CD-ROM for PC and Mac, $49.99)* This *7th Guest*-style logic game is the debut title from Robert De Niro's multimedia house. It features the voices of Cher, James Belushi, and Christopher Reeve. But the real star is the skin crawling design from album illustrator Mark Ryden.

OUR SECRET CENTURY

15 *(Voyager, CD-ROM for PC and Mac, $29.95)* Voyager may have collapsed under the weight of consumer indifference this fall, but the company leaves a legacy of rich, thought-

THE WORST

SMASHING PUMPKINS ONLINE CONCERT

1 THE INTERNET'S very own Altamont. As the Pumpkins played Dublin's Point Theatre May 11, fans at home heard Billy Corgan try to calm the rampaging crowd as a 17-year-old was crushed to death.

WEBSTOCK

2 (*www.webstock96.com*) Exhibit A in multimedia's not-ready-for-prime-time status in Hollywood. Webstock billed itself as a four-day online "fair" that would mix celeb appearances with community-empowerment info. The result was a Woodstock in which no one knew how to plug in the amps.

FLOP DISC: Spielberg stiffs

STEVEN SPIELBERG'S DIRECTOR'S CHAIR

3 EXHIBIT B in multimedia's not-ready-for-prime-time status in Hollywood—the assumption being that if you put enough big names on the CD-ROM box (Jennifer Aniston, Quentin Tarantino), it'll make for a good product. But rearranging segments shot by Spielberg is an experience more Pavlovian than creative.

DEVO: ADVENTURES OF THE SMART PATROL

4 A CD-ROM from the '80s rockers encrusted with clichés, and not just the toothlessly campy sci-fi ones Devo is still flogging. *Smart Patrol* ossifies the conventions of in-your-face multimedia: overbearing jargon, annoying complexity, diluted film noir. Whip it—right out of your disc drive.

LOSER *PATROL*: Devo take a dive

ELECTION '96

5 WASN'T THIS the year the Internet was going to revolutionize the electoral process? So why was it the most substance-free election yet? Sites like CNN/Time's AllPolitics were groundbreaking one-stop resources. And Bob Dole did mention his home page (*www.dolekemp96.org*) during the second debate. Too bad most people ended up at the parody site (*www.dole.org*).

---

provoking discs. Especially pungent was Rick Prelinger's interactive tour of bizarre old promotional and educational films.

JAZZ CENTRAL STATION

16 (*http://jazzcentralstation.com*) Historical reference, audio clips, featured artists, festival listings, bulletin boards, and one jumpin' Java live-chat toy make this the Superchief of music sites.

COMEDY CENTRAL SITE

17 (*www.comcentral.com*) Yeah, it's a promo site for a cable channel. But it manages to poke fun at both cable *and* the Web, with screen grabs of whatever's on CC at any particular nanosecond, a hilarious update of the old Operation game with Boris Yeltsin as patient, and a chance to build Michael Jackson's baby.

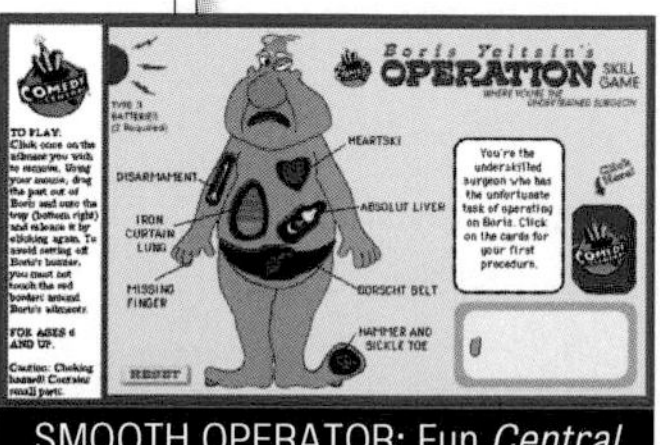

SMOOTH OPERATOR: Fun *Central*

PYST

18 (*Parroty Interactive, CD-ROM for PC and Mac, $14.95*) This lovingly mean parody of the best-selling *Myst* is for those who never could get the rocket ship to take off. Featuring a slovenly John Goodman as King Mattruss.

WOMEN WE LOVE: Film herstory with Foster

REEL WOMEN

19 (*Enteractive, CD-ROM for PC, $19.95*) The CD-ROM medium is a natural for historical reclamation projects: Witness this breezy, eye-opening adaptation of Ally Acker's book on creative women throughout the Hollywood decades. Hosted, appropriately, by Jodie Foster.

EPICURIOUS

20 (*www.epicurious.com*) This Condé Nast site hosts the online versions of *Gourmet* and *Bon Appétit*, but such Internet extras as a metric conversion chart, a weekly guide to what's ripe in various cities, a recipe file, help for the herbally impaired, and a cooking dictionary are what really feed your cravings.

BEST KIDS' CD-ROM'S

DISNEY'S ACTIVITY CENTER: TOY STORY

1 *(Disney Interactive, CD-ROM for PC and Mac, $35)* This follow-up to the *Toy Story Animated Storybook* recasts the familiar computer-animated characters (including Buzz, Woody, and the Spider Baby) in fun, point-and-click games for kids, including a nifty mix-and-match doll factory.

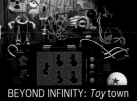

BEYOND INFINITY: *Toy town*

SIMTUNES

2 *(Maxis, CD-ROM for PC, $34.95)* In the most innovative activity game of the year, kids paint colored notes onto a grid, which are then turned into cacophonous music by tiny instruments that amble back and forth across the screen. Oddly, these random compositions often sound better than Top 40 radio.

KIDPIX STUDIO

3 *(Brøderbund, CD-ROM for PC and Mac, $29.95)* Specifically designed for the grade-school set, Kidpix augments the usual PC painting options with psychedelic patterns and creatively destructive ways to erase works in progress (such as blowing them up with dynamite).

HOLLYWOOD HIGH

4 *(Theatrix, CD-ROM for PC and Mac, $34.95)* If your kids can hunt and peck on the keyboard, they'll have a ball with this easy-to-use movie making program, which turns written dialogue into actual spoken words and adds in tons of goofy sound effects and music.

KAI'S POWER GOO

5 *(MetaTools, CD-ROM for PC and Mac, $49.95)* It's not exactly a game, but this wacky photo-manipulation program—which allows users to stretch, warp, and otherwise wreak havoc on scanned images—is sure to be a big hit with the *Ren & Stimpy* set. —*Bob Strauss*

This is me.
I love to dance.
My name is Megan.

STUDIO SYSTEM: No-mess art for budding Picassos

MULTIMEDIA

CHART-TOPPERS

MULTIMEDIA EMPEROR Bill Gates continued his domination of the software universe as Microsoft's *Windows 95 Upgrade* climbed to the top of the year-end CD-ROM heap, matching last year's chart-topping *Windows 95*. Although sales of the original operating system slowed after its launch, Win 95 proved as powerful a gaming operating system as DOS. Its stronghold was sealed when Microsoft and other companies released 178 Win 95 games in '96, pushing sales of *Upgrade* over one million. *Myst* also stayed in the top five (for the third year in a row), despite being one of the first games on the market. And *Duke Nukem 3D* satisfied gamers' thirst for blood, selling more than half a million units by year's end and landing at No. 4. —*KC*

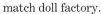

	TOP 25 CD-ROM'S	NO. OF UNITS SOLD
1	MICROSOFT WINDOWS 95 UPGRADE	1,087,578
2	WARCRAFT II: TIDES OF DARKNESS Davidson	732,322
3	MYST Brøderbund	515,685
4	DUKE NUKEM 3D GT Interactive	507,180
5	QUICKEN DELUXE Intuit	491,296
6	COREL PRINTHOUSE	478,431
7	TURBOTAX DELUXE Intuit	408,931
8	CIVILIZATION II Microprose	395,002
9	TOY STORY ANIMATED STORYBOOK Disney	389,678
10	MICROSOFT PLUS	383,927
11	MICROSOFT FLIGHT SIMULATOR	352,725
12	MICROSOFT ENCARTA	339,180
13	COREL WORDPERFECT SUITE UPGRADE	289,395
14	COMMAND & CONQUER Virgin	284,738
15	MECHWARRIOR II ActiVision	274,038
16	STAR WARS REBEL ASSAULT II LucasArts	266,142
17	HALLMARK CONNECTIONS CARD STUDIO Micrografx	262,578
18	TRIPMAKER Rand McNally	259,776
19	MATHEMATICS Sofsource	257,867
20	MICROSOFT PUBLISHER	253,769
21	FAMILY TREE MAKER DELUXE Brøderbund	246,558
22	MATH BLASTER: IN SEARCH OF SPOT Davidson	242,680
23	ULTIMATE DOOM: THY FLESH... GT Interactive	225,449
24	POCAHONTAS ANIMATED STORYBOOK Disney	214,169
25	PRINT SHOP ENSEMBLE III Brøderbund	211,815

SOURCE: PC DATA; JAN. 1, 1996–NOV. 30, 1996

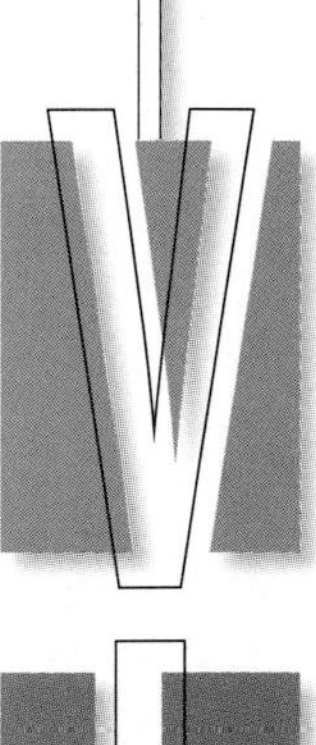
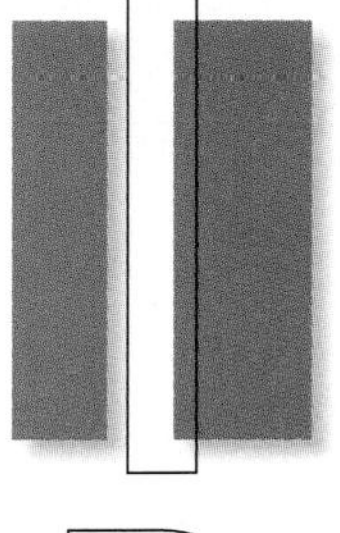
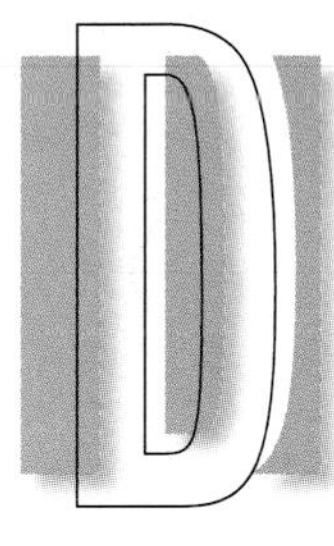

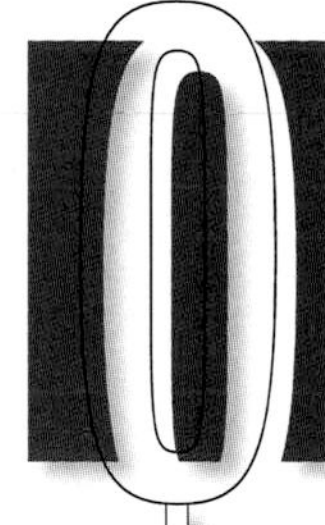

LIVING IN

OBLIVION

THE GREATEST pleasure of home video is the unexpected discovery—the tape you rent when every copy of *Seven* is out that expands into a surprise party on your TV. In theory, *Living in Oblivion* (1995, Columbia TriStar, R, priced for rental) is just another no-budget movie about the perils of making no-budget movies.

1 In practice, writer-director Tom DiCillo has crafted an achingly funny dance of egos on a soundstage. Steve Buscemi plays a director who argues with his eye-patch-wearing cinematographer (Dermot Mulroney) about close-ups, with his dwarf extra about motivation, and with himself over whether to declare his love for his leading lady (the radiant Catharine Keener). Best of all is James LeGros as Chad Palamino, a brainless hunk who may represent DiCillo's revenge on the star of his last film, one William Bradley Pitt. *Oblivion* is a beautifully observed valentine to the dysfunctional family that is every film crew. **BY TY BURR**

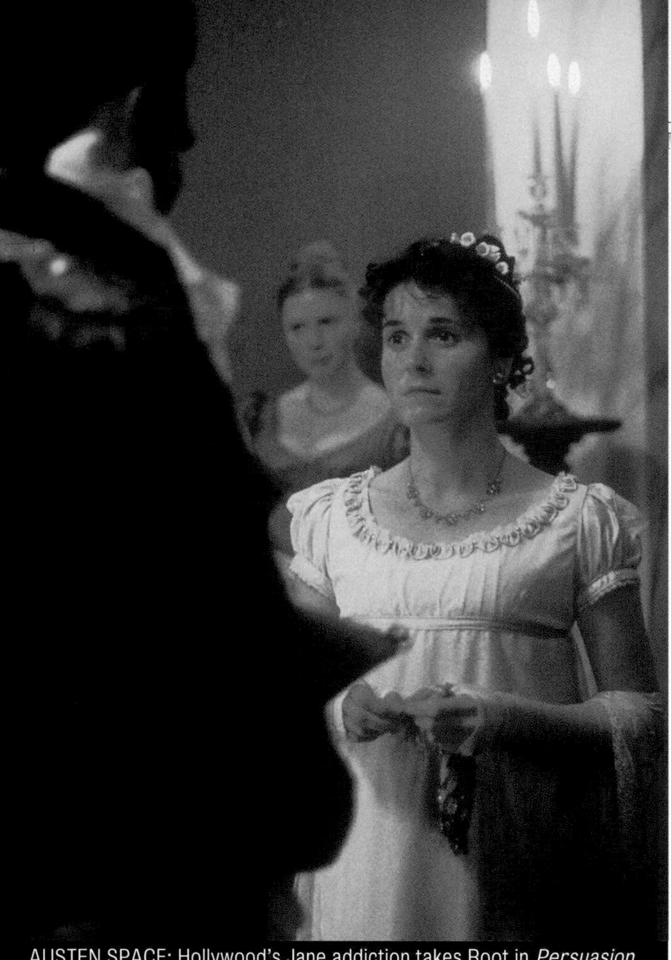

AUSTEN SPACE: Hollywood's Jane addiction takes Root in *Persuasion*

PERSUASION

2 *(1995, Columbia TriStar, PG, priced for rental)* With *Emma, Sense and Sensibility,* and *Clueless* all hitting screens in the past two years, Jane Austen deserves a posthumous power table at Drai's. So how come this British TV movie (released here theatrically) is the only one that rises above the *Masterpiece Theatre* topiary, getting at Austen's bone-dry ironies and knowledge of the heart? As the 27-year-old "spinster" who stands to rekindle a long-dead flame, Amanda Root gracefully embodies the Austen heroine: perceptive, kind, proper, and gleaming with hidden longings.

BRAZIL

3 *(1985, Voyager, unrated, $149.95)* Even if you're not a huge fan of Terry Gilliam's looking-glass fantasy—in which a bureaucratic sad sack (Jonathan Pryce) gets lost in a byzantine future—this laserdisc boxed set is a revelatory chunk of Hollywood history. In addition to a new edit of the film, featuring dazzling visual clarity and pinprick sound, there's an hour-long documentary about the skirmishes surrounding *Brazil*'s theatrical release and—included with fitting perversity—the watered-down cut of the film that Universal initially foisted on the director and the public.

THEREMIN: AN ELECTRONIC ODYSSEY

4 *(1995, Orion, PG, $19.98)* Leon Theremin's most famous invention—an electronic musical instrument responsible for the *ooo-EEE-ooo* on the Beach Boys' "Good Vibrations" and countless '50s sci-fi movies—was weird enough. His life was weirder still: fleeing Lenin's Russia for the high life in Jazz Age New York, getting kidnapped back home, and being forced to develop surveillance technology for the KGB. At the end of this lucidly bizarre documentary, when the 94-year-old Theremin reunites with his New York circle, it's as though a secret history of the 20th century has reached closure.

THE USUAL SUSPECTS

5 *(1995, PolyGram, R, $19.95)* On video you can truly savor the delights of one of the most fiendishly scripted puzzle-box movies of all time. In fact, once you get to the final scene, you'll probably want to rewind and start all over again, just to see if you missed the clues that point to the real identity of arch villain Keyser Söze.

JAMES AND THE GIANT PEACH

6 *(1996, Walt Disney, PG, $22.99)* Great, twisted minds think alike, and in the case of *Peach*'s collaborators, the late children's book author Roald Dahl, producer Tim Burton, and director Henry Selick (*The Nightmare Before Christmas*), the result is a dreamlike film of a seemingly unfilmable classic. This journey aboard a humongous fruit begins and ends in live action, but the midsection is an animated whirlpool of feverish, delightful imagery.

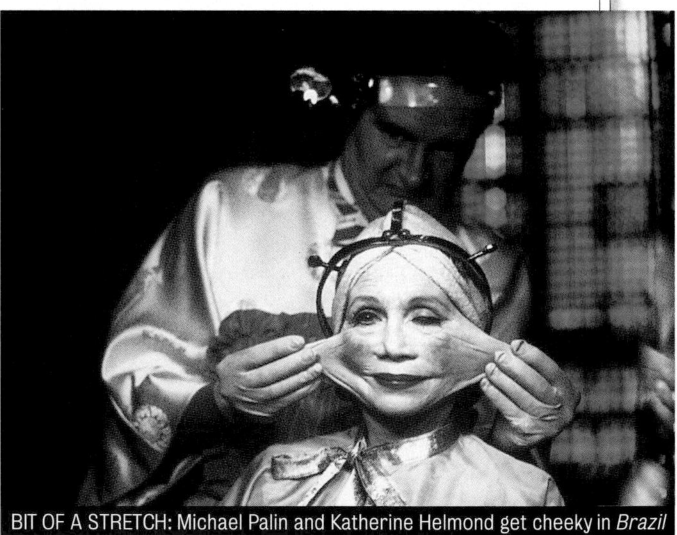

BIT OF A STRETCH: Michael Palin and Katherine Helmond get cheeky in *Brazil*

STRANGE VIBRATIONS: The inventor and his creation in *Theremin*

SMOKE/BLUE IN THE FACE

7 *(1995, Miramax, R, priced for rental) Smoke*, written by novelist Paul Auster and directed by Wayne Wang, is a lovely Brooklyn fable about belonging and redemption starring Harvey Keitel and William Hurt; *Blue in the Face* is the impromptu gabfest that resulted when the filmmakers kept the cameras rolling and invited friends like Madonna, Lou Reed, and Michael J. Fox to stop by. Both films have the fluky, guarded sincerity of New York at its most genial, and watching them on a double bill makes for a wondrous video experience.

MR. BEAN

8 *(1996, PolyGram, unrated, $19.95 each tape)* In these six sidesplitting videos—repackaging 12 episodes of his latest British telly show—*Four Weddings and a Funeral*'s Rowan Atkinson single-handedly revives the tradition of silent clowns Charlie Chaplin and Jacques Tati with an added edge of pointed Pythonesque nonsense. If you can sample only one tape, go for the holiday special "Merry Mishaps" (on Vol. 5), in which petulant, bumbling snoop Mr. Bean reenacts *Jurassic Park* in a department store crèche and manages to get his head stuck inside a Christmas turkey. Sublimely silly.

WHAT A TREAT: Atkinson

THE BEATLES ANTHOLOGY

9 *(1996, Turner, unrated, $159.99)* Thought you saw the entire 4½-hour documentary when it aired on television last year, after the release of the first *Beatles Anthology* CD? Here's the original 10-hour British edit that was subsequently whittled down for the American broadcast on ABC. Even if it doesn't put the story of John, Paul, George, and Ringo into the larger cultural perspective that they helped create, this eight-tape boxed set is still bursting with loads of rare concert footage and previously unseen outtakes.

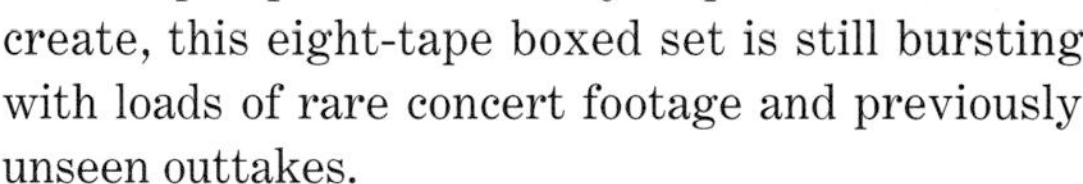

ALADDIN AND THE KING OF THIEVES

10 *(1996, Walt Disney, G, $24.99)* Atoning for the drab 1994 *Aladdin* sequel, *The Return of Jafar* (in which the big blue Genie is voiced by Dan Castellaneta, a.k.a. Homer Simpson), this second of Disney's video-only follow-ups features the return of Robin Williams to what may well be his liveliest, most representative role. The story's a little

A WEBBED FEAT: In the dazzling *Giant Peach*, James finds solace in Spider's nest

sticky—Aladdin bonds with his nogoodnik dad—and the animation looks slightly second-rate, but we'll take full-on Williams wherever we can get him.

12 MONKEYS

11 *(1995, MCA/Universal, R, $19.98)* In which director Terry Gilliam returns to *Brazil* and finds it a far nastier place than he originally thought. Like *The Usual Suspects*, *Monkeys* benefits from the rewind button: The herky-jerky time travels of James Cole (Bruce Willis) have a fetid richness that deserves to be plumbed for its details. As a bonus, Willis turns in his least smug performance to date.

BRIAN WILSON: I JUST WASN'T MADE FOR THESE TIMES

12 *(1995, LIVE, unrated, $19.98)* Record producer Don Was' tribute to the creative force of the Beach Boys could be overshadowed on video shelves by Terry Zwigoff's *Crumb*: Both documentaries examine the tormented families and ongoing survival of key '60s artists. The difference is that Robert Crumb has always maintained a sardonic distance, while Wilson now looks like the noble wreck of his ideals and fancies. An essential look at a still-beleaguered innocent.

THE TURBAN-ATOR: *Hype*'s Jackson is a ring king

LONG AND SHORT OF IT: *Cats & Dogs*' Thurman, Garofalo

THE GREAT WHITE HYPE

13 *(1996, FoxVideo, R, priced for rental)* There's a certain sophistication missing from the script, cowritten by the usually precise Ron Shelton (*Tin Cup*, *Bull Durham*). But since the subject we're wheeler-dealing with here is that sideshow called professional boxing, hilarious vulgarity is definitely called for. Samuel L. Jackson is a turbaned, effervescent sight to behold as an unscrupulous promoter (Don King, call your lawyer).

THE TRUTH ABOUT CATS & DOGS

14 *(1996, FoxVideo, PG-13, priced for rental)* Once, director Michael Lehmann made a terrific black comedy called *Heathers*. Then he made a turkey called *Hudson Hawk*. Now all is forgiven with this romantic charmer, in which Janeane Garofalo gets the starring role she deserves as a mildly schlumpy radio veterinarian who falls for cute Ben Chaplin and hides beyond bombshell neighbor Uma Thurman. Rent it with the Steve Martin vehicle *Roxanne* for a double bill of *Cyrano* updates.

THE BIG CLOCK

15 *(1948, MCA/Universal, unrated, $14.98)* If you liked the 1987 Kevin Costner–Gene Hackman thriller *No Way Out*, you'll love the offbeat 1948 original, at last out on video. The setting is a publishing company instead of the Pentagon, but magazine editor Ray Milland (*The Lost Weekend*) still has to solve a murder committed by his tyrannical boss (Charles Laughton) as the evidence increasingly mounts against Milland. Laughton's drolly evil performance is the best thing in either this or the remake.

SHANGHAI TRIAD

16 *(1995, Columbia TriStar, unrated, priced for rental)* China's top director, Zhang Yimou, and his longtime leading lady, Gong Li, tackle the gangster genre with eye-popping, imaginatively swanky results. Get past the subtitles and you'll find a melodramatic swooner worthy of Joan Crawford. It's a treat to see the exquisite Gong go wild at last as a prostitute-turned-moll called Jewel.

SHANGHAI SURPRISE: As a moll girl, Gong (with Shun Chun) finally lets go

EXECUTIVE DECISION

17 *(1996, Warner, R, priced for rental)* Out of a thousand action-packed *Die Hard* rip-offs over the past few years, *Decision* is the only one to favor meat-and-potatoes storytelling over macho posturing. Kurt Russell plays the policy consultant who ends up sneaking a SWAT team aboard an airplane hijacked by terrorists—in mid-flight, no less. The film gets bonus points for killing off costar Steven Seagal in the first half hour.

TICKED OFF: Maureen O'Sullivan and Milland kill time in *The Big Clock*

CLEAN, SHAVEN

18 *(1995, Orion, unrated, priced for rental)* Charismatic and controversial—his on-set heroin abuse making *The Rich Man's Wife* was chronicled in a recent magazine article—Peter Greene played a psycho in that ridiculous '96 thriller, but he turns in a far more unnerving performance in this little-seen tale about a terrified and terrifying schizophrenic wending his way back to the daughter who was taken from him. More of a case study than narrative, *Clean*, directed by Lodge H. Kerrigan, deftly balances horror and sympathy, ultimately getting into its protagonist's head like a madman prying off his own fingernail.

ANGELS & INSECTS

19 *(1996, Evergreen, unrated, priced for rental)* If David Lynch made a Merchant Ivory film, it might look like this. Adapting A.S. Byatt's cold-eyed novel of entomology and eroticism among the Victorian gentry, filmmakers Philip and Belinda Haas (he directs, they both write) subtly underline the sexual bugginess of the human species. Patsy Kensit and Kristin Scott Thomas play very different yet equally bewitching women whose secrets ultimately come to light like emerging pupae.

FARGO

20 *(1996, PolyGram, R, priced for rental)* It's no coincidence that the Coen brothers' best movie since *Raising Arizona* likewise deigns to care about its characters. Well, not all of them: The killers, played by Steve Buscemi (again) and Peter Stormare, are a Mutt and Jeff for *America's Most Wanted*. But there's a sadness to William H. Macy's car salesman—locked helplessly in heartland bonhomie as he schemes to have his wife kidnapped—and a blessed serenity to his pregnant small-town pursuer, Sgt. Marge Gunderson (Frances McDormand), that resonate after you've hit rewind.

AIR OF DISTINCTION: *Decision*'s Halle Berry, Russell in flight

THE WORST

THEODORE REX

1 *(1996, New Line, PG, priced for rental)* Used to be that when a star made an out-and-out turkey, the studio would bury it in Europe or shelve the thing. Now it gets a video premiere. Watching this Whoopi Goldberg atrocity—whose $35 million budget makes it the most expensive direct-to-video product ever—is like gawking at a 10-car pileup. And it's hard to decide which is worse: the lame future-cop-partners-with-reconstituted–T. rex plot or the Precambrian production values. Even kiddie dino fans will wish this one extinct.

REX 'N' F/X: Goldberg and pal

GORDY

2 *(1995, Walt Disney, G, $14.99)* Let the buyer beware: This one's about a cute talking pig, and the box art even looks suspiciously familiar. But we know *Babe,* and this, sir, is no *Babe.* Instead it's a broad-as-a-barn country comedy (with Nashville vets Roy Clark and Mickey Gilley in small roles) that trots out its anthropomorphic critters like geeks in a freak show. If *Babe* is the *Citizen Kane* of animal movies, this must be *Ernest Goes to Jail.*

O.J. SIMPSON: THE INTERVIEW

3 *(1996, H&K, unrated, $29.99)* In which the star of the nation's longest-running tragi-sitcom importunes us on the subject of his innocence from his living room, then guides us on a tour through his house and points out where he left the bags. If you think he didn't do it, this is still one ugly piece of home-video exploitation. If you think he did, *The Interview* opens up the possibility that Simpson may in fact be a better actor than we thought.

UP CLOSE & PERSONAL

4 *(1996, Touchstone, PG-13, priced for rental)* Television news has become so shallow in the past decade that it deserves a movie this craven. *Up Close & Personal* takes the true story of self-destructive newswoman Jessica Savitch, guts it of any meaning, and turns it into a zombie remake of *A Star Is Born.* Michelle Pfeiffer plods gamely through; as for costar Robert Redford, here's hoping he was paid enough to keep Sundance in business for a few more years.

CLOSE, NO CIGAR: Pfeiffer, Redford

HACKERS

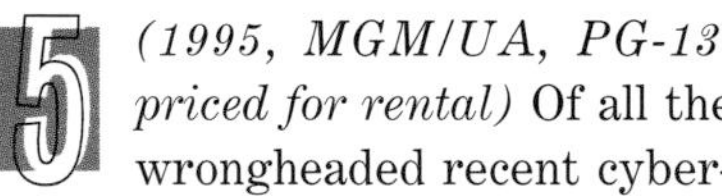

5 *(1995, MGM/UA, PG-13, priced for rental)* Of all the wrongheaded recent cyberthrillers (*The Net, Virtuosity,* ad nauseam), why would we pick this as the runt of the litter? Maybe because its vision of young, amoral computer whizzes has everything to do with mass-media stereotypes and nothing to do with non-virtual reality. It's the modern equivalent of Ike-era teen cash-ins with titles like *Rock, Pretty Baby.*

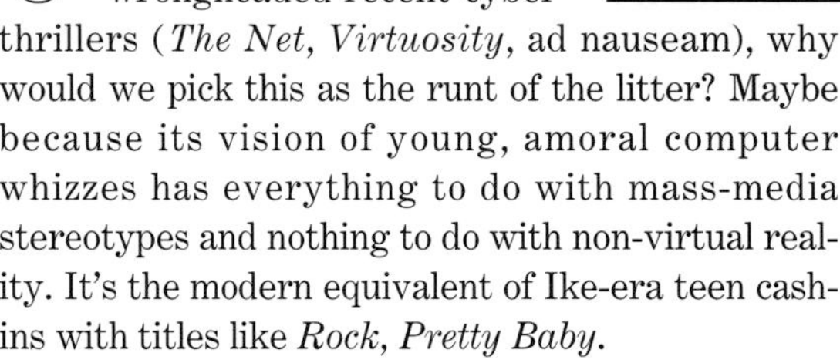

BHAJI ON THE BEACH

21 *(1994, Columbia TriStar, R, priced for rental)* It sounds like something to screen for a high school social-studies class: An eclectic group of Indian women living in England take a day trip to the beach at Blackpool. But director Gurinder Chadha's *Bhaji* finds a universal humanity in the larky teenagers and fussy older ladies and abused wives and pregnant career women on this particular bus. A *bhaji* is a pungently tasty snack; so is the movie.

CLASH BY NIGHT

22 *(1952, Turner, unrated, $19.98)* For years one of the last video holdouts in Marilyn Monroe's filmography, this melodrama from a Clifford Odets play shows the young M.M. in an unusually naturalistic mode. Star Barbara Stanwyck plays a fishmonger's wife who dabbles in adultery with Robert Ryan, but Monroe has a woozy

MAGIC BUS: The day-trippers of *Bhaji on the Beach*

RED, FAT, AND BLUE: Talbert looms large as *Angus*

kitchen-sink sexiness that really makes you wish she'd made more films outside of Twentieth Century Fox (this was her only one for RKO).

ANGUS

23 *(1995, Turner, PG-13, $14.98)* The best high-school-misfit movie since 1986's similarly titled *Lucas*, and like that film it avoids both cynicism and sentiment. Charlie Talbert is the title teen: His mom (Kathy Bates) says he's from "hearty stock," but *he* knows he's just fat. How Angus gets the girl of his dreams away from the nasty class golden boy is told with a wry wit that will evoke sighs of recognition in anyone who didn't fit in as an adolescent (i.e., everyone).

I SHOT ANDY WARHOL

24 *(1996, Evergreen, unrated, priced for rental)* Beneath the title's tabloid come-on is the roisterously sad tale of Valerie Solanas, a Factory misfit who got her 15 minutes of fame when she tried to kill the Pop-art maestro himself. Lili Taylor finds the scabrous proto-punk humor under Solanas' demented feminism, and Jared Harris (Richard's son) puckishly makes Warhol a wallflower at his own party—a vacuum to be filled with meaning or bullets. And what a soundtrack, featuring Pavement and Yo La Tengo.

THE JUROR

25 *(1996, Columbia TriStar, R, $19.95)* Of course it's another lousy Demi Moore film, this one adapted from a beach read so preposterous the video box practically comes with an embossed cover. But it's worth renting for Alec Baldwin's high-as-a-kite performance as a Mafia hitman with a penchant for dum-dum Zen koans. Baldwin is a greatly underrated actor, and until he gets respect he clearly intends to have fun.

DATA SOURCE: *VIDEO BUSINESS*; FIGURES FOR VIDEO SPECIALTY STORES ONLY

VIDEO

CHART-TOPPERS

THE BEST PICTURE and Best Director Oscars—and the film's early-in-the-year video release—certainly helped catapult Mel Gibson's $75 million-grossing *Braveheart* to the top of this year's rentals chart (but the movie's amusing exposé of what went on under all those kilts didn't hurt either). As for the year's biggest video triumph, the latecomer *Independence Day* surged from behind within six weeks of its Nov. 22 release, commandeering rock-solid rental numbers *and* the top sales spot, with FoxVideo shipping a record 21,954,575 tapes. Blasting past *Jurassic Park* and *Forrest Gump* (both of which have moved fewer than 17 million copies), the phenomenally successful pop-corn flick is primed to become the best-selling live-action video ever. —*Erin Richter*

TOP 15 TAPE RENTALS	RENTALS PER STORE
1 **BRAVEHEART** Mel Gibson, *Paramount*	403
2 **SEVEN** Brad Pitt, *New Line*	397
3 **TWISTER** Helen Hunt, *Warner*	390
4 **DANGEROUS MINDS** Michelle Pfeiffer, *Hollywood*	340
5 **JUMANJI** Robin Williams, *Columbia TriStar*	334
6 **ACE VENTURA: WHEN NATURE CALLS** Jim Carrey, *Warner*	329
7 **HAPPY GILMORE** Adam Sandler, *Universal*	319
8 **12 MONKEYS** Bruce Willis, *Universal*	309
9 **INDEPENDENCE DAY** Bill Pullman, *FoxVideo*	308
10 **BROKEN ARROW** John Travolta, *FoxVideo*	306
11 **CASINO** Robert De Niro, *Universal*	304
12 **THE NET** Sandra Bullock, *Columbia TriStar*	302
13 **EXECUTIVE DECISION** Kurt Russell, *Warner*	300
14 **THE NUTTY PROFESSOR** Eddie Murphy, *Universal*	284
15 **MR. HOLLAND'S OPUS** Richard Dreyfuss, *Hollywood*	281

TOP 10 TAPE SALES	TAPES SOLD PER STORE
1 **INDEPENDENCE DAY** Bill Pullman, *FoxVideo*, $22.98	533
2 **TOY STORY** Animated, *Disney*, $26.99	451
3 **BABE** *Universal*, $22.98	347
4 **POCAHONTAS** Animated, *Disney*, $26.99	287
5 **TWISTER** Helen Hunt, *Warner*, $22.96	268
6 **THE NUTTY PROFESSOR** Eddie Murphy, *Universal*, $22.98	239
7 **THE ARISTOCATS** Animated, *Walt Disney*, $26.99	204
8 **MISSION: IMPOSSIBLE** Tom Cruise, *Paramount*, $22.95	179
9 **ALADDIN AND THE KING OF THIEVES** Animated, *Walt Disney*, $24.99	131
10 **JUMANJI** Robin Williams, *Columbia TriStar*, $19.95	129

BOWING OUT

DON SIMPSON, 52

(died Jan. 19) As notorious for his offscreen excesses as his on-screen successes, he was half of the highly profitable Simpson-Bruckheimer production team that blasted out such high-testosterone hits as *Beverly Hills Cop* and *Top Gun.*

GERRY MULLIGAN, 68

(d. Jan. 20) First brought to widespread attention through his work on Miles Davis' seminal *Birth of the Cool* album, baritone saxophonist Mulligan became a pioneer of West Coast cool jazz in the 1950s.

JONATHAN LARSON, 35

(d. Jan. 25) Renown came too late for the composer, who died of an aortic aneurysm just before his high-energy rock musical *Rent* opened to raves off Broadway. Larson's East Village update of *La Bohème* soon moved to Broadway and won four Tonys and a Pulitzer Prize.

JOSEPH BRODSKY, 55

(d. Jan. 28) The 1987 Nobel Prize-winning poet settled in the United States after being expelled from Russia in 1972. Five years before his death, Brodsky became his adopted country's first foreign-born poet laureate.

GENE KELLY, 83

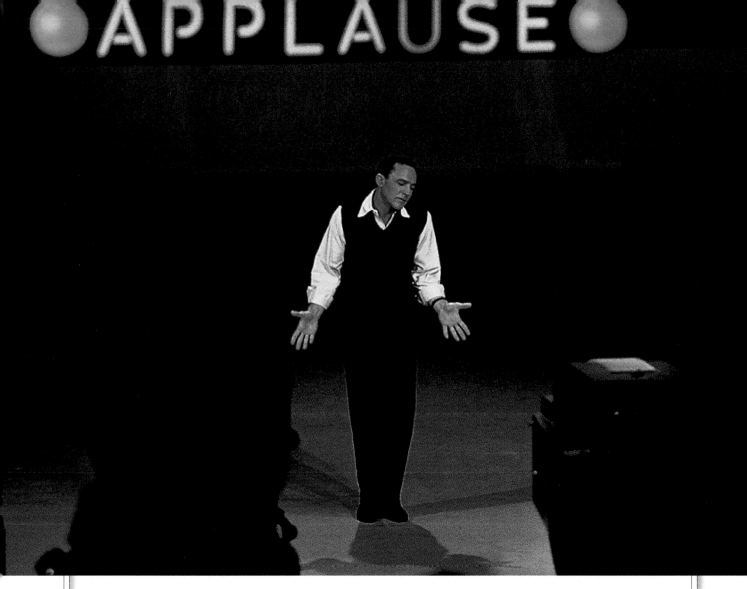

(d. Feb. 2) The T-shirt-wearing guy next door, Kelly brought joy and exuberance to dancing—a hobby he took up as a kid in Pittsburgh. In 1952, he sang—and danced—in the rain. Only he could make getting soaked look so fun, and so sexy.

AUDREY MEADOWS, 71

(d. Feb. 3) TV wife of Jackie Gleason, Meadows won small-screen immortality as *The Honeymooners'* Alice Kramden. Though her bus driver husband, Ralph, often threatened to send her "to the moon," feisty Alice gave as good as she got.

MARTIN BALSAM, 76

(d. Feb. 13) It's Balsam's face, not his name, that you'll remember from this consummate character actor's long list of classic films: *Psycho*, *On the Waterfront*, *All the President's Men*, and his Oscar-winning supporting role as a hardworking family man in 1965's gem *A Thousand Clowns*.

MCLEAN STEVENSON, 66

(d. Feb. 15) After appearing on *The Smothers Brothers' Comedy Hour* and *The Doris Day Show*, Stevenson found an unforgettable role as the absent-minded Lieut. Col. Henry Blake on TV's *M*A*S*H* from 1972 to 1975.

MINNIE PEARL, 83

(d. March 4) With a $1.98 price tag swinging from her straw hat, the queen of country—and corn—at the Grand Ole Opry and on *Hee Haw* was actually a finishing-school graduate named Sarah Cannon from a well-to-do Southern family.

GEORGE BURNS, 100

(d. March 9) He became a star only after hooking up with his beloved Gracie, but Burns' comedy spanned the history of modern show business, from vaudeville to the small screen to the silver screen, where he won an Oscar at age 79 for *The Sunshine Boys*.

VINCE EDWARDS, 67

(d. March 11) As Dr. Ben Casey, he fueled TV's *first* medical craze, in the early '60s, with his dark, brooding antidote to Richard Chamberlain's blond, pretty-boy Dr. Kildare.

GREER GARSON, 92

(d. April 6) The Irish-born actress personified the noble, stalwart woman of the '30s and '40s. She also made history with the longest Oscar acceptance speech (it clocked in at 5½ minutes) for Best Actress in 1942's *Mrs. Miniver*.

SAUL BASS, 75

(d. April 25) Graphic designer Bass turned opening-title sequences into a film-within-a-film art form. Just recall the beginnings of *Vertigo*, *West Side Story*, and *The Age of Innocence*, and you know you're beholding the work of a master.

JACK WESTON, 71

(d. May 3) The curmudgeonly actor landed his first film two days after arriving in L.A. (1960's *Please Don't Eat the Daisies*), then played bit parts until his memorable 1981 turn as the whiny dentist in *The Four Seasons*.

TIMOTHY LEARY, 75

(d. May 31) An ex-Harvard professor, fired for turning students on to LSD and jailed for drug charges, Leary was a '60s icon, Winona Ryder's godfather, a lecturer, and a proselytizer for the Internet ("the LSD of the future"), on which he posted a daily log of his final illness.

ELLA FITZGERALD, 79

(d. June 15) During a 60-plus year career, the First Lady of Song—and acclaimed voice of jazz—recorded more than 100 albums and won 18 Grammys but still could ask shyly after a concert, "Did I do all right?"

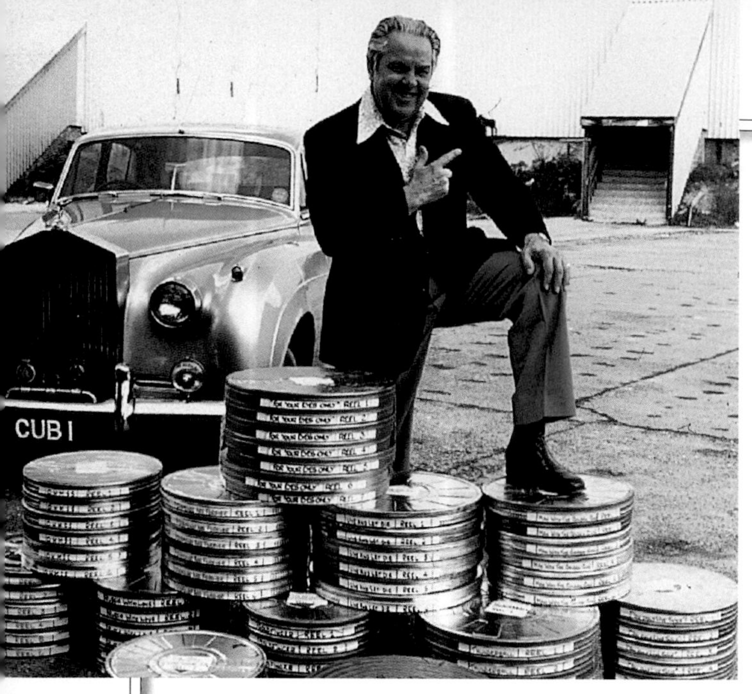

ALBERT "CUBBY" BROCCOLI, 87

(d. June 27) A descendant of the Italian immigrant family that introduced its namesake green vegetable to America, Broccoli started as a gofer for Howard Hughes in 1940 and went on to produce 17 James Bond movies.

MARGAUX HEMINGWAY, 41

(d. July 1) At 19, the six-foot stunner became a million-dollar spokesmodel. Her acting career (*Lipstick*) was less towering, and after battling bulimia, alcoholism, depression, and epilepsy, she followed grandfather Ernest Hemingway in suicide.

JOHN CHANCELLOR, 68

(d. July 12) His long journalistic résumé included a 1961 stint serving as *Today*'s host and getting booted from the 1964 Republican Convention, microphone in hand. The respected newsman went on to anchor the *NBC Nightly News* before his retirement in 1993.

CLAUDETTE COLBERT, 92

(d. July 30) She's best known as the runaway heiress who showed Clark Gable how to hitch in her Oscar-winning role in 1934's *It Happened One Night*. The throaty-voiced Paris native bowed out of films in 1961, a lady to the end.

GREG MORRIS, 61

(d. Aug. 27) One of the first African-American actors with a regular role in a TV drama series, Morris played high-tech wizard Barney Collier on *Mission: Impossible*. His job? To save the day by creating yet another wild gadget.

BILL MONROE, 84

(d. Sept. 9) When "high lonesome" tenor Monroe formed the Blue Grass Boys in 1939, he had no idea he would be credited with the creation of a musical genre. The Father of Bluegrass sold more than 40 million records.

JOANNE DRU, 74

(d. Sept. 10) The older sister of game-show host Peter Marshall, Dru made her mark as a spirited pioneer woman in Westerns such as Howard Hawks' *Red River* (1948) and *She Wore a Yellow Ribbon* (1949) with John Wayne.

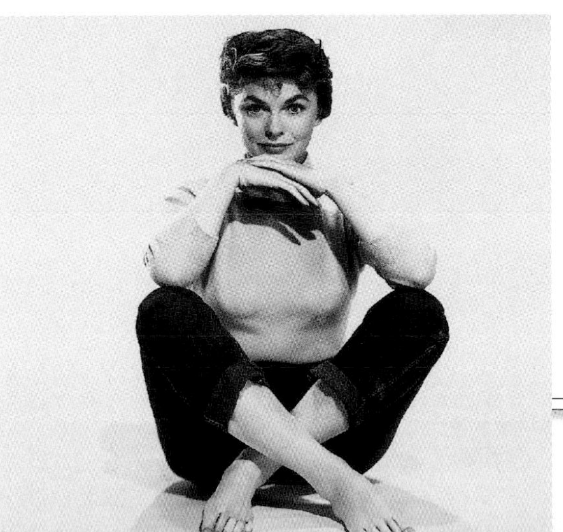

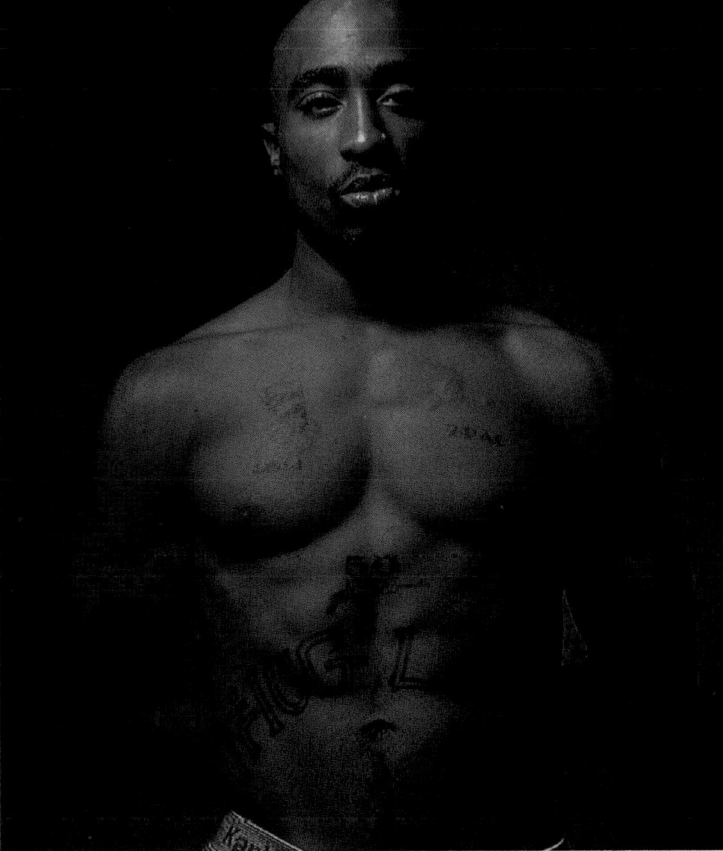

TUPAC SHAKUR, 25

(d. Sept. 13) With a rap sheet to accompany his "gangsta" rap songs, the multi-platinum star (*All Eyez on Me*, *Me Against the World*) and up-and-coming actor (*Juice*, *Poetic Justice*) was shot to death while cruising down Flamingo Road in Las Vegas.

JULIETTE PROWSE, 59

(d. Sept. 14) The lithe and leggy actress-dancer-choreographer from South Africa made her Hollywood debut high-kicking in the 1960 musical *Can-Can*, where she met fleeting fiancé Frank Sinatra.

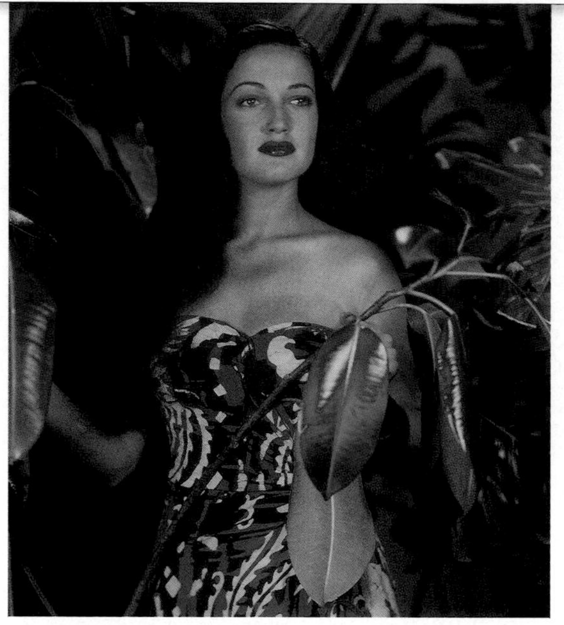

DOROTHY LAMOUR, 81

(d. Sept. 22) The nation's first official pinup (her sarong hangs in the Smithsonian), Lamour played the sexy straight woman to Bob Hope and Bing Crosby's juvenile jokesters in seven *Road* movie comedies (*Road to Morocco*, *Road to Rio*, et al.).

TED BESSELL, 61

(d. Oct. 6) *That Girl*'s devoted guy, Bessell played "Oh, Donald!" Hollinger to Marlo Thomas' plucky single gal (1966–1971) and went on to work behind the scenes as a TV director and Emmy-winning producer of *The Tracey Ullman Show*.

MOREY AMSTERDAM, 87

(d. Oct. 27) The former vaudevillian still appears most nights on Nickelodeon as Buddy, the wisecracking TV writer on *The Dick Van Dyke Show*.

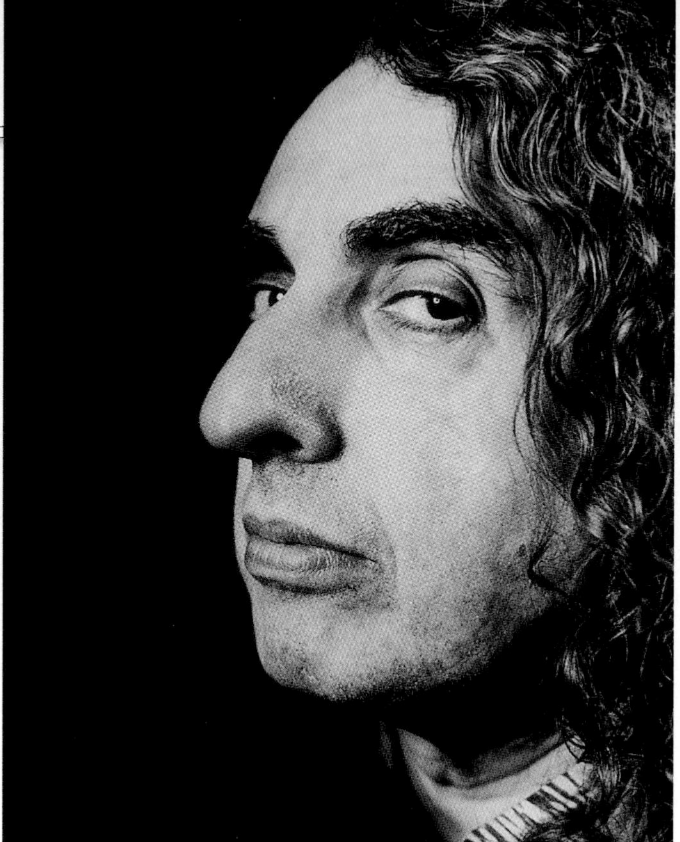

TINY TIM, 64

(d. Nov. 30) His age was as hard to figure as his fame. In 1968 the ukulele strummer hit the charts with the falsettoed "Tip-Toe Thru' the Tulips" and married his first wife, Miss Vicki, before 45 million viewers on *The Tonight Show*.

HOWARD ROLLINS, 46

(d. Dec. 8) After earning a Best Supporting Oscar for 1981's *Ragtime*, Rollins ricocheted between creative highs and deep lows. Drug problems ended his run on TV's *In the Heat of the Night*, yet he had completed the movie *Drunks* and a PBS drama before his death.

MARCELLO MASTROIANNI, 72

(d. Dec. 19) He rocketed to international fame with 1960's *La Dolce Vita* as the jaded journalist who frolicked in a Roman fountain with Anita Ekberg. Known as the Face of Italy, he personified European masculinity in more than 120 films and earned three Oscar nominations.

CARL SAGAN, 62

(d. Dec. 20) With his TV show *Cosmos* and his 26 appearances on *The Tonight Show*, the Pulitzer Prize-winning author and astronomer became a household name by popularizing the "billions and billions" of stars in the sky.

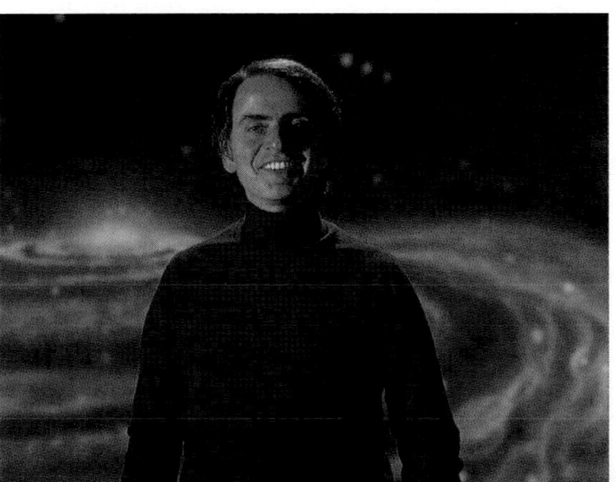

LEW AYRES, 88

(d. Dec. 30) Reaching stardom in his third movie, 1930's *All Quiet on the Western Front*, Ayres had a sporadic film career that included the original *Dr. Kildare* and his Oscar-nominated turn as another doc in 1948's *Johnny Belinda*.

CREDITS

COVERS Anderson: Malone/Retna; Bullock: Aslan/Sipa; Cage: Davenport/Outline; Clooney: Davis/Shooting Star; Cosby & Rashad: T. Esparza; Crow: Preston/A&M Records; Cruise: Miller/Archive Photos; DeGeneres: Jeffery Newbury; Downey Jr.: Barrett/Globe Photos; *Evita*: Everett Collection; Fitzgerald: Shooting Star; Gibson: Smeal/Galella Ltd.; *Hunchback*: the Walt Disney Co.; Hunt: Neal Peters Collection; *ID4*: n/c; Jackson: Factor/Visages; Kiss: Jeff Jacobson; Lane: L. Sebastian; Lithgow: Trapper/Sygma; Love: Visages; Morissette: Corio/Retna; *Nutty Professor*: B. McBroom; O'Donnell: Jesse Frohman; Paltrow & Pitt: Davila/Retna; Shakur mural: Beckman/Retna; Smashing Pumpkins: Page/Retna; *That Thing You Do!* trio: Edward Gajdel; Tyler: Thurnher/Outline; Washington: Sanchez/Outline; Williams: L. Sebastian **6–7:** Polly Becker

THE YEAR IN ENTERTAINMENT

CALENDAR *Cruise Patrol* illustrations: Ross MacDonald; *Pamelapalooza* illustrations: Steven Salerno; *Woody Watch* illustrations: Elliott Banfield **38–39:** (clockwise from bottom left) Hanoch Piven; Robert DeMichiell; Globe Photos; Preston/Retna; AP/Wide World Photos; Tim Carroll (2); n/c; Tim Carroll; J. Wolfe; P. Caruso **40–41:** (clockwise from top left) David Jensen; J. Fitzgerald; AP/Wide World Photos; Tom Bachtell (2); AP/Wide World Photos; Tom Bachtell; C. Coote; G. LaMana; Ortega/Galella Ltd.; Michael Lavine **42–43:** (clockwise from bottom left) Sean Kelly; Berman/Sipa; Baker/*L.A. Daily News*/Sygma (2); AP/Wide World Photos (2); Brook Meinhardt (2); R. Torres; Everett Collection; John Kascht **44–45:** (clockwise from far left) Katrin Thomas (3); n/c; R. Tom; Orban/Sygma; Harry Campbell (2); the JFK Library; the Dynamic Duo; AP/Wide World Photos; M. Wallace **46–47:** (clockwise from far left) AP/Wide World Photos; Laszlo/CoMedia; Regan/Camera 5; Robert DeMichiell; Paul Corio; Everett Collection; Paul Corio (2); Photofest; Harry Campbell; Glynis Sweeny **48–49:** (clockwise from far left) Mazur/LFI; AP/Wide World Photos; Michal Daniel; Tim Carroll; Halfin/Retna; Photofest; W. Chin; Haley/ Sipa **50–51:** (clockwise from bottom left) Kyle Baker; n/c; Matthew Martin; AP/Wide World Photos; David Scott Sinclair; Mark Matcho (2); Mhlambi/Sygma; Mark Matcho; Spencer/Retna; AP/Wide World Photos **52–53:** (clockwise from far left) AP/Wide World Photos; Ad McCauley; Fineman/Sygma; Preston/Retna; Matthew Martin (2); C. Haston; Harry Campbell; Schwartzwald/Sygma; Blakesberg/Retna **54–55:** (clockwise from top left) Corjoni/Outline; Hanoch Piven; Smeal/Galella Ltd.; David Scott Sinclair; Paul Corio; Matt Campbell; A. Hall; Paul Corio; Robert DeMichiell; G. Kraychyk; S. Green/Courtesy Harpo Inc. **56–57:** (clockwise from top left) Greg Clarke; Jordan/Photoreporters; Winter/Celebrity Photo; Flores/Celebrity Photo; Paul Corio; Matt Campbell; Mark Matcho; Everett Collection; Hansen/LFI; Brook Meinhardt **58–59:** (clockwise from top left) Stephen Kroninger; Barrett/Globe Photos; Soqui/Sygma; Sean Kelly (2); Richard Beckerman; n/c; Cuffaro/Outline; L. Sebastian **60–61:** (clockwise from top left) Kyle Baker; Elliott Banfield; Juliette Borda; Everett Collection; S. Emerson; n/c; Tom Bachtell; Pope/Retna; Holz/Outline **66–67:** (clockwise from bottom left) Winter/Celebrity Photo; Smeal/Galella Ltd. (2); Paschal/Celebrity Photo; Aaron/Celebrity Photo; Spellman/Retna; Smeal/Galella Ltd.; Gallo/Retna; Shen/Celebrity Photo; Smeal/Galella Ltd.; Paschal/Celebrity Photo; Granitz/Retna; Paschal/Celebrity Photo; Mayer/Star File; Gough/Celebrity Photo; Granitz/Retna; Elgar/LFI; Renault/Globe Photos; Ferreira/Globe Photos; DeGuire/LFI; Downie/Celebrity Photo; Spellman/Retna **68:** (clockwise from top left) Roth/Retna; DeGuire/LFI; Henny Garfunkel; the Walt Disney Co./Everett Collection; Photofest (2); Gough/Celebrity Photo; Smeal/Galella Ltd. (2); Ferguson/Galella Ltd.; Ferreira/Globe Photos; Spellman/Retna; AP/Wide World Photos **69:** (clockwise from top left) Starr/Saba; Jordan/Photoreporters; n/c (5); Arroyo/Celebrity Photo; D. Appleby **72:** Winslet: *Orange County Register*/Saba; Alex Berliner/Berliner Studio (4) **73:** (clockwise from top left) Henny Garfunkel (4); Prouser/Sipa; DeGuire/LFI; Trupp/Celebrity Photo; Acikalin/Sipa; Spencer/Retna **74:** (clockwise from top left) Laszlo/CoMedia; Barrett/Globe Photos; Pat/Retna; Jeff Jacobson; Frank Micelotta; Jay Blakesberg; Smeal/Galella Ltd.; Mazur/LFI; Ferguson/Galella Ltd. **75:** (clockwise from top left) Shen/Celebrity Photo; Celebrity Photo; Downie/Celebrity Photo; Paschal/Celebrity Photo; Berman/Sipa; Mazur/LFI

ENTERTAINERS OF THE YEAR

79: Jesse Frohman **80:** Courtesy *The Rosie O'Donnell Show* **81:** Katz/Gamma-Liaison/Courtesy *Smoke* magazine **82:** Laurita/Visages **83:** Andrew Brusso **84:** Anton Corbijn **85:** Edward Gajdel **86:** Alistair Morrison **87:** Regan/Saba **88:** Cates/Sygma **89:** Holz/Outline **90:** Parry/Katz Pictures/Outline **91:** Robert Trachtenberg **92–93:** (clockwise from top left) Walls/Outline; Kristine Larsen; Schoerner; Levine/Sygma; Todd Eberle; Sennett/Outline **94–95:** (clockwise from far left) Jon Ragel; Alison Shirk; Buck/Outline; Eika Aoshima; Matthew Welch; F. Scott Schafer

THE YEAR IN REVIEWS

98–99: Photofest **100–101:** (clockwise from top left) Photofest; B. Wetcher; Everett Collection; R. Batzdorff; B. Foley; L. Longman **102–103:** (l–r) S. Baldwin; Everett Collection; Neal Peters Collection; n/c **104:** (top to bottom) Photofest (2); n/c; L. Sebastian **105:** (top to bottom) the Walt Disney Co.; B. Wetcher; n/c **106–107:** (l–r) P. Vinet; M. Wallace; C. Barius; R. Tepper; T. Collins **108:** (l–r) N. Goode; M. Tillie; P. Morrissey **109:** (clockwise from top left) A. Cooper; Smeal/Galella Ltd.; David Sheldon; Galella/Galella Ltd.; Strong/Sipa; Smeal/Galella Ltd.; Rose/Globe Photos **110–111:** M. Ginsburg **112–113:** (l-r) K. Staniforth; D. Cadette; *The Simpsons* © & TM 20th Century Fox Film Corp. **114–115:** (l–r) W. Maloney; M. Williams; L. Watson; G. D'Alema **116–117:** (l–r) M. Yarish; R. Tepper; *Superman* TM DC Comics; n/c **118:** (top to bottom) Archive Photos; n/c; Photofest **119:** (clockwise from top left) n/c; Trapper/Sygma; David Sheldon; Smeal/Galella Ltd.; Smith/Retna; Smeal/Galella Ltd.; P. Drinkwater **120–121:** Janet Wooley **122–123:** (clockwise from top left) Lavine/Outline; Lixenberg/Outline; Allen/Retna; n/c; Ramirez/Retna **124–125:** (l–r) Steen Sunderland; n/c; Busacca/Retna; Bart Everly; Kino/Retna **126–127:** (l–r) S. McGuire; Buck/Outline; Dyer/Montage; David Gahr; David Sheldon **128–129:** Scofield/PEOPLE WEEKLY **130–131:** (l–r) Edward Gajdel; Jill Krementz; Borris/Outline **132–133:** (clockwise from top left) Fineman/Sygma; Susan Shacter; Cates/Sygma; Hirschfeld; Culver Pictures **135:** (r) David Sheldon **136–137:** Ian Pollock **140:** Spielberg: B. Marshak **141:** (l–r) the Walt Disney Co./Pixar; n/c; David Sheldon **145:** (bottom) the Walt Disney Co. **146–147:** (l–r) n/c; M. Wallace; Foto Fantasies; n/c (2) **148–149:** (l–r) S. Hanover; n/c; Regan/Camera 5; n/c; David Sheldon

BOWING OUT

150–151: (clockwise from far left) Camp/Outline; Anthony Rapp; Willoughby/MPTV; Haas/Magnum; Kahana/Shooting Star; Archive Photos; Hartman/Globe Photos **152–153:** (clockwise from top left) Sedlik/Outline; Everett Collection; Rose/Globe Photos; Metronome Collection/Archive Photos: Wolman/Retna; Bull/Everett Collection; the Kobal Collection; Camp/Outline; Rona/MPTV **154–155:** (clockwise from top left) James/Sygma; Little/Outline; Photofest; Clinch/Outline; Frank Driggs Collection/Archive Photos; Shooting Star; Everett Collection (2); Kirkland/Sygma **156–157:** (clockwise from top left) Photofest; G.A. Archives/Shooting Star; Neal Peters Collection; the Kobal Collection; Sygma; Globe Photos; Rona/MPTV; Everett Collection

INDEX

(Numbers in OCHRE indicate photographs.)